FROM

CAPE COD

TO

DIXIE AND THE TROPICS.

BY

J. MILTON MACKIE,

AUTHOR OF "COSAS DE ESPAÑA," ETC.

"Toward the Sun!"
Old Motto.

NEW YORK:
G. P. PUTNAM, 441 BROADWAY.
1864.

JOHN F. TROW,
PRINTER AND STEREOTYPER,
50 Greene Street.

PREFACE.

THESE sketches of travel were written before the breaking out of the present rebellion in the Southern States; but as, on the occurrence of this event, letters very properly yielded to arms, they were withheld from publication.

Now, however, when the public mind is turning to books for momentary relief from the long-drawn story of battles and campaigns, it may not be ill-timed to give to the press an account of a pleasure journey, made, in part, through the Southern States; and a portion of which may serve as a memento of the happy days—not soon to return, I fear—when there existed between the inhabitants of the Northern and Southern sections of the country a free interchange of services and hospitalities.

It is, indeed, the great business of the nation,

at the present crisis, to bring back to the Union by force of arms its erring, misguided members; but, while we of the North are intent on subduing them, there is a satisfaction in showing that we neither hate nor despise them; and I am happy to contribute my humble mite in proof that we cherish pleasant reminiscences of our former friendship, and shall be ready, on the restoration of peace, to give to the returning States every right and privilege consistent with the safety, dignity, and welfare of the united republic.

Great Barrington, Mass., *April*, 1864.

CONTENTS.

CHAPTER I.

The Start.

"WE will go a little nearer to the sun," said I to the gentle one by my side, the morning after marriage—and, at the same time, looking vacantly enough at a huge porcelain stove, across the room, an heirloom of a once-noted Puritan.

"For the stove," I went on soliloquizing, "the stove is an invention the mother of which—not a doubt of it—was necessity. Nor is your furnace any other contrivance than a poor imitation of that great subterranean fire we do not much like to think of. And, finally, to live by hickory through this Northern winter, would realize, at least, as great an impossibility as a small forest brought to Dunsinane. My dear, 'tis better we set off toward the sun."

"By the next train?" was her soft, consenting reply.

"By the doves, rather, at once. Cupid, put in the doves!"

"And, boy," said I—seeing that everything had been nicely packed in, and we two happy mortals were "all aboard"—"boy, swing your torch!"

Had the doves been horses, how their hoofs would have resounded as they went down the frozen, icy road! Every hair in my head, and buffalo, bristled with electricity. Every point of everything that had a point was converted, for the time being, into a small lightning rod. Crack went the whip; and, indeed, everything cracked. The ice cracked, till it groaned; the snow, till it crackled. The white hills looked as though they could be broken into pieces as easily as pipetails. All nature snapped, and was almost snappish — ourselves excepted, because we were going toward the sun, you see. Old Boreas, too, I will take out of that category, who was, indeed, in his element, and rode gayly on the ends of the horsetails—that is to say, on the wings of the doves. Young Jack Frost, also, seated only too firmly astride my mustache, with arms akimbo, was as merry as ever was Puck, or Santa Claus. It was, truly, the very morning of all the winter when the polar bear—if he ever did such a thing—would be sure to put his paws in his mouth, to keep them from freezing. And if Samson, I could but say to my wife, had only selected this day for setting firebrands to the tails of the foxes, it would have been, indeed, a comfort to them, and just the thing they wanted.

We reached New York, at last, in safety—thanks to the prairie buffalo for the use of his skin. But during the last half hour of the drive, I remember trying to say, in a hoarse whisper, to my companion:

"My dear, I am the happiest man this side heaven; only, if you have any intention, during the coverture, to box my ears for me, I wish you would do it now. The tingling might not be so bad as the frost-bite."

The reply was a smile from out the furs, as radiant and as soft as the aurora which flashes athwart the gloom of night within the circle of the pole. And, ere it had entirely faded, we descended at the ——— House.

CHAPTER II.

Washington.

ARRIVED at Washington, the Mecca of our politicians, their wives, and daughters, I was glad to find a half-new hotel; though not surprised to observe that its timbers shook a little under my feet, as I ascended to the story next to heaven. Crowds of fine ladies and gentlemen were encountered on the stairway, together with a fellow having a bag and long rope in his hand, apparently going up to hang and bag somebody.

The stairway of the hotel—if I may stop on it long enough to add one observation more—was, as I afterward remarked, rather a favorite place with the young ladies from certain sections of the country, for receiving the attentions of their admirers; probably on account of its being a little less exposed to the glare of the gaslights than were the parlors. At any rate, I noticed a young belle from Kentucky, and one that rang as loud as any other in the house, receiving the homage of an M. C., while sitting, herself, in all her graces and paraphernalia, on the steps.

The new chambers had a neat look; yet no wardrobe or closet was anywhere visible, nor even so much as a peg to hang a hat on. There was a marble wash basin; but the water was of the color of snuff. Silver-plated bell knobs there were, though nobody came at the ringing. Hot water seemed to be an impossibility; and, indeed, it was self-evident that I was here to be monarch of all I surveyed, and of nothing more. However, if one attain to gentility in Washington, he ought to be willing to dispense with a little comfort.

After a hasty survey of the premises, and a no less hasty toilet—for it was late in the evening—I descended to the supper room, where I found a large company of well-dressed gentlemen and ladies, but a set of waiters looking, at the end of their day's work, not much cleaner than their table covers. One of them, after some little delay, was engaged to bring me stewed oysters. He brought me two tablespoonfuls. I called twice for the salt, and as many times for the pepper; though the salt, when I got it, had begun to lose its savor, and the pepper had been made from buckwheat hulls. And no sooner was any dish or castor placed before me, than it was abstracted by some prowling, pilfering waiter. While I was turning my head, it was gone. However, in justice to the menials, I hasten to add, that the next day, after having received their fees, they were very attentive; so much so that, at breakfast, one of them politely asked if he should open my boiled egg for me. Had I given him another dollar, he would have offered, no doubt, to feed me with a spoon.

The greater part of the guests appeared to be worthy, respectable people, who had come up from the provincial towns where they had been living in quiet all their days, and were now committing, in a visit to the capital, their first great indiscretion. Where I starved, they supped well; and altogether better than they "hopped" afterward. For, while some of the waltzing was good enough, I could but observe that only a few of the ladies knew how to walk, and fewer of the gentlemen how to stand still. It was as if a person should undertake to read before having learned his letters.

Soon satisfied with both seeing and hearing, I retired from the scene to enjoy a good night's rest; but, at the end of a couple of hours or more, I was waked by a blundering porter, who, when asked what he wanted, replied:

"Are you going by the early train, sir?"

"No, you scoundrel!"

"All right, sir," continued the fellow, in a tone of voice equally complacent and unfeeling.

"All wrong!" I muttered to myself, as, turning on my side, I endeavored to go to sleep again.

The next morning, I observed that the unsocial French custom of helping out the breakfast with newspapers instead of chitchat, had become fully established here. The members of Congress were intently reading the reports of their speeches; the ladies were looking through the penny papers to see what the letter writers said of the belles of Washington; while opposite me sat a couple of newly wedded lovers solacing themselves each with a copy of the New York *Herald.* But there were some exceptions to the prevailing silence, not to say moroseness, of the company at table; and one of the prettiest young ladies in the house talked loud enough to disturb all readers not gifted with considerable powers of abstraction. This high-toned style of conversation is, indeed, common enough in mixed company, the habit being unconsciously formed by many even of our handsomest and most agreeable ladies, in consequence, it may be, of their being obliged every night to elevate their voices high enough to be heard in crowded balls and parties. Surrounded by a circle of admirers two or three deep, the young miss gives tongue with all her might, in order that she may be heard by the entire crowd; and if she be overheard, also, by some of her rivals, so much the better. The noise is supposed to give her consequence. Indeed, the merit of a low voice in woman would seem to be in danger of being lost sight of in a society where, the more beautiful the belle, the louder her scream. At this rate, our young ladies will soon have to go to parties with small speaking-trumpets in their pockets.

At dinner, it was itself an entertainment to see in what fashion some of our Congressmen, the great politicans, and stump orators of the country, dine. The first thing done by a certain class of the men sent up to Washington to represent their constituents, and do as they would do themselves, is, after taking seats at table, to thrust their hands into the adjacent dishes of nuts, and lay down a handful of them by the side of their plates. In altogether a greater hurry to get at the end of the dinner than they usually are to arrive at that of their speeches, these lawmakers skip either soup or fish, or both, and plunge at once into the *medias res*, the thick of the eating. Even there, however, they make short work of it. Before a quiet man has tasted his soup, and gradually worked his way through a small plate of fish, these energetic feeders are calling loudly for almonds and raisins. But the dessert once reached, all their hurry seemed to be over. They ate pie and pecan nuts by the half hour, and so leisurely, that one who had gone deliberately through all the courses, came out neck and neck with them at the coffee. Yet were they not quite satisfied; but many of the ladies left the table with either an apple or an orange in hand, while some of the gentlemen's pockets were half filled with various gimcracks. These sweets taken from the table are generally supposed to go to the small children, the babes in the nursery. They must fare well—the little fellows! And, indeed, I remember once hearing of a lady who said she always stopped at a certain hotel in New York, because there were so many nice things on the table for the dessert, that she was able to send home every week such a love of a package to the children.

On the whole, the crowd of guests appeared to be well entertained; and evidently thought it a fine thing to visit Washington at the height of the season, and be lodged in this great caravansary. To be sure, a person of quiet habits might be tempted to say that the hotel seemed to him to be full of boots, and gentlemen in them, who appeared to estimate the degree of their personal consideration by that of the noise made by their heels. But by far the greater number of persons were evidently living on the excitement of being in a crowd, and found the confusion and hurly-burly as entertaining as it is at the menagerie when the lion roars, the donkey brays, the horse laughs, the elephant sneezes, and the monkey hangs by the tail, all at the same time. What matters it if they have a room at the top of the house, containing one window and a cracked looking-glass, a table on three legs, and a rocking chair tied up with red tape and twine ends—what of it, so long as they sit down to dinner every day in company with a thousand guests, all Congressmen, and Congressmen's wives and daughters; and if, after dinner, they all promenade together and jostle each other in two small parlors, and a hall fifteen feet by forty? Some few of the visitors, however, moved about the house with the look of persons who had seen too much of a good thing, and who would be happier than ever in their lives before, when once more returned to the quiet of their comfortable though unpretending homes.

Whoever goes to Washington without seeing the President of the United States, runs the risk of being thought next to nobody. Accordingly, the White House being thrown open for the reception of visitors the day after my arrival, I did not fail to make my appearance there. It was a beautiful April morning dropped down into the early part of February, as I strolled through the grounds, and up the steps of the far-famed Presidential mansion; being in a mood to be pleased with everything, and especially with the great father of the universal Yankee nation.

But what is this I see before me at the threshold? Is it a spittoon? By my troth, an enormous one! A perfect monster in capacity, suggestive of quids of the very largest size, and a great many of them. A gentle hint, this, no doubt, to the stranger just arrived from Texas, or the Upper Mississippi, that he will please unpack his cheek before coming into the presence of democratic Majesty.

But here are more spittoons in the anteroom! It would seem, then, that it is not expected that the American people, on coming to pay their respects to their chief upper servant, should for a moment relinquish their right to chew tobacco whenever and wherever it may please them; and they are accordingly provided with conveniences for expectoration within five-and-forty feet of the foot of the throne. This is as it should be—and strongly democratic. If there be anything wrong about it, it is, perhaps, that there are not vessels of this kind enough to supply the demand for them; and I would most respectfully suggest that the principal avenue to the White House should be lined with rows of them, as the approaches to European palaces are set out with rare plants and flowers.

I saw the spittoons; but, as ill luck would have it, not the President. He sent word to the sovereign people, and their wives, who had called on him that morning, that he was too busy to see them. The guests, therefore, were obliged to entertain themselves as best they could with inspecting the Presidential parlors and upholstery. This they did pretty thoroughly. They admired the ceilings, the chandeliers, the chairs, the tables, the curtains; and gazed at the carpets, as Moloch at the golden pavement of heaven. Some of the ladies lingered before the mirrors, taking that opportunity to survey their *toilettes;* some of the gentlemen eyed the mahogany, and the sideboards ; and one demagogue I observed inquisitively looking up chimney.

After the survey of the premises, it remained only for the company to look at each other. This, also, was done. Everybody stared at everybody; and, finally, all either went home, or looked into the grounds to see the Presidential flock of fat turkeys. Next to the great Southern belle, a dashing young widow in ermine and point lace, and in possession, as it was whispered about, of an annual income of two hundred bales of cotton, there was one cock turkey which made the handsomest and proudest display of the morning. In fact, I was better pleased with his showing off, which was done in the very best style of turkeys, than with the widow's. His strut was regal; and the way in which he made himself big with feathers, quite took the hoop out of all the crinolines, causing them to look scarcely bigger than so many folded umbrellas. Nor did I fail to notice the propriety, since the spread eagle has possession of the national escutcheon, of maintaining in the grounds of the chief magistrate of the country this brother bird, with distended wings and tail, and throat red with gobbling.

CHAPTER III.

The Virginia Springs.

AFTER having crossed the mountains of Virginia by rail, the old-fashioned stage coach took me up a short distance from the Warm Springs; and, a few hours afterward, a smart crack of the whip under the flank of the off leader brought the carriage handsomely round to the door of the hotel. As I alighted, no sooner had my feet touched the ground, than I was recognized by one of the black boys, who had waited on me, two summers before, at the White Sulphur; and was at once claimed by him as "his gentle'um." The fellow was, indeed, in a perfect ecstasy over the arrival of "his gentle'um from York;" while I, seeing no difference in his wool from that of a dozen other negroes standing by, had not the slightest recollection of ever having enjoyed the pleasure of his acquaintance, and looked upon him simply as a darkey suddenly gone mad.

"Bery glad to see massa once more in de moun-t'ns," said he, rubbing his hands briskly, and grinning from ear to ear. "Do massa no remember Custopol ob de White Sulphur, two summers gone back?"

I looked again, and saw that it was, indeed, Custy. Could any other black boy in Virginia be so black as he? His nose was scarcely less flat than the pancakes he used to bring me at breakfast. His mouth was full half an inch in advance of it, and so large that, when he kissed any of the yellow girls, in going through the reel, the report was like that of a big popgun. His teeth were grinders all round; and, with his jawbone, a bold man could cut down as large a host of enemies as he could with that of an ass. But when it came to comparing foreheads, Custy was lacking there. In his brows there was no presence. The wool grew down over them; and, cut ever so close, it would have sufficed to throw them into the shade, were they not already blacker than any shadow. Custy's phrenological developments were to be sought for elsewhere—even to his heels. Moreover, though his shoulders were broad, his back was hollow, and his waist a mere finger bowl. So that when, on a Sunday, Custy drew his bands tight, and cocked his hat a little on one side of his head—in his bright yellow waistcoat, tall red cravat, and a gentleman's cast-off blue coat, set off with brass buttons, and cut with a broad roll in the collar—he was as jaunty a gallant as ever "picked" a banjo.

I went directly in to breakfast, being prepared for it by a drive outside the coach since daylight, and told Custopol to bring along his hoecakes.

"Nice ven'son steak, massa," said Custy.

"Very well," I replied; "hoecakes and venison steak."

"Butter made in de house, massa!"

"Exactly—hoecakes, and venison steak, and fresh butter."

"Hot milk?"

"No; give me the cold cream. No such cream as this in York, Custy!"

"Me believe dat. People must come back to Old Virginny for to see de right yaller milk."

"And the yellow girls, too, Custy?"

"He! he! he! ha! ha! ha!" replied my colored Adonis, and wiped the water out of his mouth on the edge of his apron.

But when Custopol laughed, I made it a rule to stop the conversation. His grinning was all very fine, and brought out his ivory, and the white of his eyes, to admiration; but when it came to laughing, I was always afraid lest he might so far forget himself as to blow his steam whistle, which would certainly bring down the whole house about my ears.

Venison steaks twice a day, and my black boy perpetually on the grin to see me eat them! Indeed, he would have been delighted to serve them as many times more; while his cakes, morning and evening, were as hot as the hearth from which they came. Bread, alone, answers a poor purpose; but on corn cakes, venison, and mountain air—with a drop of the dew, now and then—a man, whose conscience is easy, will as surely thrive as cows on clover. From the very first day of this regimen his ribs feel heavier; while on the piazza stand the scales, for the purpose of enabling him daily to note the happy progress he is making toward one hundred stone. The thin dyspeptic, on arriving in these mountains, no longer weighs his food, but himself; and, after every meal, kicks the beam one notch higher. If, then, at night, he will also give a boy a quarter to "pick" the banjo under his window, and sing "Going over Jordan," and "Jim crack Corn," he will end his day with perfect stomachic satisfaction, falling sound asleep in the very act of ha-ha-ing, and dreaming of nothing short of a heaven carved in ebony.

By the way, this fondness for being weighed is universal at these Springs; at each one of which there is a pair of balances standing not far from the front door of the hotel, and offering their convenience to the guests. Accordingly, every man and woman wishes to know how many pounds he, or she, has gained in the last twenty-four hours. Nine persons out of ten, here, can tell you their exact weight. Especially is it pleasing to see the eagerness of young mothers to know how fast their babies are growing; but I scarcely ever saw one who was strictly impartial at the trial. They were always disposed to give the little fellow credit for a half pound, or so, more than he was entitled to; would daily crowd up the beam; and sometimes make such announcements that, let the baby be ever so fat, one could not refrain from believing he had, besides, a brick in his cap. Some infants, on the other hand, would make no impression whatever upon the scales, and would have to be taken out until they were a week older; or, at least, had eaten their dinner. One thin, nervous gentleman, also, with a touch of the dyspepsia, could not be induced by any amount of persuasion to get into the scales, being apparently afraid to know how light he was. Ladies of a certain age, too, were rather shy of them. Once I saw a matron turned of forty, who, in a heedless moment, had ventured to take her seat under the beam, jump out of it, on the announcement of the number one hundred and ninety-nine, as if she had been shot. But some old gents, on the other hand, who used to sit about in easy, wide-bottomed chairs, were evidently well pleased at showing off the effect of their threescore years of good living—generally taking the opportunity of giving the name of the county in which they had been "raised," and mentioning the weight of their fathers before them.

Still—to return to my muttons—it must be confessed that, since the arrival of the French cook in these hills, there is a notable falling off in the pleasures of the table. Sambo was a better spit-turner. An outcast from the Palais Royal, where he served dinners at two francs per head, the *artiste*, who arrives in the central regions of Virginia, brings with him only the knowledge of a few tricks for cheapening dishes. His grand invention is to put all meats into the pot. His roast beef is first boiled, and then toasted. So is his roast mutton. A thorough-going socialist at heart, he has even gone so far, at some of the Springs, as to boil all his meats together in one cauldron; thereby reducing them all to an equality. The saddle of venison lies—alas! to think of it—cheek by jowl with ham, and a side of bacon. Beef must fraternize with veal, and exchange juices with it. Even the pig—little innocent!—is put into water, and parboiled. Shade of Charles Lamb! that he should no more be roasted! But it has come to this in the progress of civilization, and the greedy water is allowed to suck out half the juices which made the Chinaman's fingers so savory, when, by that happy accident, he pulled out the roasted pig from the burning house by the tail, and invented a dish, the memory of which, one would suppose, the latest posterity would not willingly let die.

I know the merits of the well-educated professor of the French kitchen; but the vagabond, who has found his way into the valleys of the Blue Ridge, has nothing of the professor about him, save his paper cap. He is homesick—*régrettant la patrie*—into the bargain; and, I have not a doubt, qualifies his soups with his tears. Let no man taste them. Certainly, he has either forgotten his French, or never knew it. The other day, the landlord, proud of the outlandish look of his list of dishes, and thinking, perhaps, to pay me a compliment, in intimating that I was acquainted with the French language, said to me:

"You can read this, I suppose, sir?"

"No," I was obliged to reply. "Really, I am unable to do it."

The landlord, having shown me up to room No. 14, the appearance of which was satisfactory, said he would send a boy to wait on me. It proved not to be Custopol, but a fellow about forty-five years of age, though still a boy in Southern parlance, and destined to remain such to the day of his death. He came with the official brush in hand, and, bowing, asked:

"Will massa have his coat brushed?"

"You are to be my boy, then?" I inquired in return.

"Yes. And will massa have his coat brushed?"

"What is your name?"

"They call me Sully."

"Sully!" I exclaimed, taken suddenly with a fit of abstraction at hearing a name which had not saluted my ears since the days when, a sophomore, I was drilled in history by the college professor. "Sully! You then were once a prime minister of state! You were a duke! You were the favorite of one of the most heroic, and the most amiable kings of modern times! You were his ambassador at the English court, in the days of the great Queen Bess! And, Sully, you rogue, repeat to me some of the fine things you whispered in the greedy ear of Her Majesty!"

The Sully before me, who stood still in his shoes, without moving a hair's breadth, nor scarcely so much as winking, opened his mouth for a reply; but all he could repeat was the question:

"Will massa have his coat brushed?"

By this time, of course, I had become convinced

that it was no use trying to teach "dis nigger" history, or to persuade him that he had ever been anybody else than the boy Sully, who was "raised" in Norfolk, and belonged to a citizen there who kept an oyster shop—

> "Oh! raking 'mongst the oyster beds,
> To me it was but play"—

and who, when shellfish were out of season, hired out his servant to wait, and brush at the Springs.

After getting this short narrative—and it was about all that the boy knew respecting his history—it remained only to reply to his so-many-times-repeated interrogatory:

"Yes, Sully; you may brush my coat."

Sully, accordingly, brushed my coat—a task he continued to do daily. He brushed my shoes, also, and performed the service of my room. When he had no other work on hand, it was his duty, and his pleasure, to look after me. He brought me a match to light my cigar, if, by chance, I wanted one. He brought me my hat, my gloves, my stick. And, finally, he stood over me, at table, with a peacock's tail in his hand, to keep the flies off, when, as brushing was his favorite summer vocation, he sometimes with the tip of his feathers also brushed my tea and coffee.

As the song has it:

> "When I was young, I had to wait
> On massa's table, hand de plate;
> I pass de bottle when he's dry,
> And brush away de blue-tail fly."

But if Sully had few or no materials for the biographer, to the observer of men and things he presented a person of a size sufficient to awaken attention, and justify description. He was constructed on the principle of the curve. With nothing angular about him, he was as round as an apple, and everywhere came full circle. He was, by all odds, the fat boy of the establishment. Of course, he had no waist, and was under the natural necessity of wearing suspenders. His skin was so full, that, but for the perspiration which dropped from every pore the moment he put himself in motion, it was plain there would be a crack somewhere. He must have been in the habit of frequently opening his oyster and his mouth at the same point of time, otherwise nature could never have attained to such fulness of form, and so universally brought all her lines round till they met. And then, what was gained in winter was not lost in summer; because, he coming up at the commencement of the warm season into the pure air of the mountains, the fat of the bivalve, which had once settled on his ribs, remained there the year round.

Sully had not the least particle of vanity in his composition; at least, in studying him carefully for a fortnight, I could see no sign of any. He, accordingly, did not imitate white folks—was *sui generis.* This utter lack of vanity showed itself not only in his manners, but also in his dress. His clothes were evidently all originally made to fit his own person, and were not the thrown-aside garments of a gentleman. They, consequently, were the farthest possible removed from *chic.* There was no dash in the cravat, no fashion in the coat, and not so much as a bright red, or yellow thread in his whole wardrobe. All was either plain white, or black. Or, at least, if there were any warmer tints, they were so subdued, and ran so naturally into the two cold colors, that the prevailing tone of modest dulness was never marred. The boy's fancy seemed never to have risen higher than the simplest black and white check. This he always donned clean—in no sense could it be said that he sported it—on a Sunday.

Sully's dress corresponded with his disposition, which was not gay. I cannot conceive of his ever having danced the "breakdown." If he had ever attempted it, it must have been when, on some great festal occasion, he so far departed from his usual sobriety as to take a little whiskey. Nor could he touch the banjo. I don't believe he had ever been half a dozen times to a colored ball since he was a small boy; nor, except on rare occasions, was he ever seen looking in at the windows of the saloon in the hotel upon waltz, or cotillon. If he could only go to bed early, he wanted no other amusement, unless, indeed, it were to get up late. He, however, could doze tolerably well, even on his feet, and engaged in his ordinary avocations.

I never saw Sully make a gesture but once, and then it was entirely in keeping. It was not a pointed gesture. He did not lay his thumb against the end of his nose, with little finger projecting, nor, with extended index, count off his arguments on his digits. Much less was there any violence indicated in the motion; no doubling of the fist; no beating the breast; no rapping of the knuckles on a table. But Sully deliberately raised his hand, and deliberately brought it down again, in both instances describing a semicircle. The movement was as round as himself.

And the occasion on which Sully made this gesture was, when I asked him a question respecting his wife.

"Sully," I inquired one day, "are you a married boy?"

"Yes, massa; 'tis now gone two years."

"Picked out a young girl for your wife, Sully?"

"No; I took an old gal—a free woman—born de same year dat was me."

"And how do you like it—the married life?"

"Right well."

"But suppose you, and your wife should disagree?"

"Massa," said Sully—and it was then he made his gesture—"we should quit!"

CHAPTER IV.

Five Unprotected Ladies.

FIVE ladies, unattended by a gentleman, arrived at the Sweet Springs, in the same coach as myself. They were apparently all of the same age, and looked enough alike to be sisters. Two of them, certainly, had formerly accepted of husbands; the others, probably, not. Yet, being helpmates one of the other, they got on safely, and everywhere had their own way, spite of men, and fate. Their very number gave them force, and great advantages over a single unprotected female.

On the road, they were, indeed, not a little anxious about their baggage, fearing lest it might be cut off from the coach by robbers, while the driver was thinking of something else; and whenever we stopped, one of them, at least, generally managed to get out, for the purpose of seeing that their trunks rode comfortably. All their bandboxes were on the top of the coach, excepting one of considerable size

2*

containing caps, and another smaller one filled with homœopathic medicines, both of which were carefully carried in their laps. Whenever, therefore, the road was a little rough—and it was by no means always smooth—one eye was kept out of the window to see if, by chance, some of the boxes might not be tossed over the railing. The ladies, themselves, stood the jolting pretty well, their thoughts being mostly fixed on their valuables outside; and, indeed, the chief pleasure experienced on their travels seemed to be the satisfaction it gave them, at every stopping place, to learn from personal observation, confirmed by the testimony of the driver, that all their travelling effects were safe. That both they themselves, and all they had, should get unharmed to the end of their journey, was surely a cause for the very greatest satisfaction.

So it turned out. They were all delivered over to the landlord of the inn which had been fixed upon, months before, as the spot where they would pass the summer, safe and sound, themselves, their trunks, and their boxes—even to their umbrellas, parasols, and sticks. But I mistake—they had no sticks.

Once, however, on the journey, they had been pretty badly frightened. There was then running on the road a line of coaches in opposition to that of the mail; and, in consideration of a very considerable abatement in the price of passage, the ladies had ventured to take seats in one of the former. But the drivers sharing the spirit of rivalry between the proprietors, the Jehu of the "Lucy Dashwood"—in which the ladies had taken passage—had, from the start, made up his mind that he would take the snapper off the lash of the "old line" driver, before reaching the end of his journey. Accordingly, he managed to keep close behind his rival until they came to a place where there was room enough for a race. The main road itself, just there, was narrow, and had some sharp turns in it, so that quick driving over it required pretty steady rein, and horses well in hand. But along its side ran a creek, the bed of which also furnished a track to a driver who, at the same time, was not a bad pilot. Therefore, on reaching this place, the hindmost whip determined that he would either tip over, or get the lead. Seeing that his opponent kept to the road which was dry, he boldly dashed into the wet one.

"Good gracious!" exclaimed the ladies, all at once; and, but for being held fast, one or more of them would certainly have jumped out into the creek. Meanwhile, splash down through the torrent went coach and horses, making the water fly in at the windows as if it had been a violent rain storm. The ladies dropped both cap box and medicine chest, in order to clasp their hands in consternation. But before they had time to wring them, the horses, with the lash around the ears of the leaders, sprang out of the creek at a bound. The small boulders in the road where it left the water leaped out of it as if they had been frogs; the good, stout vehicle shook in every timber, but came out unbroken; the harness held fast, and the horses, gaining once more the smooth *terra firma*, rattled down the hill, with tails in the wind, and their dull rivals far behind.

Immediately on being set down at the inn, the five ladies took possession of the landlord, and carried him off with them, to look at his rooms; and, according to the account of the matter afterward given to me, he did not get out of their hands without some rather hard usage. They did not like his accommodations. The rooms first offered them they scarcely deigned to look at; but, after going over the whole house, and holding a consultation upon every vacant chamber in it, they finally came back to those they had so disdainfully refused at first, but which, by that time, had been taken by another party. So they were obliged to go over the whole ground a second time. One of the sisters wanted to have a bed which no man had ever slept in! Another insisted on being settled in the new part of the building, lest there should be animalculæ in the walls of the old. In all the rooms they pulled up the bed-clothes, and peered anxiously, but knowingly, into the holes in the four posts. They demanded a rocking chair, with a cushion to it, in each one of their chambers. And, finally, one thing was absolutely indispensable—the curtains at the windows were an insufficient protection; they must be reënforced by shutters, made by the carpenter.

"But, ladies," replied the good-natured landlord, "there is not a carpenter to be had in the mountains. If you think the curtains insufficient, you must pin up something."

"Indeed, we have nothing to pin up!" rejoined they all. Finally, however, seeing there was no remedy, this suggestion met with their approbation; and, either with or without what they wanted, or thought they wanted, the five ladies were, at last, all settled in their chambers.

But it was not more than ten minutes after they had taken possession of their apartments before one of the ladies rang the landlord up again. Her chimney smoked.

"That can't be, madam," said the host, "for there is no fire in it."

"So much the worse, if it smokes when there is no fire! What, then, will it do, when, on a rainy day, there are a couple of backlogs on, and I sit down to warm my feet by the fire?"

"But, madam, I don't perceive that it does smoke."

"I do. I smell it. And when there are fires built all about the house, I am sure that this chimney will smoke violently. There are now several gentlemen with their cigars on the piazza, and their smoke comes down through this fireplace. I smell it."

The landlord was a man of too much experience to argue long against the testimony of one of the seven senses—particularly in the case of a lady arrived at such years of discretion. He therefore quietly gave up his argument; the lady her chamber; and so the peace between them was not broken.

Only one thing remained to give them any uneasiness—and that was their travelling bag. For, on the journey, some inconsiderate person had remarked that he believed one of the outside passengers was just recovering from an attack of the small pox, caught at Staunton, where there had recently been several cases of it.

"Oh, our travelling bag!" exclaimed she who seemed to be rather the bellwether of the party. "The man has been sitting on our travelling bag!"

He had, in fact, been sitting, at one time, with his back against the unlucky piece of baggage; and it very naturally followed that he had given it the small pox.

What was to be done? The bag contained a part of their several wardrobes which could no more be dispensed with than shutters to the windows. What in the world was to be done?

"Have you ever been vaccinated?" first asked each of the other.

"Yes, I have been vaccinated," was the reply all round.

"Have you been revaccinated?"

"Yes, I have been revaccinated."

"Then let me see the scar."

The scars were, some of them, hard to find; but, when found, were all pronounced satisfactory. And after much debating of the point, it was finally decided that, if the bag should be well smoked, and then its contents washed, a globule from phial marked 44 being put in the tub, they would run very little, if any, risk of taking the contagion.

It is more than probable that they escaped this peril also; for there was some reason for believing that the traveller who made the remark about the outside passenger having this disease, was an evil-disposed person who could not resist the malicious pleasure of quizzing these respectable, but unprotected ladies. If so, he deserved the severest condemnation, and will no doubt find his reward reserved for him in the future.

At the close of the bathing season, on returning to the inn at the "Sweet," I inquired of the major-domo if any of the "five ladies" had had the small pox before leaving, and was glad to learn that, up to that time, the disease had not made its appearance among them. They had passed the summer, on the whole, to their satisfaction, though, on being weighed the morning of their departure, it was found that, after all their endeavors to the contrary, they had not gained a single pound. But if they had not gained, so had they not lost anything. And their dresses would not need altering.

A good many suggestions, the manager informed me, he had received from them, in the course of the summer, as to how the accommodations of his house might be improved against another season. They had, indeed, planned an entirely new cast of the whole establishment, adding an additional wing to the house, removing the stables, changing the fences, turning the current of the creek, and doing a good deal of painting and whitewashing, both indoors and out. They had, also, closely calculated, with slate and pencil, the value of the property—houses, lands, baths, and live stock—besides making an estimate of the gross and net receipts of the establishment; and, by their own showing, had run the proprietor in debt for betterments to full three times the value of his estate.

To all these suggested improvements, therefore, the innkeeper had gravely shaken his head; and, in winding up his story, he further intimated to me that, in his opinion, persons, whose wants at a hotel were the most numerous and unreasonable, did not always live any better at home than those who were more easily pleased, and took things as they came.

"However," added he, "they were very worthy ladies; and, no doubt, had been accustomed to have their own way at home—everything pat—and just so. But our servants could not get along with them at all. Poor Polly's head — she's the maid — was turned before they had been in the house a week; and Sam, the small boy who waited on them at table, was fairly brought down, the day before their departure, with what is called here the 'break-bone fever.'"

CHAPTER V.

The Warm Springs.

THE view from the top of the Warm Springs mountain is said to be the most beautiful of any in this part of the Alleghanies. Although, in either boldness of outline or grace of detail, it cannot by any means be compared with the famous scenes of the Alps or the Pyrenees, still it will well repay the trouble of the ascent. You climb to a rocky crag, whence there is a panoramic view of summits and intervening vales, far and wide, until the distant horizon is lost in mists, or ranges so remote as scarcely to be distinguished from the clouds. The shadows of passing masses of vapor lie about in black spots upon the green foliage of the forests, which cover both mountains and valleys. For everywhere here is this green veil drawn over the face of nature. Only the narrow streams, meandering through the vales, send up a silver gleam; or, here and there, a cultivated hillside is yellow with grain; or the limestone road glistens, as, like a scaly monster, it winds its coils around the breasts of the mountains; or, far below, a whitewashed cottage, with its curl of blue smoke, lends its brilliant contrast to gardens and meadows. And yet, at second look, you observe that, while the nearer summits are overspread with the numerous variations of green, from the white birch's delicate tints to those of the sombre cedar, there are on the remoter ranges such great numbers of the yellow pine, stripped of its foliage by the preceding winter's fires, and showing only its bark, that a purple hue prevails in many localities, almost deep enough to remind one of the heathery hills of Scotland.

Passing from the general view to the examination of details, you see below you, on the western side, the valley of the Warm Springs. It is as lovely as a vale in Vallambrosa—long, and moderately narrow, with several gaps in the mountains on either side, and through one of them passes out toward the west the small stream which flows down from near the head of the valley. By its side runs a carriage road, along which are scattered a few habitations; the little cluster of buildings at the bath being the principal ones. The meadows are not so low but that you can watch the mowers as they swing the scythe, or the haymakers piling up the thick stacks; and so far are the undulations of sound conveyed through the clear, elastic air, that you distinctly hear the sheep-bell tinkling from neighboring summits, the lowing of cattle on the cultivated hillsides, and even the shrill call and answer of quail whistling to each other from still lower grain fields.

The mountain situated opposite you, and on the other side of the valley, has its sides very evenly ribbed, or furrowed, the upper half being thickly wooded, and the lower under tillage. Its ridge is a gracefully undulating line; and so sharp is it that the topmost trees have the appearance of being set upon it as a fringe. When in the afternoon the sun has somewhat declined from the zenith, only the treetops between the furrows on the declivities are directly illumined by its rays, while those in the furrows themselves are dark with shade. The tall woods, also, that skirt the cultivated half of the mountain side, cast long shadows upon the green of the pastures and the yellow of the grain fields; while single elms and chestnuts, here and there, project their profiles far down into the still sun-lit valley. To this unequal distribution of light and shade the landscape owes its most pleasing effects.

Indeed, it is the charm of this scenery, that it is never seen twice the same. With every change of light and shade, in different positions of the sun, from various points of observation, in different states of the atmosphere, the aspects of this mountainous and wooded nature vary perpetually. The beholder is constantly discovering some new features in the landscape, graces before overlooked, a more true and significant expression. The mountains are a very Proteus—a chameleon, rather—and their tints change while one is looking at them. For now the distances are a deep blue, and now they are purple. The sun lights up, at one moment, the round-topped hills covered with flowering chestnuts; at another, the rays being withdrawn, the hollows of the valleys are dark as evening. Large white clouds gradually form above the higher summits, and, one by one, float off into midheaven. The mists rise, and again are dissipated. At high noon, there is not a shadow among the whole multitude of mountains; while, at early morn and evening, every peak, and crag, and rock, and lone-standing tree has its reflected image, and the forms of the landscape are multiplied twofold. This hour, the vapors, driven by the winds, are chasing each other, like wandering spirits, athwart the sky and over the mountain tops; the rain clouds gathering, dash against the summits, and break over the valleys; the thunder rattles from one end of the heavens to the other, shivering, with its bolts, the monarchs of the forest, and illumining with frequent flashes the untimely obscurity. The next, the winds are hushed; the sun bursts brightly out of the clouds, which roll away to the eastward; the bow of promise, spanning the heavens, binds together the distant mountain tops; the wet foliage of the trees glistens in the sunlight; and, at evening, the last rays of declining day spread the hue of roses over the round clouds which, here and there, elevate their gorgeous heads above the horizon. Then, in their turn, the gorgeous clouds losing the tints too fair to last, the stars light up their fires on the highest peaks; the valleys are peacefully folded in the mantle of evening; and the grim mountains sleep.

There is no luxury in water greater than that of the Warm Springs bath.

That one of these fountains used for bathing is protected by an amphitheatre, having a circular opening in the roof, for light and ventilation. You undress in an anteroom, and descend by a flight of steps into the pool, which is some forty feet in diameter. The water, generally, is about five feet deep, but may be made higher, or lower, to suit the stature of the bather—the rule being that it shall come up to his chin. A rope is stretched across the bath, and upon that one may hang, or lean. The temperature of the water is about ninety-six degrees of Fahrenheit around the edge of the pool, and ninety-eight in the centre; where, especially, it comes gushing up with innumerable gas bubbles from between the stones which cover the bottom.

On entering, everybody feels perfectly well-to-do in this bath—however he may do in the world. The water readily fraternizes with the bather's blood, both being of about the same temperature. One can promenade, or swim; he can loll on the rope, or sit meditative on the steps. In either of these cases, he is all under water, except his head, and he feels as though he could never willingly get out of it. This is, in quality, exceedingly buoyant; so that the individual, too large to get about in the air with entire comfort, here feels not much heavier than a feather, and gay enough to dance hornpipes. It is so soft that the roughest hide will seem smooth, as if anointed with myrrh and frankincense. It is, also, perfectly transparent; and the light, streaming through the circular opening in the roof, not only fills a portion of the pool with the gorgeous colors of the prism, but also furnishes the stones lying at the bottom with tints, as if they were all precious—rubies, pearls, and emeralds.

Steeped in this delightful element, the traveller forgets the aches of the road; the rheumatic feels the pains in his bones assuaged; the cripple is conscious in his chords that they are relaxing; the nervous invalid is soothed; and all, no longer oppressed by ills, whether of the body or the mind, revel in the most delicious sensations, or are transported in day-dreams into far-off, happy planets, where the inhabitants live in warm water.

But perhaps the greatest charm of the bath is its bubbles. These come up, here and there, as they will; sometimes single, then in pairs, and again in clusters—like the going off of a bouquet of rockets. As you stand up in the water, those rising from between the stones directly beneath you attach themselves, as if drawn by some magnetic influence, to your legs; and then creeping up your body, produce a species of titillation the most exquisite, surely, ever felt. They tickle you as if it were fun for them, too.

If you give the little things a serious thought, you cannot persuade yourself that they are not animated, happy existences. As they rise to the surface over the whole bath, those directly in the rays of the sun show, even on starting from the bottom, the prismatic colors, the violet predominating; while those in the shade flash through the water like balls of silver. They all come trembling, quivering, dancing up to the surface. And when they gain it, the round ball becomes a half sphere, and floats for an instant on the water. It is as though the joyous, sparkling being, after its brief dance of life from bottom to top of the water, were given one instant of more perfectly conscious delight, ere bursting into void and nought. For it is only a half-dozen seconds that the bubble reposes on the water, though some are longer lived than others; and when it breaks, the expansive force of the rupture drives a tiny circle outward with infinite grace, but quickly to disappear in the level smoothness of the surface; or oftener, mingling with other kindred circles in lines of intricate and confused harmony.

But you have time, first, to observe that the bubbles floating in the sunlight have in their centre a point of red light flashing like Mars in the heavens; while those in the shade are lit up with the softer ray of those stars whose light is white. These are the souls of the bubbles, no doubt, that burn with fires only less purely intellectual than those which shine out of the eyes of man, or beast.

Though creations of a moment's vain endurance—mere bubbles on the water—these, too, burn their tiny tapers in God's temple, as well as do the priests before their altars. Myriads upon myriads of them, without ceasing, here rise and shine, as wonderful in formation as the sun and moon; all obedient, in form and motion, to the great laws of the universe; each perfect in its kind, and without spot. And yet how few of the multitudes who lave their weary or enfeebled limbs in this pool of healing—alas! how few—ever care for these poor bubbles!

The manners here are those of the South, and decidedly suited to the summer watering place. There is nothing townish about them. All the men and women seem as much at home as if they had been brought up here, mingling in rustic scenes with natural grace, unconstrained, simple, and happy, without too much excitement. If a lady finds it convenient to dine in a morning dress, she is at liberty to do so. There is no objection to calico at a picnic. The evening's dance will, indeed, bring out a few short sleeves and low necks, where arms and shoulders are so very pretty; but all sorts of styles are admissible; and, while the gardens are rifled of roses, pinks, and honeysuckles, to twine in the young girls' tresses, I scarcely ever saw an artificial flower in the mountains. Sometimes, the first day after her arrival, a lady will come down to dinner looking sufficiently stiff and uncomfortable; but the next, she also gives her stays a little more string, leaves off the heavy silk, and begins to learn some of the artless grace of nature in these vales.

At the Northern spas, most of the ladies look as though they were not out of town. Their style of dress, not being expressly adapted to the bathing place, like that of English ladies, reminds one constantly of balls in the Fifth Avenue, and of the boxes of the Academy of Music. There is as much whalebone around the heart of the belle, in a hop at the "Ocean House," or the "United States," as if the public room of a summer tavern were an Almack's, or the drawing room of Queen Victoria. The graces which attend her steps are not rustic, surely.

The manners of our Southern friends have a peculiar adaptation to the spas, from the fact that their life at home is mainly rural. This gives them an air of naturalness at these places, and enables them, also, to pass their time pleasantly, without bringing thither the routine of morning calls and card leaving, the giving of balls and dinners, with formal invitations, and refreshments sent by express from town.

Has not, perhaps, the presence of the colored race at the Southern baths something to do with this air of simple, natural, hearty enjoyment of the country, which prevails there? Sambo on his travels, in his best doublet and hose, riding on the top of stage coaches, smitten at every different bath with the face of some new Phyllis, and realizing, at last, the fond burden of his song of "Oh, carry me back to old Virginny," wears a face in which the wrinkles are, none of care, and all of merriment. The carbonic acid he drinks in the mineral waters has upon him the effect of the exhilarating gas; while the lively air of the hills makes him as cheery as though he had been drinking whiskey toddy. He takes his summer life easily; and, in his simplicity, enjoys the succession of passing events—though but the arrival of the stage coach, or the simple carrying a glass of mint julep with a straw in it to his master—to such a degree that these Springs, constantly giving back the picture of his grinning face, might better be called the Laughing Waters than those of the Upper Mississippi.

On the other hand, the Irish immigrant, who mostly performs the service of our Northern hotels, carries in his face no sign of summer-day satisfaction —much less, any excess of radiance to reflect on society. Patrick has no banjo; and can no more sing a song than a Jew by the waters of Babylon. The donkey that stands at the hotel door has much more drollery in his head than this exile from beyond seas, who is a mere scrub, and scullion, not even possessed of wit enough to make a good flunky. His mulish physiognomy suggests no visions of rural enjoyment, and the life Arcadian. On the contrary, the very sight of these coarse-handed waiters, and wenches unkempt, is enough to disenchant all the illusions with which one may have come down into the country respecting the purity of life in the midst of nature, and the chances of meeting nymphs in the woods. Who, forsooth, ever saw a naiad in fountains when Bridget was drinking at them?

It really does make a difference, and that in favor of the Southern spa, this thrumming of the banjo in the evening twilight, together with an occasional melody heard from under the gum trees—for banjos are as numerous in Virginia, if not quite as romantic, as guitars in Spain. And one "picked" under my windows, on the evening of the full moon in the month of August, I remember with especial pleasure. No sooner had the musician—I think his name was Pompey—struck up his tune, than all the colored amateurs within hearing flocked around. At first, two or three small black boys, unable to restrain their heels, began to shuffle on the pavement with might and main. But straightway an older negro, crying to these small boys to get out of the way, and, at the same time, frightening them off the walk by blowing a low note from his steam whistle, took up himself the jig. He wore a slouched felt hat, turned up, however, both before and behind, like the ancient cocked one, and which, for band, was tied around with a long gray garter, that hung down over his left shoulder. Having on a heavy pair of boots, worn outside his breeches, he at once made the pavement ring; scraping it furiously with his soles, and knocking it sharply and rapidly with his heels. All the while the double joints in his knees were in full play, as also his shoulders; and, in fact, every bone and muscle in his whole body. Now, his feet were thrown nearly as high as his head, and his arms a good deal higher. Now, his legs were extended like a dancing girl's; and, again, the hinges in his knees were bent double. From time to time, I could see his eyes, when he turned them upward, flash with the excitement of the fling, though in the dark; his ivory shone through his mouth like the moon out of clouds; the half-suppressed cry of triumph—a sort of horse laugh—would occasionally break from his throat; and when, at length, he came to stamp out the finale of the "breakdown," the blowing of his steam whistle might have been heard at the distance of half a mile.

A public table is a very good place for showing off the bringing up of children. One small boy, four or five years of age, who had a seat directly opposite mine, one day gave me an opportunity of making an observation or two on the effects of the discipline of the Virginia nursery. He was a determined-looking little fellow, evidently accustomed to carrying things at home with a high hand, and kicking all the little negroes about, right and left.

He began his dinner with a dish of almonds, which happened to be standing before him, and at which he made a sudden grab the moment he was in his chair. No squirrel ever put nuts into his mouth faster than he did for about a couple of minutes, at the end of which time he began filling his pockets.

At length, the waiter asked him what he would have for dinner.

"Give me chicken," said he, sharply.

The chicken was brought.

"Give me jelly."

The currant jelly, also, was brought.

But, very soon, something going wrong, the youth began to cry. His mother, however, appeased him; and, stopping his noise, he called in a mild tone of voice for some milk.

"Give me milk."

This furnished, he did not withdraw his nose from the cup until it had touched the bottom; and when he did, there was still a drop pendent at its tip. This, however, fell off, as, throwing his head back against the chair, he drew a loud, long breath, as if his dinner were done, and he himself completely exhausted.

But a few moments' rest revived him, when he "returned to his muttons." Yet, nothing within sight suiting him, he sat, for the next five minutes, grumbling and whining, and in a humor decidedly unfavorable to the digestion of his almonds, chicken, jelly, and milk. But, at length, having made himself and his parents sufficiently uncomfortable, he knew what he wanted, and cried out, boldly:

"Give me 'lasses!"

"Molasses, Sammy!" replied his father. "You don't want molasses at dinner."

This paternal reproof brought the blood into the face of the heir, and, gathering up all the strength of his lungs for one burst of wrath, he bawled out, high above the clatter of knives and forks:

"'Lasses! 'lasses! corn-dodger, and 'lasses!"

The molasses was produced—if for no other purpose, to stop the young wretch's mouth. But corn-dodger being a breakfast cake, he was cajoled into substituting a piece of bread for it. This he now amused himself with working around in the molasses until the bread was well soaked through, and more or less broken to pieces. How then to get these fragments into his mouth, was the next question. A spoon did not altogether suit him; and, finally, in went the fingers. These carried him successfully through the job; though, at the end of it, his face was as well smeared, from ear to ear, as if he had been sucking at the bunghole of the original hogshead. He was now told to wipe his face on his napkin; but I think he did it on the table cloth.

To all appearances, the little gourmand was satiated. He leaned back in his chair, braced his feet against the table, and seemed as quiet as if he had been the fattest boy in the State, instead of being, as he was, as lean as a stick.

But he was not through his dinner yet. Giving the rickety table a sudden push with his feet, which overturned a good-sized dish of custards, he resumed his upright position, and cried out:

"Beef—give me beef!"

"Oh, sonny!" exclaimed the mother, "you have eaten enough."

"No, no, no!" was the indignant reply. "Give me beef! give me beef!"

What was to be done with the little rascal? He kicked, squirmed, threw up his napkin, and still cried for beef. He would have it.

Well, the beef, too, was brought. But he wouldn't touch it—didn't want it—and sat pouting with one finger in his mouth. In fact, he could eat no more. But as nobody said a word to him, he was the more indignant; and, bursting into a rage, he threw the plate containing the beef into his father's lap, that containing the remainder of the molasses into his mother's, and himself, at the same time, under the table.

"Cæsar," called out the father, "take away this blackguard!"

And, before Sammy had time to catch his breath, and scream twice, Cæsar had him out of the dining hall.

Little Sammy was, indeed, an exceptional child; but I have seen his yokefellow in these mountains. The one was in the highest class of society; the other, in the lowest. One day, when I was going by stage coach from the White Sulphur to the Sweet Springs, the driver took up by the roadside a couple of natives, having with them a child about four years of age. They were of the most vulgar order of persons to be met with in this, or any other of the States; foul in language, and not clean in appearance, both half tipsy, and disposed to be loquacious. But without further description of them, suffice it to say that the child was a little monster, being of almost twice the size natural for his years, and having the manners of a boy approaching his teens. Already, he had taken to the bottle, and sucked whiskey as another child would pap. The little barbarian also imitated his parents in another bad habit—he swore like a pirate. I did not see him chew tobacco; but doubt not he will smoke his "long nine" before he is a couple of years older. The only way of keeping him quiet was to ply him with sugar candy, and give him, now and then, a taste of the whiskey. But at last, being tired of the motion of the carriage, and out of sorts from the regimen he had adopted, he swore, at one of the stopping places, that he would go no farther.

"I no go beyond dis place, nohow," said he to his parents. "See you both d——d fust!"

Children, whether of the rich, or the poor, are not too well brought up in this country. In those states of Europe which have made the greatest progress in civilization, especially in England, the care of children is much more methodical, and painstaking, than in this newer part of the world. English children are provided with simpler food, suited to their years, and are not allowed to partake of the stimulating diet of their elders. The bone and sinew of the tall Scotchman come from the oat porridge he ate when a boy. British children are kept in subjection to rules; they are made regularly to say their prayers, and the catechism; they are early instructed by tutors, and governesses; and afterward, the boys are well whipped at Eton. But our "Young America" enjoys quite too much infantile independence; is too much left to servants and negroes; gets his religion from the Sunday school—which is, I fear, a poor substitute for parental supervision and the catechizing of the parson; uses his leading strings as a slow match—*un mechon*—to light his cigars with; makes a byword of "Does your mother know you're out?" and, first thing you know, joins the Order of the "Know Nothings," for which, indeed, he has every qualification.

CHAPTER VI.

The White Sulphur.

IN the height of the season, there are a hundred arrivals a day at the White Sulphur. Then, when nobody can get accommodations, everybody will insist on being there; for, in the month of August, the most beautiful ladies of Virginia and the South hold their court of love at this fountain; and, their fame going abroad through the mountains, the guests of the other Springs hasten to this centre of attraction. All the generals and judges of the Southern country, too, then come to drink at these white waters. Nobody is of a lower grade than a colonel; and, to be called esquire, would argue a man of doubtful consideration.

To the Northerner, this sounds a little singular; and, if he happens to be a peaceful scholar, for example, who has scarcely pulled a trigger in his life, and knows only so much of arms as is contained in the

"Arma virumque——"

of the poet, it is not without a certain degree of surprise, and a keen sense of the ludicrous, that he hears himself respectfully dubbed a colonel.

But not even the being addressed by the very highest titles, will, at this part of the season, save a single man the necessity of sleeping—two in a chamber. There are no adequate accommodations for all these fine ladies and gentlemen. At night, the floors of drawing rooms and parlors are strewn with mattresses; and lucky is the guest who can secure one. Trunks are piled up, ceiling high, in the halls and passages; so that, excepting the fortunate inmates of the pretty private cottages, the thousand and one visitors at the White Sulphur are, of all men, by no means the most miserable, but, probably, the most uncomfortable.*

One August morning, as I was standing in the doorway of the office, a well-dressed gentleman drove up in a buggy, and, getting out, asked for a room.

"We cannot accommodate you, sir," said the clerk, looking at the stranger with an air of disinterested unconcern.

* A new hotel has since been erected.

"But you can give me a mattress, or a sofa?" was the confident rejoinder.

"Impossible! not one left; and the last three chairs in the house taken half an hour ago!"

"Boy," said the rejected, but not disconcerted new comer, turning his quid from one cheek to the other, at the same time that he turned on his heel toward a servant, "unstrap my trunk."

"It really is of no use, sir," continued the clerk, calmly; "we cannot accommodate you."

"Carry my trunk under that oak tree, yonder," no less quietly added the stranger, and still addressing the black boy.

"Now," said he, sitting down on the trunk, which had been deposited under the protection of the branches, "fetch my buffalo robe; and I'll be d——d if I can't sleep here!"

This proof of pluck was an indirect appeal to the generous and hospitable sentiments which no true Virginian could withstand. There was a general clapping of hands on the utterance of this Diogenic resolution to take things as they came, and the luck of the pot with them; and one of the bystanders immediately stepping forward, politely offered to share his quarters with the tenant of the buffalo robe, who, accordingly, instead of living under an oak, like a Druid, now found himself the fortunate possessor of an apartment in one of the prettiest cottages on the grounds.

In the very height of the season there is no such thing as dining satisfactorily at some of the Springs, however well a person may fare there at all other times. Then, you fee the waiters, and still they bring you nothing. Poor fellows, they have nothing to bring! for the flour has given out; the cows have been milked dry; the mutton has run off into the mountains; and the chief cook has gone distracted! If you can manage to seize upon a bit of beef, and a slice of bread, 'tis your main chance, and hold on to it. Do not run any risks in looking about for vegetables, much less for side dishes, or pepper, or salt. For, while you are vainly endeavoring to accomplish impossibilities, some light-fingered waiter, under pretence of changing your plate, will run off with your only chance of a dinner.

The scene presents a most ludicrous struggle for bones, and cold potatoes. Or, rather, it is fearful to witness such a desperate handling of the knife; to see so many faces red with rage at getting nothing; and ladies' cheeks pale with waiting; and starving gourmands looking stupefied into the vacuum of the platters before them; and disappointed dyspeptics leaving the table with an expression on their faces of "I'll go hang myself." Add, besides, to what one sees, that which he hears—the maledictions heaped liberally upon the heads of cook, and provider; the clatter of what knives and forks succeed in getting brought into action; the whistling and roaring of Sambo, and the rattling of his heels; with, now and then, an awful crash of chinaware, a slide of plates, or an avalanche of whips and custards; for, where there are several dozens of waiters running up and down the hall, like race horses, there must be occasional collisions; and these, again, lead to fights, at least once, or more, in the season, when a couple of strapping black boys knock each other's noses flatter, and make their mutual wool fly. Truly, the Frenchman who dines on the hair of his mustache, and the end of his toothpick, in front of the *Café de Paris*, is a lucky fellow, and has something under his jacket, compared with these boarders at two dollars per diem.

But it is still worse dining, when it rains. The ancient roofs of some of these halls and piazzas are not made of caoutchouc; and you cannot then sit at meat without two black boys at your back—one to keep off the flies, and the other to hold over your head an umbrella. There is a good excuse for the soup being thin on such days. 'Tis, in fact, mere rain water, with, possibly, a fly, or two, in it.

All the doctors lay down the rule, that the patient

must drink mineral waters on an empty stomach; and, by my troth, it is easy following it, during the height of the season, at some of these Springs. That organ is rarely so much occupied in its legitimate business as to be in an unfit state to receive a glass from the fountain. It is said that Chinamen, when hard pushed for other articles of food, can subsist tolerably well on water diet; and, in spending the month of August here, one comes gradually to comprehend how the thing can be done.

"Eat a little milk, a little mush, or a very thin soup," said the mineral-water doctor, at one of the Springs, after he had looked at my tongue, and was still gravely holding me by the pulse, "and drink the water *ad libitum*."

"It is well to diet a little, while drinking the spring water," said the landlord to me, soon afterward, in the course of some conversation with him.

"They both agree in their views," said I to myself; "and what is sworn to by two disinterested witnesses ought certainly to be true. I'll live on bread and milk for the next fortnight."

Luckily for myself, I did not die in the attempt—though the price of three or four private dinners, which afterward appeared in my bill, indicated that I must have felt very "far gone" when I ordered them. Indeed, such rules are preposterous, and can only be observed with such a long list of exceptions as completely disproves them. If I were a doctor—peace! ghost of Abernethy—I would say to my patient:

"Drink thy sulphur water before breakfast, O man! if thou wilt; but if thou expect ever to derive any benefit from it, have a saddle of mutton, or good fat steaks, and sherris-sack, for dinner!"

Still, one likes to be at the fashionable Springs when the crowd is greatest. At the others, it is not so. There, he wishes to be well accommodated—to have a large, airy apartment—to be well served at the table—and to enjoy his quiet, and the society of a small circle of friends; but here, he desires to be in the midst of the grand movement. The more colonels, the better. The more pretty ladies, the gayer. He wants to talk upon politics with all the judges; attack or defend Sebastopol with all the generals; dance attendance on all the well-bred dames, and waltz with all their daughters. Half the pleasure is in the excitement which proceeds from the great number of persons collected together. Let the fashionable crowd dwindle down to a few dozens, and you leave also. Then you can have an entire suite of rooms, and excellent dinners, with a waiter at each elbow. But, no. When you see the trunks brought down, and hear the farewells said, you are as homesick as anybody, and crowd into the ninth place in the coach, rather than run the risk of being the last man to leave the mountains. So unreasonable are we all.

"Miss," said the maid of the belle of the White Sulphur—it was not her own, as it happened—"dey say you be de most handsome young lady in de Springs!"

"Who says that, Molly?" inquired the beauty, as she stood surveying the slope of her shoulders in the mirror, previously to their being veiled in muslin.

"Dat say de tall gentle'um from de Kentuck State—him wid de black mustachy."

"You're mistaken, Molly."

"Can't be, miss; dat be true as Baptist preachin' in de Caroline. I stand in de winder, and see miss and dat gentle'um eatin' chicken salad togeder; and what de gentle'um say, a'most make miss choke herself—he! he! he!"

"Nonsense! And what, Molly, do you think of the thin gentleman from the North, with the small, blue eyes?"

"I see him, tu, at de Spring, afore breakfast; and he so stare at miss, over de top of he's tumbler, and sigh so in he's sulph' water, dat I know'd de case be done gone wid him."

"And the short young man, with reddish whiskers?"

"Oh, miss! him's nice; him's sweet as 'taters! When he make love, never look back."

"Molly, you are very foolish. There is nobody in love with me."

"Can't be so, miss; for, Jim tell me, dat Tom tell him, dat when miss tuk her steps in de ballroom, last night, all de young gentle'um—and some of de ole gentle'um, tu—look gone distract', and a-sinkin' through de floor."

And well they might; for this young lady was of good height, symmetrically formed, with small hands and feet; and while most persons would say she was slender, others, again, pronounced her plump. There was the faintest possible blush of red in her cheeks, and just enough to relieve the exceedingly delicate, yet rich, brown tint, which Southern suns had lent to her complexion. The auburn ringlets fell in graceful profusion till they swept her shoulders. Her large hazel eye was as soft as that of a fawn in these mountains. In the prevailing expression of her face, delicacy and sweetness, intelligence and affection, were equally blended. Her manners, ordinarily, were so gentle that they might almost be characterized as languid; and yet, at times, there was a degree of vivacity in look and motion, a sprightly play of emotions about the flexible mouth, and even a dance, a very masquerade and merry-making of wits and fancies in her eyes, which gave to her whole person such an airy, buoyant expression, that the next moment you half expected to see her soar upward, as easily as a hawk to the clouds.

Surely, the "old families" of Virginia and South Carolina are no fable. One sees in their daughters that high-born air, that easy grace, that feminine delicacy, which shows their blood is gentle; and, like oft-decanted wine, has been refined by being poured through the veins of at least three well-born generations. A native modesty, self-possessed; and startled only by the advances of rudeness, or indelicacy, indicates an education obtained more in the sweet privacy of a rural home, than in the public academies of cities—more in the society of relatives and familiar friends, than in the company to be met with at fashionable hotels and the world's rendezvous. I have nowhere seen young ladies whose presence was more hedged about with privacy. And yet there is no lack of natural freedom and the play of native instinct in their manners. The laugh is gay; the word leaps from the heart; the confidence is given without a suspicion of the possibility of betrayal. It is an artlessness guarded by no premeditation. But there is, at the same time, a quick, nice sense of maidenly propriety, which, though never intrusive, still is always putting a gentle restraint upon the action of the impulses, always keeping a rein, fine as gossamer, upon the swift running of the tongue, and always guiding the burning chariot wheels of nature's passions around all the goals of early life with grace, and safety.

The accomplished belle of the White Sulphur had, to my eyes, the look of a lady who was never expecting admiration but had been ever receiving it. From her childhood up, it could not be otherwise than that she had been continually surrounded by domestic love and chivalrous courtesy. This long-continued reflection in her face, as in the mirror of the photographist, of the tenderest and noblest qualities of the heart, had finally left there the likeness of their own beautiful form and coloring. She was, herself, the very glass of love and courtesy. Whatever was gentle and amiable in her natural disposition had been drawn out and fostered by this atmosphere of affectionate respect in which she had lived—as the rose unfolds more perfectly its beauty in the well-tempered air of the conservatory than when exposed to the blight and the worm, the cold and the winds of the neglected garden. And, indeed, as there is no grace which more becomes a woman than that expression of face and manner she derives from the interchange of domestic affection, and from the adoration of men of honor and generous sentiments;

so there is nothing which so effectually withers and stains the heavenly bloom of beauty as daily contact with only the vicious and the vulgar.

As for amusements here, do they not consist in drinking the waters, bathing, and, three times a day, supplying the wants of nature by vigorous efforts with the trencher? A few persons bring their books with them as an additional source of entertainment; but most are satisfied with occasionally looking through a newspaper, a magazine, or some learned treatise that may be lying about, on the use of mineral waters. The gentlemen sit half the morning through in easy, wicker-bottom chairs, under the trees, conversing on the subject of politics, estimating the amount of the cotton and rice crops, smoking cigars, drinking juleps, commenting on a passing lady, a horse, or a stage coach. Rarely does a Virginian propose a walk. He prefers to sit, two hours together, beneath the shade. An active, inquisitive Yankee will go out, and explore a mountain, or look at a neighboring farm, and, returning, find the Southerner in the seat where he left him. An alligator in the State from which he comes, would not lie on a log longer. The Northern-born man, rising, perhaps, not much later than the sun, racing up hill and down to get what he calls a little exercise, climbing the pathless mountains for views of the scenery, and scouring the valley without any purpose whatever, unless it be the getting rid of half a day he knows not what to do with, is thought by him of the *terra caliente* a sort of madcap, flibbertigibbet, a personification of unreason. The latter will make as much effort as may be necessary to back a horse; if there is game, he will occasionally go out with dog and gun; and, in a few instances, I have seen him wet a line for trout, or it might have been catfish. At ten-pins, and at billiards, also, he will play. But, on the whole, it is an axiom with him, that too much exercise, as well as too much learning, will make a man mad. He, therefore, disparages both.

For any man living on the sunny side of the Union, to do nothing seems to be no labor; and he kills his time, apparently, without the pains of giving it a thought. After a while, indeed, all the visitors at these Springs learn more or less of the art of getting through the summer day easily. One begins with taking no note of the hour of the day, then lets his watch run down, and finally forgets the day of the week, and the month—all being alike, save Sunday. The morning papers he has ordered from town, come to hand several days old, and with such irregularity that, generally, the contradiction of the news arrives before the news itself; so that, at last, he comes to the conclusion that at the end of the watering season nothing of importance will have happened, and he sets his mind at rest.

As for the ladies, without knowing all the little ways they have of amusing themselves, one sees in their sweet faces that they are happy. They are, also, the cause of by far the greater part of the happiness there is in these watering places. If, by any strange fatality, the air of the Alleghanies should become fatal to ringlets, and the mineral waters wash the red out of the peach in the cheek, how soon would all these fair scenes revert to the original savages! But, fortunately, while woman lends a portion of her grace to the mountains, the grateful rocks repay the gift by endowing her with powers of enchantment superior even to those of old conferred on the Medea of the Caucasus. In the eyes of some man or other, every lady here is an enchantress. Scarcely was there a young man in the mountains, during the two seasons I spent there, who did not seem, at times, to be under the influence of illusions, more or less soft and roseate. Even my boy, Custopol, was obliged to confess to me, one day, that when, on the preceding Saturday night, Mary Jane came out in her yellow skirt and green bodice with a basque to it, a purple kerchief twisted round her braided hair, on her feet red morocco slippers, and gold drops pendent from her ears; and when he put his arm around her waist, and they went down the boards together, while Pompey, in the corner, "picked" his banjo, and all the "darkeys" in the place stood up and down the kitchen; and when Mary Jane, turning softly up her eyes, let him look by the half minute together into the whites of them; or, dancing round, poked her elbow in his ribs, and, grinning, pulled his whisker—even Custy was obliged to confess that he felt the tender passion.

The imagination, in fact, is as much exalted here above its ordinary level, as the mountains are higher than tide water. Hence, it will happen that a man, who, on coming to these Springs, had no more thought in his head of entering on the state of matrimony than he had of making a fortune, finds, before he has drunk and bathed a week, that he is in the most imminent danger of making proposals. Of course, there is no such thing ever dreamed of as match-making at the White Sulphur. For that presupposes coldness of blood, and a lively activity of the calculating faculties; whereas life in the mountains stimulates only the fantastic fancy, and the more romantic sentiments. No; neither party is entrapped. On the contrary, what in the world is more natural, when youth and maid drink together, every day, out of the same Sulphur Spring, than that they should have corresponding sensations in the region of the heart? They both look into the same pool; there cannot be two opinions between them respecting the taste of the water; they make precisely the same exclamations in their attempts at swallowing it; they behold the self-same expression of face reflected in each other's eyes as they set down the cup; and so, in a multitude of instances, before the lovers, feeling decidedly mawkish, if not desperately sick at heart, get back to the hotel, the momentous question is popped, and answered.

Love-making, therefore, may fairly be set down as one of the amusements of the Virginia Springs; whether it turn out to be really diverting to the parties concerned—*cela dépend.* But, in any event, there will always be somebody, who, quietly looking on from a distance, will extract more or less entertainment from the general aspects of the case, and who, especially if it is seen to go hard with the swain, as it often may, will really enjoy the agony, as one does a farce when they play tragedy at Wallack's.

Probably there is no better place in the States for the study of character and manners than these Springs—and this, too, is an amusement. Sometimes half a dozen words let fall in casual conversation will throw as much light on the dispositions of men, and the working of their institutions, as a novel in two duodecimos, the reading of which will require half a day.

"Jim," said a gentleman from Louisiana, travelling by the stage coach to the Bath Alum, "Jim, come inside here, and let me have your place up there."

"Massa," replied the negro, almost as confidently as if he had been his son, "dere's room enough here for two."

"Jim," again said the gentleman, after he had taken his seat by the side of the black boy, on the top of the coach, "to-night you will see Sally; for we shall meet Master William at the Alum."

"I'se right glad of dat," was the reply—Sally being the maid of Master William's wife, and probably a good friend of Jim's.

"Jim," said the master, once more, addressing the boy after half an hour's conversation with myself, "did you ever see mountains before?"

"Oh, yes, massa; de river mountains on de Mis'sippi."

"You mean when you were in Tennessee."

"'Xactly—dat was in Ten'see."

This same Jim, shortly afterward turning round toward another negro, like himself, about sixteen years of age, and sitting on the luggage, said:

"Cæsar, look at dat line of mount'ns yonder; up

and down—jist as reg'lar as you could draw 'em wid a piece of chalk!"

"Even the dusky soul of the poor African, then, in its better moods," said I to myself, "is capable of being touched by the grace of nature; and feels, in the presence of these mountain tops, its dull faculties aroused and strangely fascinated by the unwritten Word of God!"

Another source of pleasure upon which none of the guests can refrain from relying, more or less, is the arrival of the stage coach. Let it happen however often in the day, it is still an important event. One expects his friends; or, if not, somebody may come he has met before; at any rate he must see who is there.

Down gets the first gentleman from the coach. He is tall, with a large proportion of bone in him, and only a moderate supply of muscle. His rather long brown hair is brushed, like a Methodist minister's, off his forehead, which is a high one, but not broad. The well-tanned face indicates vigorous health, though a little sulphur water will be no disadvantage to the owner's liver. The air of calm self-possession marks the man accustomed to command; while the slow gait and quiet motions suggest the habit of overseeing work instead of performing it. The blue dress coat with brass buttons, which is neither old nor new, together with light-colored pantaloons, black satin vest, dark silk cravat, and broad-brimmed felt hat, belong evidently to a gentleman somewhat careless of personal appearance, but of independent circumstances; in short, it requires no epaulettes to convince you at a glance that the stranger is a colonel from one of the eastern counties of Virginia.

When his luggage is taken down, you will find that it consists of a leather trunk covered with small brass knobs and marked with the owner's name, in full, together with those of his county and State; on the top of it is strapped a heavy overcoat, while at one end dangle an extra pair of boots. The colonel travels without a hatbox; but has, instead, a well-worn pair of saddle bags, which are filled with the smaller articles of his wardrobe and such "traps" as he may very likely want on the journey.

On acquaintance, he proves to be a man of good plain sense, who belongs to what he denominates the Jeffersonian party in politics, tills the paternal acres very much after the fashion of his father before him, has, generally, a suit or two pending in the courts of law, but is as goodnatured as he is highminded, and really hates nobody. Once introduced, he will ask you to take a julep with him.

The general moves in more state; he arrives in

his own coach and two, or even four—for this old-fashioned turnout has not yet entirely disappeared in the progress of civilization and the rail. He may, also, have two or three outriders, in the shape of sons, on ponies, and black boys riding mares. Sons, servants, mares and horses, they are all of his own raising; but the carriage, possibly, may have belonged to his father or some of his ancestors; for it is after the ancient English model, round topped, heavily timbered, and possessing the property, like Homer's heroes, of never growing old. The trunks being piled up behind, and to them attached a water pail, the footman is obliged to squeeze himself into what of the narrow seat in front is left by the driver.

The latter is an old whip, whatever his age may be. Though without gloves, he handles the ribbons with a careful precision, as if the leaders were every moment about to spring into a run; though in shoes, his immense feet hold well by the footboard; and in a mere jacket, instead of the official capes, he produces, by means of his spread elbows, and blown-up air, scarcely less of a sensation than the coachman of my Lord Mayor of London.

When this whole affair sweeps up to the door of the hotel, the excited landlord, especially if it be a four-in-hand, rings his bell with a fury which indicates that something extraordinary has happened; and the servants come running, as if they expected to witness the arrival of a dozen stage coaches at once. But 'tis even more than that; 'tis a Virginian general, with horses and mares, black boys and maids, wife and children. The hair of every waiter in the house would stand straight on end, but for the curl in it!

The landlord opens the carriage door himself, hat in hand; and the general gets out. He is a shorter man than the colonel by a half inch, or more. He has a broader and still more open face, a wider back, and carries a respectable corporation before him. His clothes are thin, the colors light, and his face is red; while down out of his fob hangs a heavy gold chain, with two ponderous, ancestral seals, and a key between. The general takes off his white beaver courteously to the colonel, who instantly steps forward to shake him by the hand.

While these congratulations are being exchanged, down the carriage steps carefully comes Dinah. She is dressed mostly in white, and has a cotton kerchief of this color, striped with blue, tied so completely over her hair, that only enough of it remains in sight to show that it is becoming silvered o'er with the pale cast of age; while, over the kerchief and directly on the back of her head, is set a bonnet of open straw and muslin, originally made for the general's pretty daughter when she entered her teens, and so small, withal, that it serves merely to cover the good dame's cerebellum.

The baby is then handed out to Dinah; the rest follow; and when the trunks have been taken down, and the carriage pockets emptied, Cuffy, the coachman, effects his exit with a crack of the whip, such as makes not only his own horses, but all those within an eighth of a mile, jump—each one as though it were about his own ears the lash was playing.

And when, any time within the next half hour, the respectable Virginia farmer, or esquire, well-to-do at home, rides up to the hotel door on his nag, a greatcoat rolled up and tied, together with an umbrella, behind the saddle, and a pair of leathern bags, containing a scanty change of apparel, projecting beneath his thighs, the careless landlord scarcely deigns to touch the bell once. A sleepy-looking negro holds the new comer's bridle while he dismounts; another, lazily taking the saddle bags on his shoulders, and the roll under his arm, conducts him to his chamber; and there is no more noise made over the arrival, compared with the previous excitement, than might be likened to the blowing of a horn reversed.

For the rest, there are a dozen or more of these Springs. They all lie in the pretty Alleghanian valleys, within an easy day's, or half day's drive from each other—the White Sulphur being in the centre. The roads are generally good, with enough which are bad to accommodate those who require a little jolting. The stage coaches are well built; the drivers are skilful; and a dash on the outside of the carriage through these hills refreshes and invigorates, instead of fatiguing the traveller. In fact, the now almost obsolete pleasure of journeying by wheel may here be enjoyed in its perfection, with social chat, preceded by no formal introductions, with acquaintances, and, perhaps, friends made, whom it will always be a pleasure to remember, and with such good, plain fare, at roadside inns, as the sharpened appetite will pronounce better than the very *chef-d'œvres* of cooks in town.

The Springs are of all waters, having for their principal ingredients sulphur, alum, iron, magnesia, or salt. They are also tri-colored, with deposits, white, red, and blue. Some are used for drinking, and some for bathing. The invalid may have his choice; and whatever his complaint, say the doctors, it makes no difference—he is sure to be cured. The cripple is set up at the Hot Springs, and the *malade imaginaire* is made whole at the Warm. The dyspeptic is put on alum water, and the Southwesterner, with bile in his blood and jaundice in his eyes, is ordered to drink of the White Sulphur or the Salt. The Healing Spring is good for the gout; ladies, weary after the winter's dancing, are strengthened by bathing in the two Sweet Waters; the Blue Sulphur, taken before eating venison steaks, is said to be excellent against all devils of the same color; and ever since the publication of the learned Dr. Burke's book, it is every man's own fault if he don't know that the Red Sulphur is a certain cure for consumption.

The summer climate of these mountains is truly delightful. The boundless forests on their tops are, indeed, a magnet for the clouds; so that rain often occurs in the day's chapter of accidents. But it is merely a passing shower—a dash of big, fast-falling drops—soon gone over the hills and far away. The water runs immediately off the declivities, the drops hang only a few moments from leaf and flower, and the brilliant sun, dissipating the vapors, dries the surface of the ground and takes away all dampness.

It is hot in the sunlight; but you live perpetually embowered in shade. In that, the mercury daily stands square against the point of summer heat, or, occasionally, a little above it, so that one revels in fine linen; and if he makes any use of the mint which grows invitingly by every pathside, it is more as a luxury than a necessity. Sitting under the oaks, or promenading on the piazza, the summer idler finds that he can keep cool from one end of the dog days to the other, without so much as touching a straw. This, to some persons, may be rather provoking than otherwise. But with such pure air to breathe, fanned by the softest breezes, instead of being whipped by the winds of the sea-shore bathing place, and nightly refreshed by sleep beneath a blanket, if you will, but with windows wide open, and disturbed by no worse serenading than that of the banjo, a man is sufficiently happy without stimulus, or excitements of any kind. To look out upon the green pastures and the luxuriant woods—to wind gently up the hilltops, or stroll by the side of brooks—to watch the never-ceasing play of light and shade on the mountains and in the valleys, and to gaze at the fantastic shapes of the summer clouds, now drifting in fleeces through the sky, now towering in gorgeous peaks and ranges above the horizon, and, at evening, aglow with all the prismatic flames which burst from the apparent disruption of the setting sun—to do all this is, indeed, to forget the more highly scented cups of civic dissipation, as well as the rile in the mug of the world's ordinary toil, and to live in the midst of such innocent delights as by the poets are fabled to lie around its infancy.

CHAPTER VII.

Through Virginia and Carolina.

ONCE more out of the mountains, I find myself among the plantations of Eastern Virginia. It is a district of country where the soil is often of a rich yellow, or mulberry color, and brown donkeys are ploughing it early in February; where zigzag fences are laid twelve rails high, and not a stake in them; where hay and corn remain through the winter stacked in the fields; where the forests are strewn with gigantic trunks left lying as they fell, and the green foliage is sprinkled over with the white of large projecting branches which have been splintered, or twisted off by storm and tempest; where the houses often look top-heavy, and tumble down, though supported by strong chimneys of brick or stone, built on the outside; where the wagons, canvas-covered, are shaped like whale boats, and are drawn by from four to six mules, with Uncle Tom on the back of the nigh leader; where ladies travel with guitars, and gentlemen with saddle bags, negroes in white woollen blankets, and negresses in pink ribbons; where, emerging from the pine woods, young misses enter the train, robed in shawls bought at Berlin for not less money than would suffice to purchase a small negro, and the young gentlemen who accompany them, sprawl over two seats in every variety of attitude, excepting that of the Apollo Belvidere; where the traveller starts on his journey by rail at four o'clock in the morning, and stops a whole hour at seven for breakfast; where, driven to the hotel in nothing less than a 'bus and four, he is received by a cloud of negroes, the chambermaids being superb in white aprons, and variegated turbans, and all anxious to do something for "Missis;" while the boys, met at every turn, are either in danger of running down "Massa," or are sure, when wanted, to be running away from him; now making their obeisance halfway down to the floor, and the next moment laughing behind his back until mouth and ears meet; most of them oiled in the joints to such a degree as scarcely to be able to stand up, and the rest threatening to tumble down from stupidity, and sleepy-headedness.

I passed through one, and but one neat village (that of A——) on my way from the mountains to

Richmond. The latter is a thrifty town, rather picturesquely placed on hill and river side; and is made pleasant in winter by the magnolia, the arbor vitæ, and various evergreens. Here I went to see Crawford's equestrian statue of Washington. The figures of Henry and Jefferson, which stand on the base of the monument, are admirably done; the former exhibiting the impassioned orator in full action, and contrasting pleasantly with the more quiet, thoughtful attitude of the writer of the Declaration of Independence. But on seeing the figure of Washington, my first impression was that this modest, great man, if he could have been consulted about the matter, would much have preferred, instead of being elevated so high in the air, to stand more nearly on a level with the illustrious patriots below. On beholding him at that awkward height, the spectator hardly feels that he is in the presence of the father of his country; for the expression of the countenance is lost in midheaven. Whoever approaches the monument near enough to get a good view of the statues at the base, on looking up to that above, sees little else than the under side of the immense horse's belly. There may be good cause, to be sure, for placing an equestrian statue in an elevated position, as on the pediment of a temple, or on a natural eminence; but as this monument stands on high ground, where it can easily be seen at a distance, there seems to be no good reason for erecting so lofty a pedestal.

The Washington in the State House, close at hand, by Houdon, interested me more, notwithstanding its French strut, and lack of idealization. For, with these exceptions, it is the great man himself left behind in marble, and dressed, and looking as he actually did when in full life. Indeed, the figure of Washington is itself so sublime, that all attempts of art to sublimate it have hitherto not been successful.

On leaving Richmond, the traveller going South will do well to save his appetite until his arrival at Wilmington, where I can safely promise him, at least, good white Johnny-cake. Here it was, on the ninth of February, that I tasted my first shad of the season, making no bones of it. Throughout the dinner a black boy stood behind my chair, with his hands resting on the back of it; and, on receiving my orders, started suddenly to my side, as if waked out of a reverie. Then, shooting off headlong on my errand, and headlong returning, he again relapsed into his previous state of semi-somnolency, and hung suspended from the chair-back. The hotel is not exactly a fit subject for a eulogy; still I rested very comfortably in it during a day and a night.

Like so many other Southern cities, Wilmington is a town built on the sands. A seaport, it enjoys a large and profitable trade in turpentine, besides doing a lively little business in fine-cut tobacco, and various Southern "notions." It contains a few moderately well-looking houses, scattered about among a great many half-painted and dilapidated ones. I saw scarcely a wall without a brick loose, or a fence without a board off, or any work in cement that had not a crack in it. The yards in front of the houses, however, were pleasant with evergreens, and climbing plants; and the coming spring had here scattered in advance the first camellias, hyacinths, and daffodils.

The rail from Richmond to Charleston took me through a country exhibiting fewer marks of civilization than I had anticipated. To the very end of the journey, my surprise was repeatedly excited at passing through forests beyond forests, interspersed only by more or less extensive clearings. Even in these, many of the corn and cotton fields were pretty well filled with stumps and the stems of broken, half-decayed trees, left standing by the axe and the firebrand. The two Carolinas I found as rough as Ohio; while Illinois, with its cultivated prairies, might almost pass for an old country in comparison with them. Nearly the whole stretch of these Southern pine woods is as level, too, as any prairie; and many districts, in consequence of recent heavy rains, were little better than a succession of dismal swamps. Even the noble pines themselves, tall, slender, and tapering as were their stems, and sometimes beautifully spreading their tops, like the stone pines of Italy, yet being disfigured by the axe for the sake of their sap, which is manufactured into turpentine, present such conspicuous scars as to make the otherwise fair woods look ghastly enough to be the haunts of ghosts.

Indeed, the poor whites who mostly inhabit these openings in the forests are scarcely less haggard than sprites. They would be equally pale, also, but that they are so yellow. Theirs is the genuine fever-and-ague complexion, more or less modified in this rainy season by the color of the mud wherein they live, and move, and have their being. Fortunately, their hovels are made of logs instead of clay; otherwise these, too, would gradually be dissolved in water. The dress of these natives of the woods was, certainly, when I saw it, in a great many instances fast coming to nought. At best, it was coarse and neglected; while the general aspect of life was low and almost brutish.

At the end of two days of travelling, it was truly a relief to emerge from these pine-grown regions, and see, on approaching the suburbs of Charleston, a greater variety of forest trees. The oaks now preponderated, their boughs hung with gray moss and their trunks often draped with climbing evergreens. In low places, the maples were hanging out their crimson buds and fringes. At the same time, the sun, breaking through the heavy clouds which had for several days obscured the heavens, poured a flood of golden light over the tender foliage, over the city, and the bay; and, genially warming the air, gave promise that I was here to meet the spring thus far advanced on its way northward from the equator and the shores of the Caribbean.

CHAPTER VIII.

Charleston.

FIRST of all I went to the races. For I had begun to hear the February races in Charleston talked of as far north as Washington, and had been told much of the fine horses, much of the beautiful women, who, in *grande toilette*, grace these festive occasions. Unfortunately, the twelfth of February brought with it gentle showers of rain; but, heavy as was the course, I had rarely seen in the States better running. The horses were ridden by slips of black boys, whom, at first sight, I thought scarcely equal to the task, but who, in the end, proved themselves to be born Jehus. Like the steeds, they must have been bred specially for the race course. I forget, at this moment, what the time made was; but the horses were so well matched as to come in almost neck and neck.

As to the ladies, they were not to be cheated out

of their holiday by the rain. They were there in full feather; in ermine and point lace; in light brocades and cashmeres of India. They were there in the latest *nouveautés;* gay with flowers and graceful with fringes, as well as in perfect little loves of parasols, and fans fluttering with coquetry. One or two dowagers sported their diamonds and jewels more appropriate for the ballroom. Nearly all, as it seemed to me, were rather over-dressed for the occasion; though, as it is the fashion of the Charlestonians to put on new bonnets for the February races, as the Philadelphians do at Easter, perhaps the temptation to make too much of the toilet at this time might well be irresistible. Still, bright colors do not harmonize with dark skies; the reason why they are always so becoming in the *tierras calientes* of Spain and Italy being because the air there is full of resplendent light, and so many of nature's tints are high-toned. But at the Charleston race course, nothing was gorgeous save the silks and ribbons; for, while heavens of lead overhung an earth scarcely yet green, even the cheeks of the fair were pale, and their eyes lacked the lustre of the south of Europe. They were, however, sufficiently pretty and high-bred.

The lords of this part of creation, likewise, were tall and fine-looking; though it struck me that their easy morning costumes, if adapted to the occasion, were not quite in harmony with the elaborate toilets of the sex. Certain it is, that the tip-top beaux were generally dressed in overcoats, sacks, raglans, sticks, and umbrellas. I could but think, also, that many of them carried a trifle too much weight in the watch chain, and, in some instances, selected their waistcoats of a crimson slightly too emphatic for the black of their pantaloons. But, on the whole, the crowd of clubmen were well attired; and I did not see among them a single specimen of the black-satin-vest gentry.

For the rest, considering that ladies came to the race in full dress, I was a little surprised at seeing that the floor of the saloon wherein they were assembled was, in places, wet with tobacco juice, and sprinkled with nutshells. Lads, whose bringing up in the best families of the town should have taught them better, threw the shells on the floor as unceremoniously as if they had been in a beer garden, or a cockpit. Even a lady arrayed in ermine, and deep frills of Chantilly lace, who was holding a court, at the moment, consisting of four gentlemen, all in waxed mustaches, suffered two out of the four to stand in her presence munching peanuts.

It may be added, that, with few exceptions, the elegantly arrayed ladies present on this occasion to witness the running, and receive the admiration of the handsome members of the Jockey Club, were unmarried; and that the presence of a somewhat larger number of matrons would have imparted a little more dignity to the festivity, without detracting too much from its grace.

To return to town. My first impressions of Charleston were extremely agreeable. It was a pleasant thing to find an American city containing so many memorials of the times colonial, and not wearing the appearance of having been all built yesterday. The atmosphere, charged with an unusual dampness in consequence of the low position of the town on coast and river bank, helps materially to deepen the marks of years; soon discoloring the paint upon the houses and facilitating the progress of the green moss, which here is ever creeping over the northern side of roofs and walls. The whole town looks picturesquely dingy, and the greater number of buildings have assumed something of the appearance of European antiquity. The heavy brick walls and the high gateways are such as one sees in London or Paris. Many front doors and piazzas had been wrought after the graceful models brought from England in the old colonial period. The verandas, story above story, and generally looking toward the south, or the sea, form another pleasant feature in the prevailing style of building. Nor less attractive are the gardens and courtyards invariably attached to the best houses, where, in winter, the hedges are green with pitosporum and the dwarf orange; and where blow the first fragrant violets and daffodils of spring. Here, in February, I beheld with delight the open rose, and camellias so numerous as to redden the ground they fell upon; also, the wild orange bursting with white buds, and the peach tree in full blossom, as well as the humble strawberry at its foot. Stopping at one of these lofty gateways, and looking through the quaint, old-fashioned gratings, I could not help repeating the lines of Goethe

> "Ein sanfter Wind vom blauen Himmel weht,
> Die Myrte still und hoch der Lorber steht."

These charming gardens, in connection with the piazzas resting on ornamental pillars, make the whole town graceful. One sits, in the morning, in these open chambers, inhaling the refreshing air from the sea, its perfume mingled with that of the flowers below; and, at midday, closing the Venetian shutters to exclude the sun, he rests in grateful shade. Here, too, throughout the longer portion of the year, may be spread, at evening, the tea table; while the heavens still glow with the purple and amber of the sunset. And here lingers the family until the bells from the tower of St. Michael's, sweetly ringing their silver chimes through the calm, starry air, announce, at last, the hour of repose.

Many invalids from the North, delighted with these Southern balconies and these melodious evening bells, with this soft air and genial sunshine, with the lovely promenade of the ever grass-green Battery, and with the pleasing prospect of the bay, never the same with its coming and going ships, are tempted to linger here the winter through, nor go farther southward in their search for health or pleasure. But the climate of Charleston, if soft—soft, even, as that of Rome—is damp, and exceedingly variable. The consumptive invalid, therefore, should never dally long with these sea breezes, nor stay to pluck these flowers. He should proceed onward as far as St. Augustine, or inland to the dry, sandy hill country.

In winter, many of the wealthy South Carolinian planters come to Charleston to enjoy the gay season of February; and a few spend several months here for the sake of the greater advantages in educating their children. But all come to town with less parade than did the grand seigneurs of the generation preceding. For a quarter of a century, the number of coaches and four has been gradually diminishing.

Fewer outriders herald the planter's advance. The family carriage has grown a little rickety, and the worse for wear; though the horses are still well blooded, and Sambo holds the reins with cheeks as full, and shoulders as widely spreading. Comparatively few are the masters who nowadays pass through the country with a retinue of from fifteen to twenty servants; who, at a wedding, or other festive occasion, open wide their doors to all comers, entertaining troops of friends, twoscore and more, with for every one a couch, as well as for every one a month's welcome. Fiddling, indeed, has not died out; and Pompey still draws his bow, and beats his banjo with as much ardor as in the days of yore. At the merry-makings, there is dancing every night in the parlor, as well as plenty of giggling and roaring in the kitchen. Five-and-twenty varieties of corn cake may be served at breakfast; the pot of hominy, like the widow's cruse, is inexhaustible; the bacon makes the table groan; though certainly the number of pipes of wine annually laid down is getting every year less; nor do I believe there can be many nabobs left, who, in purchasing their supplies in town at the beginning of the season, do not fail to include a hogshead of castor oil for their little negroes.

The February balls in Charleston are scarcely less known to fame than the races. The most select and fashionable are those of the Saint Cecilia, and they have been given here from times running back past the memory of all the dancers now living. Only the gentry and the more favored strangers are admitted. They go at ten o'clock, and stay until three. The attendance, however, is principally confined to the younger portion of the fashionable community, who, before setting off for the dance, see the mammas and papas comfortably to bed. I observed that even the young married ladies attracted but little attention from the beaux; and, in fact, I was repeatedly told, that whenever a bride was led to the altar, she, afterward, went in society, as a matter of course, to the wall. Even the bride, who comes from other parts of the country to find in this hospitable city a home, runs imminent risk of receiving but few marks of courtesy from any gentleman not married. She may be beautiful, accomplished, and elegantly dressed; but the beaux will look at her, if they deign to look at her at all, with blank, mute admiration. This, in a city so famed as Charleston is for gallantry of manners, struck me as a little singular. I saw many fair young ladies among the dancers, and the prevailing style of toilet was characterized by simplicity as well as elegance. Some waltzing, also, I noticed, as graceful as that which may be seen in the countries where the waltz is at home. Of flowers, however, whether as an ornament for the person, or the apartments, there were quite too few; and it seemed as though the profusion with which nature, in the more genial seasons of the year, furnishes these decorations, had led to the neglect of their cultivation by artificial means in winter.

From the presence of two races, the streets of Charleston have a pepper-and-salt aspect. The blacks are almost as numerous as the whites, but are generally of smaller stature. I saw very few slaves, either male or female, who were of large size; still fewer who were good-looking. As an exception, however, in the matter of size, I noticed one portly dame striding down the street in broad brimmed hat, and staff, who appropriated to her own use nearly the whole of the sidewalk, and swaggered with an importance which plainly marked her as having authority in the kitchen of one of the proudest families of Charleston. On Sunday, the negroes I saw airing themselves on their way to church appeared to good advantage, being respectful in manners, and, for the most part, becomingly plain in dress. The aged dames were in turbans containing only a few modest stripes, though worn pretty high. The younger damsels showed, of course, more love for dressing like white folks. One dainty miss, with large, liquid eyes, and the deep red breaking through her colored cheek, like the vermilion streaming through dark clouds that lie athwart the sunset, made herself gay in a French cashmere; another displayed her jaunty modesty in Canton crape; while the principal colored belle of the promenade held up her rich black silk to exhibit an elaborately embroidered petticoat. The other sex were decently clad, and scarcely in a single instance that came under my observation, grotesquely. They showed, occasionally, a little red in their cravats—sometimes a little buff. But not even on the coach box did Pompey go much beyond a brass buckle in his hat, and purple plush in his waistcoat. On the whole, therefore, the colored palmetto gentry seemed to me to have learned demureness from their betters; though there was, perhaps, as much grinning and giggling as was decent on a Sunday.

But the next day being a half holiday, in consequence of the Governor's review, I was surprised at seeing crowds of nurses in bandanna turbans, and sable urchins in caps so gay as to need nothing but belles to set them all ringing. The sunny afternoon air was quite filled with the kites of these small black boys. Their loud, tumultuous laughter mingled pleasantly with the music of drum, and fife, and bagpipe; while, by nightfall, the circles of all eyes had grown visibly larger from gazing at the plumes and glitter of the militiamen. With special pleasure I remember the sight, on that afternoon, of a pair of brats about the size of Murillo's beggar boys, and as much like them as blacks can be like Spaniards. They occupied the same position, also, against a sunny wall, and were in the same need of having their heads combed; the one being happily intent on smoking a broken clay pipe, and the other gazing at vacancy with a degree of tranquil animal satisfaction which distended his half-shining, half-unwashed skin wellnigh to cracking.

It was but a sorry entertainment to visit the slave market; yet, one fine morning, attracted by the auctioneer's flag, I dropped in. There was but one small lot on the block, evidently a badly damaged lot of merchandise; and I did not hear a single bid for them. One old woman, however, by trade a cook, was put up for sale separately. She was, at the time, half seas over, and might very likely have been thus exposed by her master for the sake of frightening her into better behavior. But, if such had been the purpose, the failure of the experiment was complete; for, when she saw that not a single bid was made for such a sinner, she exclaimed, with a prodigiously broad leer of satisfaction, "Nobody want dis ole nigger? Well, I goes back to massa."

For piety and church-going the negroes are as remarkable as the Charlestonians themselves. They like to sing psalms and to deliver to each other the solemn word of exhortation. Their labor in prayer resembles the wrestling of Jacob with the angel; though, in this exercise, they sometimes get themselves on the hip. Their masters and mistresses, however, I am sorry to say, are in the habit of making the observation, that a negro's Sunday faith has but a loose connection with his week-day conduct. Moved, myself, one Sunday evening, to sit under colored preaching, I accepted the invitation of a friend to visit one of the conventicles attended exclusively by negroes. On entering the large and commodious building, we were politely shown up the broad aisle to a seat directly in front of the pulpit, it being the chief seat in the synagogue, and one expressly reserved for white folks. Thereupon the wink was tipped to the sable sexton, who was made to understand that, inasmuch as I was a distinguished gentleman from New York city, the performers in Divine service would be expected to do their best. At length, after a tolerably long pause of preparation, a venerable negro was called up by the clergyman to open the service with prayer. This he did with not a little solemnity, not forgetting, at the close of the exercise, to intercede expressly in behalf of the "gemman present from York." The prayer ended, a devout old negro, called Pete, immediately struck up the hymn beginning, "I'm bound for de kingdom." But old Pete had, apparently, forgotten, in his zeal, the presence of the eminent gentleman from New York, and had to be snubbed by the sexton.

"Stop dat, you nigger!" quickly exclaimed the official, looking, at the same time, sharply at the singer's face, and then, after a pause, pointing upward, he called out, authoritatively:

"Choir, sing 'Vital spark.'"

The singing was not bad; the tone of voice being pure, and the chief deficiency consisting in the lack of expression. All the other exercises, likewise, were done decently and in order.

From the negro, whether under the sounding board of the conventicle, or the hammer of the auctioneer, to Powers, the sculptor, may seem a pretty long stride; but the statue of Mr. Calhoun, by this great American bust maker, stands in the old State House, at but a short distance from either the meeting house, or the slave market. With a disposition to speak well of native art, I cannot, however, attribute to this statue of the distinguished Carolinian any high degree of merit beyond that of possessing a good head. Unfortunately, the marble, too, has the fault of being the least bit smutty at the tip of the nose, and suggests the homely idea of snuff-taking.

5*

The body is encumbered by the drapery, which, though wrought with very great pains, seems to be heavy with the water of the wet garments after which it must have been modelled. The three folds on the left shoulder are particularly stiff and monotonous. The figure, represented as stepping forward, is impeded, in so doing, by two supports, one on either side. The left arm is elevated awkwardly, to hold a scroll bearing an inscription, which, at a little distance, looks as though it were done in red chalk, and produces rather a burlesque effect than otherwise. But the weakest points in the statue are the hands and arms, which look still weaker when contrasted with the remarkable strength and boldness of the head. It was a pity, indeed, to impair the effect of so excellent a bust by adding a body to it.

Before leaving Charleston, I did not fail to take a look at its environs. On a bright, sunny afternoon, the soft southwest wind gently blowing, I was driven out by a friend to his farm, situated a few miles out of town. The rather quiet landscape was made attractive by numerous liveoaks, with sturdy, broadly spreading branches, by tall, dark-leafed magnolias, and by the graceful wild oranges, all being evergreens. Some of these trees were draped with grapevines climbing to their summits; and the hedges were green with the Cherokee rose, and the yellow jessamine. In a stroll through the gardens of a farmhouse, I gathered a nosegay of fragrant violets, snowdrops, jonquils, and Christmas berries, which, brought home, filled my apartment for hours with a sweet, summer perfume.

But the most pleasing feature of the scenery which came within my observation, on this excursion, was an avenue, or, rather, a couple of avenues, of liveoaks of unusual size and beauty. The trees being fully grown, the crooked branches stretched themselves high in the air, numerous as the masts in the crowded seaport, and strong enough to supply the joints and knees of the proudest ships of war. They stretched high overhead, and apparently halfway to heaven, until gradually lost in the tapering twigs, and evergreen leaves, and gracefully pendent mosses. The stems had the strength of the columns of some great temple in Thebes or Palmyra. And yet, I was told that these monarchs of the plain had scarcely yet attained their threescore years and ten. When the old men of Charleston were in their cradles, these oaks were tiny acorns, such as I trod under foot as I walked thoughtfully in the vast, checkered shade of these green avenues. So vigorous and rapid is the growth of vegetable forms in this clime of the sun.

On returning from the country, I drove through

the Mount Auburn of Charleston, called, from the beautiful trees interspersed through it, the Magnolia Cemetery. But, entertaining always a decided disposition to keep out of places of this sort as long as may be, I was scarcely in the mood to do justice to this promenade among the graves. As it was, the situation seemed to me little better than a collection of low sandhills, the monotony of which was varied, after the manner of the Chinese, by a few pools of standing water. The principal monuments, as is generally the case in cemeteries, had a look of more or less vain ostentation about them; their proportions being rarely good, and the carving being almost always tawdry. The simplest forms, and lines of ornament, certainly, sympathize best with heartfelt grief; and we generally raise the monument to ourselves, rather than to the dead, whenever we overdo it. Some new tombs in the Egyptian style were pointed out to me as particularly "nice;" one of them having a glass door which allowed all curious persons to look in, and see the coffins. But, thinking the sight could not possibly prove entertaining, I drove out of the grounds at as fast a walk as the regulations of the place would admit of.

Returning to town, we passed along the Battery, the principal promenade of the Charlestonians, and a truly beautiful one. Two rivers, the Cooper and the

Ashley, flow past it into the bay, which here spreads out to view a pleasant expanse of waters. Almost entirely landlocked, the Palmetto Islands bound it on the south; to the eastward project into the water the two salient points of Forts Sumter and Moultrie; while in the west, when I first saw it, lay diffused over all the beautiful tints of the sunset. And, night after night, as I returned to the Battery at that hour, the sky was ever aglow with the same hues of purple and salmon color, of saffron, rose, and green. On the first evening, too, the full moon, rising above the eastern horizon, scattered innumerable sparkling points of light in a line across the dancing waves, laying a necklace of diamonds on the bosom of the bay. A little later in the year, all the fashion of Charleston will be met, at the hour of twilight, promenading on this smoothly laid sea wall. Nightly the cool breeze from the water fans them, and refreshes their languid spirits, when May-day introduces the season of hot weather. And hence has grown up the proverb, that the Charlestonians live but during two months of the year—in February, for the sake of the races, and in May, for that of the promenade upon the Battery.

CHAPTER IX.

Savannah.

WITH pleasant regrets I took my leave of Charleston, and, passing the long Palmetto Islands, saluted once more the open, broad Atlantic. As the sun came up higher, its rays, agreeably tempered by a slight haze in the air, made for us a summer sea in February. And such the sea remained the livelong day; a soft southwest breeze just raising a ripple over the azure expanse, and the bosom of the ocean only so much heaving as when it is most at rest. It was but mere pastime for the white seagulls to follow us on lazily flapping wings; often resting poised in the air, now dipping, for a moment, in the ship's white wake of foam, and then alighting gracefully upon their watery nests, to be rocked asleep by the gently rolling waves, as from the branches of trees the birds' nests hang swinging in the summer winds. The whole day long not a sail was to be seen, making the ocean seem like an idler keeping holiday; and, at nightfall, our steamer brought us to land in the haven where we would be—that of Savannah.

Comparisons are proverbially odious; and any one that might be instituted between two such rival cities as Savannah and Charleston, would not be agreeable to the inhabitants of either of them. These two towns are well known to be antipodes in taste and opinion; whatever is most applauded by the one, being held in great disrespect by the other. The Charlestonians think well of their city on account of its fine old baronial mansions, and pride themselves upon the length of pedigree which can be shown by the families residing in them. But they of Savannah, who live in houses built in the newer style of architecture, and worship in church edifices the origin of which hardly dates so far back as the American Revolution, do not consider themselves upstarts, for all that. They put the "Pulaski" against the "Mills House;" Bull street against the Charleston Battery; Bonaventure and Thunderbolt road against the Magnolia Cemetery and the plank turnpike; their park of pines against the one palmetto; and the muddy waters of the Savannah, and the town pumps, against the bay of Charleston, its forts and islands. It is a very great pity that there should be this variance of taste between neighbors; but still I should hardly undertake to decide the large number of questions in dispute between the two parties, unless I were officially requested to do so by the town authorities, and were tendered my fees. I may, however, be allowed to say, that it happened to me, on more than one occasion, to hear residents of Savannah boasting of being the fifth or sixth in descent from some of the old, pre-revolutionary aristocrats of the more northerly metropolis. It is acknowledged, moreover, by the Savannese, that Georgia is a border land—a State of transition between the new Southwest, with its population of thrifty but recently-born cotton and sugar lords, and Carolina, settled so many generations earlier by the cavaliers of England. I speak, of course, of the southern Carolina; for, the difference in character between this and the other twin sister, has been strongly marked from its first settlement down to the present times. Whenever the Charlestonian talks of Carolina, it is of his Carolina; and in case of your alluding to the other, he shrugs his shoulders, and reminds you that that State was originally a colony of hard-fisted, bull-headed Scotchmen.

But, all invidious comparisons aside, Savannah is a pretty town, half city, half village, and well deserves its graceful name. Beautiful shade trees have been planted in the streets, most of which are wide and straight, having originally been laid out, as it would appear, by line and compass. There are not crooked ones enough to give even a little variety to the monotonous right angles. Still, it is pleasant, in this early season of the year, when the leaves are new, and the heat of the approaching sun begins to assert its great power, to take one's promenade in checkered shade. For this exercise, the street of streets is Bull street. Here reside many of the opulent families, and here walks all the fashion. Through this thoroughfare, also, roll the pleasant carriages, if a carriage can be said to roll in sand; and the young bloods canter the horses, which, a few degrees farther north, would be trained to trot.

At intervals, along this Corso, there are pretty green squares, likewise decorated with shade trees; and in the centre of each one, instead of a fountain, stands a tall wooden pump. Sufficiently conspicuous in itself, this useful ornament was made more so from the circumstance that, whenever I happened to be passing, there rarely failed to stand a negro or two, working away at the handles so lazily that the question might be raised, whether it were he that was working the pump, or the pump that was working him.

But continue your promenade to the end of Bull

street, and there you shall see the city park. It is an enclosure of a few acres, shaded by tall, resinous pines, which cast upon the green turf beneath them a pleasing shade. The place is laid out with much simplicity in paths, half sand, half shell; but you have permission, likewise to walk, or sit upon the grass and the wooden benches, and to admire the neat stone fountain, which, situated in the centre of the grove, sends a few playful though feeble streams out of the horns of sundry Tritons and sea gods. It is a pretty work of art enough, except that the water nymph, standing on the summit, has her left hip badly out of joint; as one may more distinctly see on going behind her. It is rather a pity, too, that the artist's fancy, after bringing to birth the marine divinities which grace the lower part of the fountain, should have so completely exhausted itself on reaching the principal basin, where, in utter lack of any mermaids, or lions' heads, or other artistic conceit, the water is left to run out of plain, straight pipes, no more ornamental than the town pumps. However, it is a nice little fountain; and, what with the well-dressed ladies and gentlemen who nightly come out to look at it, and the numerous children joyously romping under the trees, and the small babies that are carted out there to get their airing, brings pleasantly to the mind of the traveller the many beautiful fountains and gardens of the old countries.

On your way both to and from the park, you meet a considerable number of Northern invalids. For this city, situated in a plain of pure silex, has the advantage of a dryer climate than that to be found in any other of the great towns of the South. It cannot, however, be called a dry air, except by comparison; nor is it particularly pure or invigorating. Vexed by few high winds, indeed, the winters are mild, and much more favorable, no doubt, to certain kinds of valetudinarianism than the rigorous ones of New England. Certain it is, that the habit of invalids to come from the North to Savannah is a long-established one. In such numbers do they congregate here, that, at breakfast at the hotel tables, one hears on all sides the questions asked, "How did you sleep last night?" "How is your cough this morning?" And in walking the streets, likewise, the talk overheard is always a good deal about rheumatism and the liniments.

I could more confidently recommend Savannah as a winter residence for consumptive patients, if the hotels there were only a little better. The recent theory of physicians is, that persons afflicted with pulmonary disease should be kept on a generous, nutritious diet. But this pleasant remedy is not so easily to be obtained at the public tables in Savannah. Nor are there any good restaurants; though something might undoubtedly be done toward improving his fare, by the patient's getting up early in the morning, and doing a certain portion of marketing himself. In that way he might obtain some delicacies which waiter and cook would be only too happy, for a valuable consideration, to set before him. He may also find himself sometimes quartered in the neighborhood of noisy courtyards; for I remember that, in one upon which opened the windows of my apartment, there stood a machine for cracking ice, which, being kept in pretty constant action both by day and evening, made quite noise enough to wind up the nerves of any one who had them much unstrung. And in case this might not suffice, the addition of the music made by two small darkeys who were learning the art of drumming, the one by practising upon an empty cigar box, and the other upon a cracked tin kettle, surely would.

During the day passed in that apartment, I, Yankee-like, spent some time in making an estimate of the expense to which I should be put, in undertaking to have the amount of noise which was produced by the drums and the ice machine, manufactured for my entertainment in any other manner, by one or more black boys hired expressly for the purpose. But it was so great that I forbear mentioning it. Should, however, the prescription of whiskey, with a slight addition of water and sugar, be recommended, as it was a few years ago by many Southern practitioners, as a remedy for consumption, the Savannese guest will not have it in his power to complain that his wants in this respect have not been provided for. Indeed, let the patient travel on any of the great roads in this part of the country that he may, the supply of this remedy will not fail him; for scarcely a railroad train stops anywhere, that one does not see rudely painted in large letters, over the door of some shanty more or less well-looking, the word "Bar-room."

But, against plenty of liquor, the invalid who visits Savannah must set sandy roads and exorbitant carriage fees. I know not by what rule it happens, that horse hire in this city should be so unusually expensive, unless it be to maintain a certain proportion between the rate of charges and the depth of the silex one is driven through. Yet let me hasten to add, that any such little drawbacks to the perfect satisfaction and happiness of the invalid which I have here taken the liberty to allude to, will be more than compensated, no doubt, by the hospitality and kindness of the people among whom he comes to take up a temporary residence. In their cheerful and well-appointed houses, such petty deficiencies and discomforts will be quite forgotten. Besides intelligent and refined society, he will find, in some of them, collections of rare and valuable books, as well as of ancient and costly manuscripts, and of interesting autographs, the equals of which can be seen in few American cities, and which will furnish no little consolation to the stranger in weather not suitable for promenading in Bull street.

Whoever visits Savannah, drives, of course, out to Bonaventure. Everybody expects him to take this drive, and he expects to do it himself. He goes by the Thunderbolt road as far as the Thunderbolt road will take him; and then he turns off into a highway, where the sight of his horses' hoofs and the felloes of his carriage wheels is immediately lost in from two to four inches of sand. Still another inch of the same being suspended in the air in the form of dust, it certainly would not be libelling this road—for the privilege of passing over which a handsome little toll is collected from the traveller—to describe it as a sandy one. However, it leads through the pleasant pine woods, and has, at the end of it, in Bonaventure, what might be made, with little pains and expense, the most imposing place of sepulture to be found in the country. The spot is well known from the descriptions of travellers, the charac teristic feature of it consisting in several avenues of evergreen oaks. Planted a hundred or more years ago, they have now attained very great height, while from their branches hangs pendent a funereal pall of gray moss. The groves of the Druids were not dark with so solemn a gloom. The profoundest silence reigns in these magnificent and sombre aisles, where repose the ashes of the dead; broken only by the moaning of the treetops when the winds sweep over them, wrestling with the huge gnarled branches, and making the gray moss wave like mourners' tresses, strewn with ashes; or more cheerfully broken, in mild, sunny days, such as that wherein I first visited it, by the sweet voices of the wood birds, which build their nests and rear their young in these green, sylvan retreats. It was, indeed, a sweet, soothing requiem which these little songsters were singing on that May morning; one expressive of the tender sympathy of nature for man, when, at last, he lies down to sleep on her bosom, and suggestive of a happy existence after he shall have awaked refreshed by his slumbers.

In returning from the cemetery, we soon came upon a little garden of flowers, the blowing roses, fragrant pinks, and glowing verbenas of which made a pleasing contrast with the gloom of the grand old woods. From one place to the other was like a step from death to life, and produced a most exhilarating effect upon the spirits. The gardener gave us flowers, which, taken in the hand, put the whole party at once into holiday attire, and made us no longer thoughtful mourners, but revellers in the midst of the full life and beauty of nature. So buoyed up were all our hearts, that, in returning home, we insisted on making a diversion through Lovers' Lane, in spite of the dust and heat of the way; nor did even the celebrated but ill-jointed plank road, so called, over which we finally drove into town, suffice to finish us.

But the black boy who showed us through the flower garden I must not forget to mention, simply for the sake of his name. It was January! Can a more shocking misnomer be found anywhere on record? If left to make his own selection of a prenomen, the month which stands in the calendar for midwinter would, I am sure, have been the last he would have pitched upon, and must undoubtedly cause a cold chill to creep down his back every time he hears his name called. Name a negro after a hot month; calling him after the last one in summer, for example, Augustus—Augustus Cæsar—and his appellation will be a subject of joy and pride to him as long as he lives. But it is too cruel to call him January. I was tempted to ask the poor fellow if his wife's name were July; but, having compassion on him, I varied the question, and inquired if he did not like the hot weather. He said he did; and, of his own accord, added: "Dere be nothing so good for de nigger as to build a big fire in de rice field, and toast his shins in dog day."

The negroes, by the way, often have very odd names. The boy at the hotel who waited on me at table, answered to the name of Plenty: a name surely good enough so long as there was plenty of roast beef and plum pudding to be had for the asking; but one involving a pungent sarcasm whenever, as was sometimes the case, he brought back the guest's empty plate, with the reply, "Roast beef all gone, massa!"

However, Plenty and the other boys all waited at table to the best of their faculties, and never failed to satisfy me, except when they had partially lost their heads from mixing their toddy with a stick a trifle stiffer than it should have been. One day, I remember, when old Pete was unusually tipsy, he began with asking whether I would have soup, lobster, or pie; and afterward, when I was quietly enjoying my coffee, he disturbed my composure by the inquiry, if massa would not be pleased to be helped to some "wery nice wegetables!"

But my chamber-boy had a name which pleased

me, perhaps, as much as any other, and was certainly a source of the very greatest satisfaction to himself. He was a conscientious and most reliable black boy; but, one evening, before that fact was known to me, wishing to be awaked at an early hour on the morning following, I called the boy, and, looking doubtingly in his face, put to him the question:

"Now, can you be relied upon to wake me to-morrow morning at six o'clock?"

Whereupon, gathering all there was of himself up—for he was very short-legged—and looking at me with a face of mingled astonishment and indignation, he replied:

"Sir, my name is Chisholm (Chism)!"

CHAPTER X.

A Georgia Railway.

"AWFUL hot, madam," said a gent in the 'bus, who happened to be sitting next to the lady by my side, as we drove through the streets of Savannah to the station of the railway to Montgomery. We were early at the station, it being the custom of landlords hereabouts to speed the parting guest, and get him out of the house about an hour in advance of the time. There was, however, no lack of laggards, one of whom came to the conductor, just as the train was about to start, with the request that he would wait a few minutes, as he had some cigars coming. The conductor waited for the cigars. But, when these had arrived, a lady came running into the station house, and implored the official to wait a few minutes for her trunk.

"Oh, my!" she exclaimed, "I must go by the

train—it is a case of necessity—and the trunk will be here in a few moments! Oh, my! oh, my!"

It was absolutely certain, she said, that the trunk would be brought in a very few minutes; for a man had just gone over to the other side of the river to fetch it in a cart. Well, the gallant conductor waited for the trunk also. But when that had finally appeared, the lady's son, a lad of some five years of age, took it into his little head that he himself was not ready to go. Neither the entreaties of papa nor of mamma could induce him to do anything with his tiny feet but stamp with them vehemently upon the platform, while, with a loud voice, he cried out:

"I'm not ready—not ready! I tell you I won't go—won't go!"

But his papa insisting on his instantaneous departure, and taking him up in his arms to put him into the car, the precocious youth, bethinking himself of one more reason for delay, bellowed forth:

"But mamma's trunk—wait for the trunk!"

The conductor, however, though a little slow at the setting out, appeared to be fast enough after he had once got under way. Besides a diamond ring, and bright gilt buttons in his waistcoat, he wore for breastpin a miniature copy of a railway engine, and proved to be a very civil person—fops sometimes making good conductors. But he gave me a greasy check, bearing on its unwashed face the printed command, "Keep this in sight." Now I was not myself of the opinion that such a soiled piece of pasteboard would be ornamental to my hat ribbon; nor could I think of parading it, like an order of merit, on my coat collar. It seemed to me, that if tickets and checks of clean paper were sufficiently in harmony with our democratic institutions, they would be much preferable.

Fortunately, the small number of passengers in the train gave to the gentlemen the opportunity—so gladly improved in this part of the country—of sitting on their backs; for travellers here seem naturally to fall into sprawling attitudes. Before me sat, or rather lay, quite regardless of the presence of ladies, a gent in black broadcloth, with both feet projecting out of the window, his arms thrown back over his head, and his five-dollar beaver resting on his stomach. At my side lay another, with legs crossed, one foot resting on the seat before him, and the other raised halfway to the carriage roof. A tall Kentuckian managed actually to extend himself over three seats; his head resting on one, his back partly on the next, and partly on his portmanteau, which had been so arranged as to bridge the interval; while his legs, extending through the open back of the second seat, were long enough to bring his feet comfortably upon the third. And—poor fellow!—when he found that he could not sleep in this position as quietly as he desired, he went outside, and sat upon the platform—observing the letter only of the order which forbade passengers from standing there. How much I wished Mr. Punch had been present to take a sketch of the various postures into which these planters threw themselves! It would have sold ten thousand copies extra.

The country from Savannah to Montgomery through which the railroad passes, is, for the most part, covered with woods. It is, in fact, a wilderness of woods, with here and there a plantation opening. Most of the fields being still full of stumps, and trees killed by girdling, it wears the face of a new country, but recently reached by the pioneers of civilization. In the plantations along the road there were few buildings to be seen, excepting negro huts made of logs, and small cottages of one story occupied by the masters; though, in two or three of the towns—rather pretty and thrifty ones—I noticed a goodly number of well-built family mansions, and some large warehouses.

At midday, to vary the monotony of the journey, the train suddenly came to a full stop in the woods. This was rather ominous, and at once excited my suspicions that something had gone wrong. Nor was I kept long in suspense; for very soon the words flew from car to car, "Freight train off the track!" And, sure enough, there we were, face to face with an engine and tender which had been thrown from the rails, and now stopped the way. And how long should we be detained? Some said a couple of hours; others said six. Only one thing, however, appeared to be known with certainty—namely, that the engine, with its tender, was to be lifted upon the rails again by the help of a couple of screws, as many big trees cut down and converted into levers, and the stout arms of a dozen or two of men, the greater number of whom were negroes. It was a poor amusement, to be sure, but the best to be had, to observe how slowly and awkwardly the process of repairing the damage was carried on. There was one captain, so called, having the direction of the business; but he had so many lieutenants, every one entertaining an opinion of his own, that in the multitude of counsels there seemed to be not a little folly. Even some of the passengers had a word to say as to the best manner of raising this wheel, or of extracting that bolt. Only the negroes appeared not to know what was to be done. They looked on with faces of blank amazement and unconcern; though they did all the hard work at the levers, and did it willingly.

Fortunately, I had that morning laid in an extraordinary supply of provisions for the journey, as well as of books and papers; recent experience having taught me that it was almost as desirable to have a private larder when travelling in our Southern States, as it is in journeying through the Castiles of Old Spain.

And, indeed, what a comfort it is, when wrecked in the midst of a forest, with no habitations in sight but two or three negro cabins, and nothing eatable in these to be had save fried salt pork and cakes of Indian meal, to have a cold chicken in your basket! A smoked herring, too, is not bad; nor is a bit of cheese; nor are a few sweet Havana oranges. And in such a basket of comforts did I find, that day, both dinner and supper. The weather was luxuriously warm, the sun shining through the thick foliage down among the stems of the trees, and a summer breeze in March making all the green leaves tremble and dance for joy. How pleasant, likewise, it was to find a spring of clear, cold, bubbling water flowing fast by the scene of this breakdown! Here we quenched the thirst of the noontide with cheerful draughts; and here, as the day wore off, spreading our white napkins, we made a travellers' picnic in the woods. Nor, the while we broke our simple bread, did the tongues of the mocking birds tire in the branches overhead; they seeming to be as happy as the day was long—for so long their singing lasted. Was it not, then, a piece of good luck to be kept for six hours in these green woods, with the birds making merry over our heads, and the running waters making merry at our feet? The magnolia, which spread its branches above the spring, would hardly be able many days longer to restrain its buds from bursting. Here and there, amid the masses of emerald leaves, the eye was pleased with seeing the white flowering thorn, itself almost a tree; and, not far off, the scarcely less high Palmia, brightening the gloom with its gorgeous pink blossoms. In roaming up and down the woods, we saw also various kinds of parasitical and climbing plants in full bloom, crimson, blue, and purple. On the surface of pools floated the water lilies, white and yellow. In fact, a multitude of rare plants of the Southern clime were growing on all sides, and nature was everywhere opening her leaves and buds with the joyful exuberance of the semi-tropical spring.

And, at last, this day of detention had a most lovely setting. The sun's rays, as he sank below the horizon, burst through the clouds which obstructed the path of his going down, converting them now into amber, now into molten gold, and lastly into purple. The light had not quite faded out of this tapestry of clouds, nor out of the lines of apple green seen through their openings in the sky beyond, when the whistle of an approaching train broke upon the silence of the twilight air, and announced to us the means of deliverance, and of speedy transportation to the end of our journey.

CHAPTER XI.

Down the Alabama.

ALABAMA — a word beautiful both in sound and signification. For, when one of the Cherokee tribes, overpowered in war by its neighbors, fled for refuge into the great Southwestern wilderness, and, after many long wanderings, came, at length, to the waters of this beautiful stream, with high bluffs and luxuriantly wooded banks, the chieftain of the exhausted tribe of exiles, striking his spear, in the presence of his warriors, into one of the headlands of the river, exclaimed, "*Alabama!*"— *Here we rest!*

I cannot say, however, that I rested particularly well the first night on this river; for the pulsations sent through every plank and timber of the boat as the piston opened and shut the valves of the great, strong heart laboring in the centre of the structure, gave to my narrow couch a motion a little too much like cradle-rocking. Going down the stream, these river craft are, indeed, a little more steady and comfortable; but they ascend the river in an agony of convulsions. But the healthy, clear countenance of the captain was a pretty good guarantee against our being blown up; as were also his pantaloons, they being made in plaits, after the fashion of the Dutch. It was plain that he was not a fast man. Indeed, before starting, he waited a quarter of an hour for a gentleman who had forgotten something to go back to town for it; and would probably have stopped anywhere along the river for a good fellow to get a "drink," had the supply of liquor, by any chance, given out on board.

The company of passengers was not an interesting one.

"Don't you think, sir, it is dangerous travelling on so much water?" inquired an Alabama lady, looking over the side of the steamer, and commencing conversation with me, a perfect stranger. But I comforted her with the assurance that the vessel was both fire and steam proof.

"Came from Montgomery, sir? Going down the river, sir?" she continued, piling question upon question in a single breath.

"Going to Mobile, madam," said I.

"To visit your relations, I reckon?"

"Yes; to spend a month with my aunt."

"Well," concluded my fair unknown, "then I shall see you again."

"Most happy," said I.

At dinner, as ill luck would have it, I was placed next to a still less agreeable lady, and one who, strange to say, was a first-class passenger—had her state room, and wore her cameo. At table she went straight through everything. In such quick succession were the dishes which the waiters set before her devoured, she seemed a travelling gnome or ogress. Not only did she eat with her knife, but, from time to time, she looked me in the face with eyes so sharp and fierce, as to awaken, at last, the fearful suspicion that she was going to begin on me after having finished her chicken. Did mortal man or woman ever before empty such loaded plates of pastry, and live? Upon my word, when I saw her, an hour after dinner, on the guards of the boat, smoking a long clay pipe, and spitting right and left over the floor, I was scarcely so much surprised at the vulgarity of her manners, as at seeing the woman alive and well after so much gorging.

It is doing no more than justice to the company, however, to add, that the boat had its cotton dowager on board. What Southern steamer, in fact, would have its requisite complement of passengers, without some one or more of this quality among them? The great lady wore, as travelling dress, a rich brown brocade; while her eldest daughter, who accompanied her, was arrayed in a tissue of roses, palm leaves, and birds of paradise. The party, it may well be believed, was the great sight of the boat; as was the putting them out at their own landing the principal event of the voyage. Indeed, it was a very grand affair, this putting of them out; nothing better of the kind having happened, so far as I know, since the day when Noah went out of the ark with all his retinue. For they were put out, the planter and his wife, his sons and his daughters, his manservants and his maidservants, with their hogsheads, barrels, kegs, bags, boxes, bundles, kettles, teapots, saucepans, trunks, bandboxes, umbrellas, and bird cages.

A valiant trencher woman, it may be added, almost as valiant as my ogress herself, was this grand dowager; and repeatedly did she strike her fork into the platter of fried oysters set at the head of the table before the captain. But, fortunately, the dish so energetically attacked by the lady in brocade was too enormous in size to suffer much from her depredations. It held a good half bushel. Still, the extraordinary rapidity with which all these bivalves were distributed, would have surprised any one not accustomed to the fast manners of steamboat tables. For the waiters came for them in a perfect *furore*, with arms outstretched, and in almost as copious a perspiration as if they were running for a wager over a Magnolia race course. This set of boys had evidently been trained to rapid movement as thoroughly as any Zouaves or Turcos.

"Coffee, or tea, massa?" inquired of me one of them, in a tone of voice so quick and decided it seemed as if my everlasting destiny depended on the answer.

"Sugar, massa?" he said again, setting the bowl down with an emphasis which made every separate lump in it rattle.

And the fury of the waiters seemed to set on fire the guests; for, as fast as the former hurried up the cakes, so fast the latter hurried them down. The one, as they ran to and fro, tumbled over each other; and the other tumbled no less facetiously into the hot biscuits, the muffins, and the scratch-backs. The meal presented the appearance of an agony—yet short in duration, all over in fifteen minutes.

On the whole, it is my opinion that the only thing on this river worth coming a thousand miles to see, is its wild woods. The traveller through these solitary regions is, indeed, alone with nature; for if the cotton planter cultivates here and there a few broad fields, living himself in a small white mansion house, surrounded by slave cabins, whitewashed or brown with their natural logs; or if the poor white clears up a rod or two of the river bank, space enough to contain a couple of shanties wherein to lodge wife and children, a cow, a pig, and a donkey; or if, on some bluff a few feet out of water, there are to be seen a half dozen smokes rising above the tops of the trees, and indicating the existence of what is here called, by courtesy, a town, or city, still these few scattered tokens of the presence of man do scarcely more than render the solitude of nature still more impressive. Man is here a new comer, and looks almost like an intruder. Civilization has wrought on these rude banks none of her great triumphs; Time has left none of his consecrated, crumbling memorials; Art has raised no towers, no columns, no spires. The cotton bale is the most significant work of man's genius; and, excepting the dilapidated log cabins on the banks, the only ruins washed by the turbid waters of this great river, are the broken trees and driftwood which float down on its surface. But the wild, semi-primitive forest, seen on approaching Mobile, is, indeed, a delight to the eyes. What a perfect wilderness of verdure of every different shade, with the white and purple of the stems of trees intermingled, it is! How light and delicate the green in the oaks and cottonwoods, and how dark in the magnolias and cypresses! Even in this spring season, too, when every leaf is tender, there are soft hues in the foliage approaching nigh to browns and yellows; while out of the crowded thickets many a shrub hangs its early flowers of white, or pink, or blue.

Moreover, while surveying this pleasing scenery, the traveller enjoys the very great advantage of being on board a boat provided, not, indeed, with a band of music, but with a steam piano. This the engineer plays upon whenever he happens to be in the mood musical. Generally, on going from town, he gives a merry waltz; and on returning, if in advance of his rivals, he entertains the expectant crowd on the wharf with a far-sounding march of triumph. Occasionally, too, he will turn off a jig, or negro melody, at the stopping places along the river, just to wake up Sambo, and tickle the heels of the small negroes. And this music is entirely gratuitous, no charge being made for it in your bills, nor any hat handed around after it.

CHAPTER XII.

Mobile.

"IT is pleasant to see the world one lives in," said I to my wife, one sunny morning, after having breakfasted at the Battle House, in Mobile. The meal, indeed, had been an uncommonly good one —good toast, good chops, potatoes shaved thin, done crisp. Even the tea was not bad, taking into account that it was Southern tea; and the waiter was civil, remarkably civil, for an Irish waiter in a "crack" hotel.

But, by the way, can anybody tell why, in a country so full of good-looking black boys, born expressly to serve tables, and needing nothing but the uniform of a white jacket to make the ugliest of them look respectable, why the guests in so many public houses in this part of the Union should be waited upon by unwashed and insolent Irishmen or Germans?* The colored waiter's toilet is always made—made by nature. As his face does not show dirt, it is to be presumed that it is always washed. His hair needs no pomatum; and, dressed at birth, no barber could possibly improve its natural frizzle. The Irish head, on the contrary, is very apt to look like a haystack; or, if greased, is sure to show the candle. By nature, Patrick's face is unwashed, and no amount of scrubbing will do more than merely polish its inherent tinge of uncleanliness. His elbows, too, are always coming through his coat; he is ever outgrowing his pantaloons; and do what you will, put him in plush and gold lace even, he will still look the ditch digger.

However, the lad James, who brought up my breakfast that morning, was certainly an exceptional Irishman. He was tolerably clean, and sufficiently instructed—a very proper, well-behaved lad, who, during my residence in the inn, did not a little to preserve unruffled the placidity of my disposition, promoting my moral as well as physical well-being. And think how annoying to a guest a waiter has it in his power to be, when he is bent on sulking; when he is determined to do nothing as it ought to be done; when he will do but one thing at a time, and is forever in doing that; when he says there is no more of this, and no more of that to be had; or—which is about as bad—when he sets before you too much of everything.

But James, this morning, by a happy inspiration—and your Irishman often says and sometimes does a good thing by inspiration—James served breakfast in his very best style. He seemed pleased himself with the way in which he did it; as much so as he would have been at making a good bull, or delivering himself of something uncommonly dry and full of brogue. It evidently gave him a silent, stomachic satisfaction to see me enjoy my dishes; he knowing as well as I did that there was no indigestion, no distemper in them. And so it happened that my morning meal was attended with only pleasurable sensations, and that I arose from it prepared to do any good deed that needed to be done—prepared to enter upon any course of rational enjoyment for the day which might present itself. Accordingly, turning to my companion, I said, "It is pleasant, my dear, to see the world one lives in. Let us go to Spring Hill."

It was a balmy morning; and, seating myself in the carriage, I spoke placidly to the driver, saying:

"Now, my man, take your own time. Slow or fast, 'tis all the same to me."

Accordingly, he put his horse on that moderate pace which best suits the comfort of an idle man having no other aim than simply to get out of town into the open country. And a quiet, pleasant drive this is to Spring Hill. On either side of the way are villas, every one surrounded with its pretty yard of flowers. The grounds are divided, for the most part, by hedges, made by throwing the turf from a ditch upon one of its sides, and planting the embankment with the Cherokee rose, which, being of rapid growth, soon forms a hedge as dense as it is beautiful. This rose runs along by the roadsides, likewise, converting walls and fences into thick banks of leaves and flowers. It climbs to the tops of high trees, hanging its festoons among the branches, or letting them droop gracefully to the ground. In fact, this showy wild flower, with its five white petals and centre of gold, embedded as it is in so many brightly shining leaves of green, gives almost a bridal aspect to the spring landscape, and wellnigh makes all these citizens' boxes look like homes of the poets.

And the legend of the Cherokee rose is as pretty as the flower itself. An Indian chief of the Seminole tribe—I had the story from a lady in Mobile, as brilliant in mind as beautiful in person—taken prisoner of war by his enemies the Cherokees, and doomed to torture, fell so seriously ill that it became necessary to wait for his restoration to health before committing him to the fire. And, as he lay prostrated by disease in the cabin of the Cherokee warrior, the daughter of the latter, a young, dark-faced maid, was his nurse. She fell in love with the young chieftain, and, wishing to save his life, urged him to escape; but he would not do so unless she would flee with him. She consented. Yet, before they had gone far, impelled by soft regret at leaving her home, she asked leave of her lover to return, for the purpose of bearing away some memento of it. So, retracing her footsteps, she broke a sprig of the white rose which was climbing up the poles of her father's tent, and, preserving it during her flight through the wilderness, planted it by the door of her new home among the Seminoles. And from that day this beautiful flower has always been known, between the capes of Florida and throughout the Southern States, by the name of the Cherokee rose.

The most striking feature of the landscape seen on this road to Spring Hill, is its lofty and wide-spreading liveoaks. They make a pleasant contrast with the pines, which stand thickly clustered together, and have tall, straight, tapering stems, and crowns tufted with needles. In passing through the groves composed of these latter trees, so full of sap in this warm climate, one scents at a considerable distance the pleasantly aromatic perfume. The pine loves the sand; and there is no lack of it here. Indeed, since leaving Wilmington, I have visited no town so softly pillowed upon the sands as is Mobile. The Cape Codder who, in passing along this road, sees his carriage wheels sinking into the yielding material, may very likely feel a pang of regret, believing himself, for the moment, transported out of this Southern paradise back to his native sea beaches. The whole of the road, however, is not so heavy, the greater portion of it having been made hard with shells.

But sand makes pure air; and on arriving in Mobile, more particularly if he come from the mud of New Orleans, the traveller exclaims, "How sweet-scented is this city!" Accordingly, in passing along this road to Spring Hill, as I came in sight of some pretty little villa, peeping out of its shrubbery, with rows of orange and lime trees, of mock orange and pitosporum, of crape myrtles and jessamines from Mexico, the thought came forcibly to my mind, What a pity it is that the Northern invalids, so many of whom I have met in the course of my journey, hurrying from one uncomfortable, ill-provided hotel to another, exposed to frequent and sharp transitions of weather, and suffering from the inconveniences of crowded cars and dirty steamboats, what a pity that, instead of pursuing health over every broken road between Maine and Florida, they could not so far overcome the natural restlessness of the American character, and their own fidgety love of change and travel, as to sit down contentedly for a half or a quarter of the year, in one of these suburban cottages!

Make your home, poor, feverish man, in some of these bowers of flowers. Here you can be constantly in the open air. The noon is not too hot for a walk in the shade; nor are morning and evening too cool for a ride on horseback. The sands are dry under your feet. The exhilarating air from the gulf blows softly in at open windows, bringing with it the pleasant odors of the roses which climb up the lattice, or of the honeysuckles that hang from the piazza eaves. When the sun is hot, the cypress casts for you its dark shadows, and the liveoak spreads an ample shade. Here come with your box of books. There is a piano in the parlor for the young ladies; and the guitar case makes but one piece more of the luggage. Or is it the fair girl herself who is stricken? Then let her come here and tend the flowers. Let her tie up these scarlet lilies; repress the luxuriance of the straying verbenas; pluck nosegays of the sweet-scented violets for her bosom; and wear these blush roses in her hair. If she must die away from her home, what land can be less strange to her than this? And there will be plenty of half-opened buds in the garden wherewith to deck her shroud and strew her grave.

Alas! however, that in late summer and early autumn this Spring Hill, now so green with the newly unfolded leaves, and so gay with every kind of flowers, should not escape the ravages of that dreadful fever which annually scourges the towns situated along the shores of the gulf. One would suppose the air too pure to admit of the coming of that dire epidemic; but it is not so. The inhabitant of the suburban villa is not sheltered from the dart which strikes down the dweller in the crowded and less cleanly town. Indeed, the approach of the fatal fever is always heralded by the prevalence of unusually fine weather. When the winds are comparatively still, when the air is clear and balmy, and every one is saying to himself, How charming are these days! and the nights, moonlit or starry, are so full of light—then it is that the destroyer is at the door. The extraordinary brilliancy of the firmament is but the light reflected from the wings of the angel commissioned by Heaven to scatter pestilence throughout the abodes of the children of men. The fine weather feeds fever until the frost kills it.

But, in the springtime, nobody thinks of the pestilence of the autumn. Much as ever are the last year's dead remembered in a region of country annually rejuvenated by a new invasion of strangers from the higher latitudes. One lives here in the present moment as it flies, and pulls the roses while they blow. The past seems almost to fade out of the memory as quickly as the color every evening fades out of the sky at sunset. Perhaps it is because, in these climes nearer to the sun, the day is so full of delights, being ever fresh with early dew, and warm with the rays of noon, and cool with the evening breeze. The heart, seduced by nature's bounty and unceasing goodness to share her sympathy, and enter into her joys, soon forgets its own sorrow. The men of business, too, lose themselves in present and pressing affairs in these trading towns, as Mobile and New Orleans, even more than elsewhere. While the season for business lasts, they work diligently in their vocation, striving every day to add as many dollars as possible to that heap of gold which is to be their fortune. But once this raised to the necessary elevation, they set off to enjoy it in their native North. Hence the feeling of home attachment is very feeble in these communities, where men reside but half a year, and for half a life. Hence all great public improvements are made slowly, and with difficulty. The ties of family are more easily severed, and the condition of life is less favorable to good morals.

Spring Hill is, of course, a hill—a slight natural elevation on these sandy shores and level plains of woods. From its summit, looking over an intervening distance of green tops of trees, one sees the city of Mobile; and, beyond, Lake Pontchartrain. Getting out of his carriage, he strolls for a few minutes in the pleasant shade, and breathes the hilltop air, pure from all odors unless it be that of flowers. Returning through the little cluster of villas called Somerville, he again descends from his carriage; for who could pass these magnificent liveoaks, these lofty pines, with bark of purple and foliage so deeply green, and these poplars growing as vigorously here as in their native Lombardy, without lingering to admire the luxuriant display of vegetation? He wishes also to inspect more closely the roses of the Cloth of Gold, and the white Lamarques. The Malmaison, too, is so delicately tinted, and its petals are so gracefully folded, that the lover of flowers is never tired of looking at it. How effulgently the Giant of Battles glows, spotting the surrounding green with crimson! And here the Lady Bank climbs the China trees, adding its yellow to their blue. How sweetly sleeps the sunlight of the noon on these beds of flowers! reposing on rose leaves; lying hid in the cups of the lilies; basking on the crimson carpet of the verbenas; poised on the outspread calyxes of the pinks; and cradled in the large blossoms of the magnolias, which on the tops of the trees are gently swinging in the wind.

I could have spent the whole morning in these lanes and gardens; but, the morning being already gone, I returned to town.

Nor is the drive along the shore of the bay scarcely less pleasant. Take it on a warm day, when, as you go, you will be fanned by the sea breeze, freshly blowing from gulf and lake. The Mobilites drive over this shore road to cool their blood, to dry the locks moistened by perspiration, and to relax the mind overwearied by affairs. I selected, however, for this excursion, a very idle, dreamy morning, when the sun, sluggishly mounting the hazy zenith, seemed almost too lazy to shine. The lake, along the shore of which the road winds, lay in a slumber too profound to be interrupted by the faint ripples which came softly creeping up from the direction of the sea beyond. With carriage top thrown back, and myself reclining indolently upon the cushions, I was borne slowly along this winding way; the horses going at their own gait, and the driver's whip dangling idly from its socket. With a temperature just soft enough, and a breeze which barely kept me company, and the sun's rays shorn by the gathered vapors of their glare, the luxury of this driving was almost as great as of sailing in a gondola upon the canals of Venice. As I passed along the road, the gardener was listlessly trimming his flowers; the farmer stopped work to see the stranger go by; the negro stood leaning against the side of the house, with both hands in his pockets; and, before the hour of noon, the laborers who had been employed in covering the road with shells had knocked off work, and, sitting on logs beneath the trees, were peacefully eating their dinner. And so I jogged on for half a dozen miles between the farms and villas, through groves of pines, and oaks, and magnolias. The Cherokee rose followed me on the hedges, and the white flowering blackberry crept after along the roadsides. Were not the tall magnolia trees, with all their dark, glossy leaves, and white buds ready to burst, made beautiful enough by nature, that she needed also to hang them with the grace of the wild grapevines? Nor were the pitch-yielding pines fair enough to the sight, with their purple bark and needles of green, that they must be climbed by such pretty parasites? How lovely are the flowers of this tulip tree! The branches, so profusely decked by them, overhang the road, and can almost be reached by the hand. I stop the carriage, and, climbing the fence which skirts the way, break off an inviting bough. The flowers are green externally, having spots of orange and a delicate shade of yellow within. In shape they resemble the cup of the white water-lily. But they have no fragrance.

And now, passed the magnolia grove and the Magnolia race course, we turn the horses' heads about—not, however, changing their pace. Then, in the depths of the forest, I saw Morpheus just lying down to take his siesta, and was almost tempted to ask him to join our company: for the carriage was an easy one, the shell road smooth, and the horses' hoofs beat the ground with a regular, monotonous cadence. The coachman on his box, I am sure, had but one eye open, the other having the night before been bunged. It being now the height of noon, the small birds merely whispered to each other in the trees; there was not even the lowest murmuring of waves on the shore; and the cocks of the barnyards, if wide awake enough to crow, still did it drawlingly, and with a tone of voice inducing sleep rather than disturbing it. Such days as these it is, said I, that make the idlers of the South; something in the very atmosphere inviting a man to sit down to smoke his cigar and waste the time. They favor lounging, loafing. Under such influences from the skies, the ladies, instead of walking, loll in carriages; and the gentlemen cannot sit upright in their chairs, but must recline with heels higher than head, thereby acquiring the stoop of the counting house as effectually as from leaning over the legers.

On my return to town, the very streets seemed to

be struck with a certain degree of stupor. There was no stir in them. Men were walking slowly up and down, or were lounging at the shop and hotel doors, all looking as though their work were done for the season.

"Rather sleepy here to-day," said I to the landlord.

"Yes," he replied; "we are apt to have dull weather at this time. Business slackens now that the cotton is all down; and people are beginning to leave for the North."

CHAPTER XIII.

The Lower Mississippi.

THE weather, after my departure from Mobile, became warmer, and, in fact, perfectly tropical. Sunshine perpetual, or effulgent moonlight, accompanied me all the way across the azure gulf; but on the bar of the Mississippi a fog came out of the north, with rain, and wind, and cold, and thunder and lightning. Climate and clothing, I made a change of both on this bar. I was let down out of heaven and stuck in the mud in one and the same moment. During the voyage, our steamer had managed to attain a speed of eight knots the hour; but here, with her keel three feet deep in the sand and slime of the river, she made only about eight inches. How, for half a day, her paddles made the yellow porridge of the Mississippi boil! The wonder was that she got through into deep water even at the end of that time. Doubtless there was a snail at her stern helping her.

Charming sight it was to look upon the banks of black mud, barely rising above the level of the waters, and somewhat resembling huge leviathans lying at anchor, or alligators asleep on the surface! It would have reminded one who had been a passenger in Noah's ark, of the appearance of the world the morning after the Deluge. Only, instead of doves bringing olive branches, there was but the flight of a few lazy sea gulls. Gradually, however, this primeval aspect of things gave place to that of the dry and solid earth. From mud islands, we came to others covered with reeds and rushes. Next succeeded the wild grasses. Blackbirds and buzzards shared the sky with the sea gulls. Then appeared the mammalia, wild hogs, half-tamed horses, cows browsing in pastures which lay a foot deep under water, and, finally, man—that is to say, the fisherman, living in a hut built on piles. Here, also, dwelt the lighthouse keeper, and, strange to say, the worker of the telegraph. The quarantine ground—I might almost say water—came into view a little later, being wellnigh submerged, and looking like a pet nursery of fever and pestilence. I was strongly tempted to inquire of the doctor respecting the health of his own family, and express an affectionate hope that he himself had not an ague; for the man was thin in the cheeks, and sallow, and, in fact, looked quite ashamed of performing the duty of feeling anybody's pulse on board the steamer. I also wished to congratulate him on his boat; as, in case the river should rise still a little higher, it might be the saving of himself and his household.

Every inhabitant of this part of the river, I afterward observed, was the owner of a similar boat, which he used for rowing himself about his small estate, and fishing for snappers in his fields, when the water was too deep to dig potatoes. The dwellings all had the appearance of being bath houses; built, in the lower part of the river, of logs, and thatched; higher up the stream, shingled; and, higher still, slated. But near the mouth, I could hardly have believed it a Christian land we were entering, had we not pretty soon come to a fort. This was an unmistakable evidence of civilization; and the extensive orange plantations, which afterward began to peep out of the primeval forests skirting the river side, still more favored the idea that we were entering the gates of a great country.

The quantity of driftwood in the stream was an indication, to be sure, of interminable forests higher up on its banks; but, on the other hand, the numerous floating casks, barrels, and bottles, proved that we were approaching some large emporium of commerce. Might it not also be the seat of a prodigal luxury, a city flowing not only with milk and honey, but with ready-made cobblers and cocktails? For the yellow, foaming river really seemed to be running with egg-nogg—and it certainly did not run straight.

CHAPTER XIV.

New Orleans.

THE first thing I saw, on the morning of my arrival in New Orleans, was the quays; and the second was the cotton on them. Acres upon acres, indeed, of cotton bales and sugar boxes I saw on the quays; and, on the river, broad forests of masts and steamers' smoke pipes, the steamers being piled five stories high, the smoke pipes projecting into midheaven, and the whole structure, in fact, carried to such an altitude, that, when there is an explosion, one can hardly be said to be blown up, but, on the contrary, blown down. Yet I did not fully realize the fact of being in the Crescent City and emporium of the Southwest, until the waiter at the hotel brought me a pitcher of water for shaving. This made it as clear as mud that I had reached the celebrated and turbid Mississippi. The natives pretend that this river water, when properly filtered, is the third best drinking water in the world. I suspect, however, that if a person will use water rather than the other beverages in more general favor here, that which falls from the skies, and is preserved in tanks above ground, is preferable. The bath, certainly, nowhere looks less inviting than in this city. One's linen must be washed in it, as the laundress cannot use a more expensive liquid; though, if lager beer could be obtained at a little lower price, it might be questioned whether the clothes would not come out of it looking whiter.

The impression which the stranger is likely to get of life in New Orleans, is, that it is sufficiently *bizarre.* In no other large American city does it seem so full of incongruities and irreconcilable contrasts. Here are half a dozen different races, and half a dozen different colors of the skin. In one quarter of the town live the Americans; in the other, the French Creoles. The latter keep themselves, in fact, so distinct from the former, that some of them are said never to pass the division line of Canal street. In ballrooms, too, the Creole ladies—and lovely creatures they are, French in dress, manners, and ideas, and pleasantly transitional between the women of the tropics and those of the States—retain a portion of the floor exclusively for themselves; though always happy, I am told, to receive the visits of the American gentlemen from the other side of the hall; and even giving them a preference over the beaux of their own caste, the greater part of whom distinguish themselves rather in dancing, smoking, drinking, and playing billiards, than in more manly accomplishments and occupations. Among the quadroons I saw less beauty than corresponds with the reports of travellers; while the lower class of the French part of the population surprised me by the roughness and almost insolence of its manners. Many fine, manly forms may be noticed among the merchants at the Exchange, and other principal centres of business; but the general type of face is rather coarse than refined, more furrowed and knit with cares than expanded with generous sentiments.

Dust, or mud, abound everywhere in this city. It does not always rain; but the sun cannot burn out the stains of mould and damp on the older house walls. The buildings, excepting those recently erected, look dingy. One-story tenements stand by the side of lofty warehouses, no law of harmony prevailing; so that it takes all the finery of the shop windows, the painted names, and the glittering signboards, to make even the most crowded streets a little picturesque. On these boards the names are written in different languages, and you constantly overhear, on the promenades, various foreign accents. In the principal cathedral the service is read in French; you buy fruit at stalls kept by Spaniards; the German at the market place spreads out his wares in a booth; the Jew offers to sell you cigars at half the street corners; and, in some quarters of the town, you can have a Chinese for a bootblack.

There is style and dash enough here, but little completeness of design or harmony of effects. In all the streets most marked contrasts abound. One meets coaches washed with gaudy and superfluous silver, but the coachman not washed at all. You pass over pavements lying deep in mud, and along sidewalks lined with gutters either stagnant, or creeping only by the aid of machinery; and yet you meet ladies taking their morning walks in ermine, and ball dresses. The promenade of the most fashionable streets is almost as much encumbered with boxes of merchandise as in New York are the *trottoirs* of Dey street. The corners, too, are beset with gents, loafers, orange women, and venders of roasted chestnuts—the latter not bad. But nowhere in all its course does the American sun behold so high-colored muslins, such flaunting silks and roseate ribbons. New York has no show of millinery to compare with it. Such nosegays of hats, such cobwebs of laces, such loves of fans, such shawls, such brocades, such tissues! They make this city a perfect little heaven for all the wives and daughters of Louisiana, Mississippi, and Arkansas. And of this heaven the queen is, or was, Madame Olympe. Every box she orders from Paris produces, when opened, the effect of another Pandora's, turning half the ladies' heads in the Mississippi country, and emptying all their purses. This, to be sure, is saying a good deal; for when the cotton or sugar planter brings down his wife and daughters to this metropolis, he means they shall have a good time, and furnishes them with money enough to buy all the millinery they can stand under.

The Englishman who, having come over in a Cunarder, takes lodgings at the St. Nicholas Hotel in New York, pronounces its drawing rooms *stunnin'*. But as much more magnificent as was its bridal chamber than its bedrooms in the fifth story, so much does the one parlor of the St. Charles in New Orleans exceed in splendor the whole suite of showrooms of the New York caravansary. For, when all the cotton widows and cotton girls have bought their new dresses in Canal or Chartres street, they display them at once in the St. Charles parlor. Every chair and sofa is set out with the new silks and satins. You hear it whispered about, that the dress of white point lace worn by the young belle standing before you cost papa two thousand dollars;

and that the lady by her side, from Red River, flames with twenty thousand dollars' worth of jewelry. Yonder miss has hidden herself in the corner, because, for the embroidered muslin she has on, Madame Olympe did not charge but two hundred dollars. The Mississippi widow, bent on making a sensation, will not come down to the breakfast table in anything short of diamond brooches, and lace from the high altar; while even then the dowager from Baton Rouge wins the general stare from her by planting herself *vis-à-vis* in pearls, and supplementary puffs made by the barber.

But in order to carry out the contrasts of this Southwestern life, by the side of the fair women decked in all this finery you may, perhaps, see sitting the captain of a river steamboat, or even his purser. Indeed, a considerable number of the gentlemen in attendance on these gorgeous belles have the look of men who might once have been head waiters, or, at least, have carried from town to town their bag of samples. Every one of them wears an enormous diamond pin stuck in his shirt bosom; and some have either Niagara Falls, or the course of the Mississippi, or all the cards in the pack, pictured in the stripes of their pantaloons. They are of that class of men who, at home, if they cannot make themselves famous in any other way, will drive a team of elks *tandem ;* and take their wives to the ball in furniture wagons, in order to give them room to spread themselves.

But perhaps the most striking instance of the incongruities of Southwestern life may be seen at the hotel tables. You pay three dollars per day for drinking your coffee out of china embellished with the head of General Cass, or of some similar worthy, who has made himself a great name at Washington. And this cup is brought to you, not by a good-looking Sambo with white teeth, eyes, and apron, but by some rude, ungainly German or Irishman, who tells you that there are no fried oysters, that the plantains are gone, the French rolls gone, and, bringing two fins on a plate, informs you that it is the last of the red snappers.

"I hope I am not too late for tea, Patrick?"

"Yes, you are. No tea after eight o'clock, sir."

"Bridget, send me the chambermaid."

"The chambermaid is off duty, ma'am, at six o'clock."

"But are you not a chambermaid?"

"No, ma'am; I'm higher. There is a girl on watch—only she has gone to tea; she will be back in an hour. You can call her."

The mistake you made consisted in taking a waiting for a chamber maid, though in a most untidy dress and soiled satin slippers.

However, you can breakfast very well on stewed redfish, whenever you can get it; and you can dine very well off roasted turkey, fed on peanuts, when you can get that. But the epicure should come to New Orleans in the crab season, and enjoy this delicacy done in rice and curry *à la Creole.*

If the time of crabs be not fully come, let him rather wait a month or two before making his visit; and, indeed, in case they are lean in any particular year, let him not come at all. He must not expect to eat green peas in March; but will be lucky even to get salad. It is not for early greens, or any such delicacies, that he pays his twenty-one dollars per week, but because the hotel has been built at an expense of a million, one quarter of it laid out on a portico with tall Grecian pillars, as if the edifice were a temple, not a tavern.

For the rest, this seems to be a city of bar and billiard rooms, of bowling and pistol alleys. Bar, billiards, and bowling are the three Bs of New Orleans. There is no room in the hotel so large as that wherein the liquor is dispensed. It being also an auction room, handbills of the sales lie about the house, and on all the public tables, those of the parlor not excepted. You can look on scarcely any street wall without being informed that, in the barroom of such a hotel, there will be, on such a day, at such an hour, a sale of negroes, or other merchandise. The hammers of the auctioneers make as much noise here as do the fighting cocks in Cuba.

But, to escape this clatter, you can take a drive to the southern part of the city, which is made beautiful by flowers. It is the garden of the town. Here every house is built in an enclosure well filled with ornamental shrubs and trees, which, during the spring season, are fresh with green leaves and fair with blossoms. From the liveoak hung with moss, to the blue violet which scents the air, all the forms of vegetation are full of sap and vigor. The flowering trees are of many colors—white, blue, yellow, purple, crimson. The roses grow on tall stems, or climb to the roofs of the houses. The walls and trellises are covered with the blushes of these most lovely of flowers; or they are straw-colored; or they peep out of the green leaves in spotted white. And in the midst of them stands the solemn, graceful cypress, making strong contrast with oleanders and pitosporums. How gracefully the locust hangs out its tassels in the air; the orange trees glow with the yellow of our sweet maples in autumn; the Chinese viburnums are only less fair in their dress of green and white; while the mocking birds in cages mock the wild birds which sing to their young in the tall laurel trees.

This is the bright side of the town; and the stranger should appropriate a sunny day to seeing it. Unfortunately, there are not so many such in the New Orleans spring as one might suppose from the reports of the local journalists, who seem to form an Admiration Society for the purpose of glorifying the city and its climate. The beauty of every bright, genial day is elaborately puffed by them in print. So is the coming of all the early fruits of the season. The arrival of the first pompano makes an epoch; the first strawberry moistens the mouth of every citizen who reads the account of it in the newspapers; the first dish of green peas in the market is sent as a present to the printer; and, in the same way, all the changing delights of New Orleans life, its balls, its races, its theatrical shows, get an extraordinary amount of puffing. But let not the New Yorker, who, sitting down in the month of March to warm his toes before the anthracite, is entertained with one of these high-flown bursts of admiration, copied into the papers of his own city, let him not disturb the digestion of his metropolitan breakfast by sighing for the possession of such premature luxuries as fall to the lot of mortals inhabiting the Crescent City. Especially let him not be tempted to set hastily off for the Gulf of Mexico, in order to regale himself with these semi-tropical delicacies. But if so completely infatuated by their description that he must needs go in pursuit of them, let him be persuaded, at least, to take his anthracite along with him; for he will need it. True, the day of his arrival may very likely be so sultry as to tempt him into white linen; but the day after he will shiver in flannels. Does he wish to breakfast on pompanos? Certainly, they are in the market, but not in the bill of fare of the St. Charles Hotel. They are to be had for two dollars and a half apiece, and grease money to the cook. He would like a dessert of large, ripe strawberries, such as he read of in the papers before leaving New York. He will be able to find them, no doubt, by going to the confectioner's in Canal street.

"How much for strawberries?"

"Twenty dollars the gallon, sir. Have some?"

However, it must be acknowledged that the extraordinary things that the New Yorker will see at the St. Charles will go far toward repaying him for the trouble of his journey. He will see gentlemen in purple pantaloons. Twice in the twenty-four hours all the magnificence of Red River and Arkansas empties itself—a perfect flood of jewels, laces, painted silks, and muslins—into the parlor. He will see that. Indeed, let him look sharp at these ladies; for, among them, he will find some with not less than four thousand cotton bales a year, and others who run two sets of sugar kettles. "Look at 'em straight, to see if you like 'em," as the orange boy said to me on the Mississippi steamer, when I stopped him for the purpose of making an investment in the contents of his baskets. And when the gorgeous tide is out of the parlor, our New Yorker may be entertained, by chance, with the sight of a couple of lovers on a sofa, sucking each an orange, while they estimate the value of their respective crops for the next season, and speculate on the probable price of negroes. Then, when he goes to dinner, it will be an amusement for him to divine the character and occupation of the gentleman sitting opposite, with such an imposing countenance, with hair artistically combed back, with so grand an air, so much deference toward the lady sitting by his side. Is he a cotton lord, or a sugar lord, or some foreign potentate on his travels? —a question which may well occupy the mind for a half hour, at the end of which time our traveller, on going down to the barroom for his *petit verre* of Cognac, gets the solution. His *vis-à-vis* is a tapman, and mixes juleps.

And, finally, the New Yorker who has come down to New Orleans to eat early strawberries, will undoubtedly be asked to spend a week on some plantation up the river, where he will enjoy the great treat of hunting the bear. This of itself will repay him for the trouble of having travelled a thousand miles, and even make him, on his return to the North, as famous as the English cockney, who, after the tour of the States, returns to London.

"Well, Colonel," says every friend he meets, "you've returned from America, at last?"

"Why, ya-a-s."

"Do anything there?"

"Why, ya-a-s; I shot a few bear!"

CHAPTER XV.

Lake Pontchartrain.

I MADE the inevitable excursion to Lake Pontchartrain. And, after a few days in town, it was a pleasant change to pass beyond the suburbs into the open fields, where, instead of the careworn faces of the Exchange, and the painted faces of Canal street, I saw herds of cows and oxen placidly grazing in the pastures. It is true that I very soon came to the great New Orleans swamp; but even that was interesting as a specimen of that kind of natural scenery of which there is so much along the course of the Mississippi. I found it full of tall trees and tangled thickets, the former of which soon come to maturity, and soon go to decay; so that the naked, dead branches and the leafy young twigs are everywhere interlaced. It is the beauty of the garden and the desolation of the waste combined. Huge trunks lie mouldering in all directions on the ground,

8

which is half submerged in water; while out of every dry spot springs an infinite variety of shrubbery, and plants bearing flowers. One hears the birds singing in the trees where they are building their nests; and, at the same time, looks in the mud-holes for water snakes and alligators.

But, now that you are at the lake, what do you propose to do? Will you walk out upon the wharf, which projects far into the water? The sun is too hot. Will you take a bath? The bathing house is not open until later in the season, when the water is lukewarm; and, besides, it is as yellow as that of the Mississippi, or the Tiber. Will you take a boat, and amuse yourself by sailing? But there is no wind. What, then, can be done? The New Orleanist knows very well what to do. He walks into the hotel, takes a drink, and orders a fish dinner. He has come out here expressly to have a feast, and, perhaps, to gorge himself with pompanos, like a pike with frogs. He will also eat croakers, or *court-bouillon* of redfish, or tenderloin trout; and the odds are that they will be quite tender enough. Yet it may be a very nice thing, a fish dinner at the lake; for everybody seems to think so. For my part, however, I preferred spending my time in exploring the neighboring swamp for mud turtles and alligators.

But after having eaten your fish, if you will, and

seen the wharf, and seen the row of shanties along the shore, and fired a few rounds in the pistol gallery, and shot, of course, your alligator, you return by the way of the swamp to the city. There is absolutely nothing else to be done or enjoyed at Lake Pontchartrain.

But, I pray you, stop, on your return, at Carrollton; for there is a garden there full of fair flowers, and attached to it a gardener skilful in arranging them in bouquets. What an infinite beauty of colors and graceful forms we brought to town in a single nosegay! It made the foul streets fragrant, as we passed along, and transformed our sombre hotel chamber into a rustic bower or cottage piazza. How lovely these roses of Ophir, of blended pink and straw-color! how full of odor these orange blossoms, mignonettes, and jessamines! And a cheap pleasure it is. For two or three paltry shillings one buys a great feast and entertainment, greater than can be purchased in our Northern towns for as many dollars.

CHAPTER XVI.

Up the Mississippi.

I WENT up the Mississippi in one of the very "crackest" boats on the river. The captain, as described in the editorial column of a morning paper, was an Esq. well known in the community; and the clerk "a gentleman with whom it is a pleasure to travel." Strange to say, I found this description very nearly true. The captain, at least, was a brave and good-looking fellow; while the clerk, when I mentioned to him the name of the plantation to which I was going, said he regretted that he should have to put me on shore at daybreak, but would give orders to the engineer to make noise enough, on approaching the landing, to wake up all the negroes on the place.

Like all the best boats, this one was five stories high, and had the appearance of being as much out of the water as a duck. From one end of the cabin to the other there extended a long vista, made longer by a mirror at the stern. In the forward part of this saloon were congregated the gentlemen, discussing politics, cobblers, and polka; in the aft sat the ladies on sofas and Yankee rocking chairs. A small apartment in the extremest stern accommodated the maids and duennas; and, though a situation the farthest possible removed from danger in case of explosion, I happened to notice that one of these colored dames said a prayer and crossed herself between each of the half-dozen cups of tea she drank at supper. No doubt she expected to be blown up before morning.

This boat was celebrated for her fleetness; and it was amusing to see her shoot across the bows of two or three rivals which had left the city a little in advance of her. The captain apparently took pride in passing as near to the other boat as it was possible to go without coming into actual contact. There was some danger, to be sure, in two steamers running at full speed within ten feet of each other; but it gave a good opportunity to the jocose officers, waiters, and crews on board of both vessels to bandy pleasant words together.

"Captain," said I, "your ship seems to be rather fast."

"Yes, sir," he replied; "she is able to take the skin off the nose of any craft on this river."

I believed him; for the boat was driven through the water with a force so great it seemed that another inch of steam would certainly split everything. The huge framework shook, from the violent efforts of the engine, as if it had the ague. The floor shook beneath my feet; the table shook, and all the dishes on it. Every door, also—every window and pane of glass in the enormous structure rattled; while all the passengers seemed to feel very much as doughnuts do when shaken in the goodwife's saucepan. Surely, at the expiration of six or seven days and nights on the river, one would have quite enough of this mode of travelling, bepraised as it is in these parts; and, even before that time, might well pray for a good thick fog to compel the boat to lie at anchor for twenty-four or forty-eight hours, thereby restoring quiet.

My stateroom was neat, commodious, and of large size; yet the air was too warm, and not too pure. Indeed, what is to prevent the odors from the tables, which are spread half the day long, and the odors from the barroom, pungent enough at all times, from constantly passing aft, and perfuming the ladies' cabin, and rooms adjoining?

However, I dined better and more comfortably than I remember ever to have dined on any river-going steamer before, the Rhine boats only excepted.

The neatly painted cabin made a handsome dining room. The tables, divided into small ones, were spread with linen immaculately clean. The waiters, who were all black boys in white jackets, served the guests with less clatter of the heels, and less running, and foaming at the mouth, than I have before witnessed in any similar crowd of attendants. My boy, whenever I wanted him, was always at my elbow. Whenever sent for any dish, he did not stop to rest his bones by the way. He also remembered what he was sent for, and did not come back with chicken instead of turkey, or mashed potato instead of green peas. He and all his fellows were evidently well officered, and had been subjected to a system of drilling second only to that of West Point.

But the excellence of the dinner did not consist entirely in the clean linen and the good service. There was a master in the art of cooking below decks, who sent up his dishes in a style which put the cooks of the great hotels on shore *nowhere*. Think of having your choice, on board a steamboat, between three different kinds of such fish as boiled sheep's head, baked snapper, and barbecued redfish —not to mention side dishes, like oyster pie and stuffed crabs! Think, too, of such extraordinary dishes on a steamboat table as calves' feet cooked as they are cooked in Portugal, and ox tongue done as they do it in Macedonia! Think, also, of boned calves' head, of maccaroni *timbale*, of briskets of pork *à la Perigord*, and of veal in a blanket of mushrooms! Think, finally, of no less than seventeen different dishes of sweets, many of them with strange names and stranger aspect!

But in order not to represent the feast as absolutely perfect, it must be confessed that the tables did shake a little—that the custards were in a state of perpetual churning—and that the forms of jelly, trembling, threatened to jump overboard. If there was none of the risk experienced in sea-going steamers, of having the soup transferred from plate to lap, one could, at least, not help thinking that he would feel more secure of his dinner if well lashed to it. Nobody, I observed, dared drink any stronger wine than the ordinary claret, which was furnished as a part of the dinner; the guests seeming to consider how easy a thing it would be to tumble from such uneasy chairs under the table.

As the captain did not land me until an hour or two after daylight, there was no need of any extra noise to wake up the negroes. But from the amount of whistling and screaming the engines performed during the night, whether on stopping at way stations for the accommodation of mails and passengers, or in saluting other boats and river craft, I should say that there could not have been much sleeping on the banks of the river, except by persons whose ears were very familiar with steam music.

Put out in the early morning upon the levee, I was left there without a soul to help me—not one compassionate cabman even. My arrival not being expected at that hour, the family coach, of course, was not in waiting. What, then, was I to do with either myself or my luggage? Clearly, I was to do as Southern people do—wait; and, what was better, enjoy the freshness of the beautiful morning by this broad river side.

The wild fowl were flying, with cheerful cry, hither and thither over the water; or feeding and gambolling on shallow places near the shore, unscared by the fowler. The river hurried by, never resting; while all nature, on that still morning, lay in repose. The grass upon the banks and fields was a soft green; as far as the eye could reach beyond ran the level woods; and, over all, the sun just risen shed the mild light of a morning in spring. I waited, but not impatiently—enjoying the satisfaction, besides, of knowing that the solid ground beneath my feet could not be shaken by anything short of an earthquake.

At last, a black boy of tender years came from the mansion house, having been sent to ascertain the cause of the boat's stopping. He was just big enough to carry my small "traps;" and, leaving the trunks on the shore, I walked slowly on behind the little guide. But before going far, a stout negress came trotting toward me, to see who was coming; nor had I received her salutations before a negro on horseback hove in sight. My escort increased at every step, until I arrived at the gate of the mansion, where still another small negro bade me welcome, and asked me to walk in.

CHAPTER XVII.

A Sugar Plantation.

THIS plantation is one of the largest on the Mississippi. It lies lower, indeed, than the river, as do the others all the way to New Orleans; the water being kept in its channel by an embankment ten or more feet in height. The whole estate, extending three or four miles back from the river, is wellnigh as level as a house floor. Its soil is cultivated by two or three hundred negroes, male and female, and almost half as many mules and horses. Just now they are planting the sugar cane, ploughing with six mules and two negroes—one of the latter driving, and the other holding the plough. There are smaller teams, however, in the lighter ground, consisting of two mules, and one man or woman. One sees a whole acre of blacks of both sexes at work with hoes, covering the canes. They labor from dawn until dusk, with a couple of hours of rest at noon; and, being behind in their planting on account of the wet state of the lands, they are now working very briskly, and do not rest on Sunday. They have, however, plenty of the "hog and hominy" which the negro so much delights in; are remarkably healthy looking, and wear, for the most part, good-natured, happy faces.

There is a whole yardful of little ones, who are kept colonized apart from their elders, and number about sixty. A bright, roguish set they are, as merry as so many blackbirds, and far blacker. Ranged in a row before us, they stood all the while giggling, and stretching their mouths at each other. A portion of them were also made to dance on a platform, which they did with a will, shuffling with their heels, and singing, in full chorus, "Oh! wait for de wagon," and "Ole Dan Tucker."

After inspecting the little negroes, we looked at the other live stock. At the call of an old woman, turkeys, hens, chickens, geese, peacocks, and guinea fowls came running and flying to get their dinner. Then a nimble black boy was sent over the fence to run among the trees and bushes, for the purpose of driving into the open ground a herd of tame deer, which we had the pleasure of seeing leap and run from one end of the park to the other.

This plantation is a little world of itself. Corn,

as well as sugar, is raised here, and is ground in a steam mill into the whitest of hominy. Here are herds of horses, mules, and cows, and flocks of sheep. There is no lack of milk for the children, and butter is churned every morning by a little negress in a stone pot almost as tall as she is. Her mistress says she sometimes goes to sleep at the task, though still keeping up the churning. Several mechanical trades, likewise, are carried on, as the carpenter's, the smith's, the cooper's. There are a dozen outhouses of all kinds in the yard—icehouse, hencoop, terrapin pen, laundry, dairy, &c. At a little distance from the mansion stands the sugar mill; and connected with it is a small village of negro houses, all neatly whitewashed.

During our visit, there occurred a succession of beautiful days, beautiful as pearls upon the string. The sunrise, so praised by the poets, we here found to be no fable; and all that had been said by this fibbing class of writers respecting the beauty of the early dewdrops, nestled in rose petals pendent from honeysuckles, cradled in the hollows of leaves, and flashing like gems from every spear of grass and blade of clover, we discovered to be simple verity. It was the freshness of the Northern spring morning, but warm and soft as the morning of the Northern summer. And what a sweet fellowship of life was it to breathe the same air as the roses and the honeysuckles! What calmness of joy to walk in these paths where the myrtle blooms, and the sweet-scented violet! The wild olive, also, is fragrant, and so is the banana shrub, bearing corollas chocolate-colored. Here, on these lawns, is a perfect harmony of flowers of every hue; and here, besides, grow great numbers of strange, semi-tropical plants, and trees which love the sun. At the same time, the ear is captivated with a chorus of mocking birds, and other sweet-throated songsters; for the birds all fly to these gardens, taking delight, apparently, in this beauty of foliage and flower, and made also more cheerful themselves from the addition they bring to the happiness of man. Such mornings are like nosegays, which never fade, and live forever in the memory.

Nor is the spring noontide on the banks of the Mississippi scarcely less pleasing. The thermometer seems at fault when it indicates a temperature of eighty-five degrees of Fahrenheit; for the air is quite cool and fresh. One is comfortable in thin woollen. Light, capricious breezes are humming, at intervals, in the tops of the cypresses, and softly caressing the roses which hang swinging from the branches of the China trees. Sitting in the pleasant shade, one is fanned by them as gently as by peacock feathers waved over his head by slaves. Indeed, these airs seem to take as much delight in idling away the noontide as we ourselves do, swinging from treetop to treetop, balancing themselves on the poplar leaves, and finding sufficient occupation, as they come from this side or from that, in bringing us now the scent of roses, or pinks, or violets, and now the incense of orange blossoms or honeysuckles. The voices of the hundred mocking birds in these groves and thickets are softly subdued, at this hour of the day, their superabundant joy getting vent only in undertones and half notes. The drowsy humming of the bees is almost audible. And how sweetly the low bleating of the lambs, as they nibble the white blossoms of the clover pastures, harmonizes with this calm of the Southern noontide; while the shrill crowing of the cock on a neighboring plantation suggests to the ear almost a discord! The cattle, tired of cropping the luxuriant lawn, now lie huddled in the shade of the broad liveoaks; the negro gardeners, who have been mowing the fragrant grass, or trimming the too adventurous climbing plants, now eat their midday meal, sitting with their backs against the fence, or lie sleeping after it in the full sunlight; while we, pleasure seekers, wish for no better entertainment than to spend the sunny hours on the cool piazza, turning some pleasant, desultory pages; or, in gentle converse, strolling idly up and down, plucking now a rose from its cloth of gold, hung down from the balcony, and now a honeysuckle from its bright tapestry of purple and scarlet. Is not this the perfection of still life? Surely it is its ecstasy.

Fortunate is the traveller who, after weeks and months spent in hotels, is received as a guest in such a house as this, to be entertained by the sight of cheerful, affectionate faces, and to take up his quarters, for the time being, in a clean, well-furnished chamber looking toward the sunrise! What a luxury there is in white linen again, and carpets soft to the feet! Welcome is the sight of French porcelain, powder puff, and pomatum! And what an air of good nature pervades the house, the service of which is performed by Africans, whose mouths are ready to grin with cheerful ivory at the first kind word addressed to them!

The day's routine is as follows: In the morning, being a wise man, one rises with the sun, and saunters through the grounds to enjoy the cool of the day; or he gets into the saddle, appropriating to his use the legs of a horse, who cradles him about for an hour or two over the estate, or up and down the river bank. Breakfast by this time being more a necessity than a luxury, he will relish corn cakes and hominy, eggs and bacon, butter newly churned and greens from the garden. The plantation breakfast is a simple one, to eat which requires vigorous digestive powers rather than any particular refinement of palate. After this meal it is the regular order of sugar-planting life to begin the day's smoking—though it would seem as if cigars were better suited to a country where there are fewer flowers. But either cigar in mouth or rose in buttonhole—one can have his choice. At this period of the day, also, it is proper to read or write; only doing so in moderation, and breaking up the continuity of labor by frequent intervals of idling, talking, listening to the mocking birds, observing the soaring of the turkey vultures, and the gay, fluttering apparition of the butterflies. The lovers of the dog and gun, too, may go out for birds, or bears; for there is plenty of game in the swamp, and there is a swamp attached to every plantation.

Your dinner you will eat when it is ready; and that may be, very likely, an hour behind time. For it is two o'clock on a plantation until it is three, and three until it is four, and so through the round of all the twenty-four hours. You ought to get very good gumbo in this part of the world; and on feast days you are entitled to terrapin, no plantation yard being perfect without a terrapin pen in it. The beef is good, provided it come down the river from St. Louis, and the Western prairies; but where there are no hills there can be no mountain mutton. Corn cakes are current at every meal. The ham is as sure to be on the table as are its legs to be under it. In March, green peas and strawberries are seasonable; and if they are not forthcoming at that time, the gardener will always have a good excuse for it. Pecan nuts will not fail you; for they grow abundantly in this region, and are picked by the negroes at halves. Your claret comes from New Orleans in the cask, and is well worth the three hundred dollars which has been paid for it. So, on the whole, your fare is satisfactory, and to be accepted with thankfulness.

After dinner there is but one thing to be done. You are put into the coach; and, after having ridden over all the country without ceremony in the morning, you will be driven over the same, after dinner, in state. The family coach is always a respectable vehicle, if an old one; but may be a little flashy if bran new. The coachman, however, is a simple black boy, in a glazed hat, without tag or tassel; and, behind, sits with dangling heels a smaller one, in a straw hat and neatly patched breeches. Nor is this last boy by any means the fifth wheel in the coach. On the contrary, he makes himself exceedingly useful in opening doors and gates, and doing all your bidding.

And so goes the day. So goes every day; for there is little variety in this kind of life. When there is a fine sunset, of course you look at it; but beware of the evenings, which are damp—often chilly. Do not expect to enjoy them as in Cuba; but, there being neither ball nor opera, draw your nightcap over your eyes at an early hour, and be sure that no windows looking toward the north are left open. From any other point of the compass air may be allowed to come into the bedchamber during the night without risk to health; but out of the north star come sudden and very dangerous changes of weather in this climate.

On these banks of the Mississippi the home is not quite so permanent an institution as one might suppose from the large size of the estates. For the business of sugar growing being of such a nature that it can be profitably managed only by a single directing mind, it often happens, on the death of the planter, that no convenient disposition can be made of the property among the heirs, except by its sale. The equal distribution of estates among the children of the deceased has the effect to turn them all out of the house and home which was their father's, no one being rich enough to receive it as his portion.

Hence sugar planters rarely can afford to erect costly mansion houses; and, if they do build them, such property is liable to come into the possession of strangers, rather than to be retained by the family during a succession of generations. Hence, also, these homes can be expected to contain but few heirlooms of the past, or costly works of art, or large libraries, or valuable furniture. Much as ever will they be shaded by tall, ancestral trees, or surrounded by fine old parks and extensive pleasure grounds. Generally, the house must be a cheap, wooden one, situated in a small lawn and yard of flowers; and, indeed, it should be so built that it can be torn down without too much trouble; for our new democratic generations must have new houses. The only pity is, that the old family associations have to be broken up, and scattered with the old rafters and doorposts.

CHAPTER XVIII.

A Western Hotel.

IT was late on a rainy evening that I arrived at the great Western city of ——. On entering the hotel which had been recommended to me, I found the hall filled like a merchant's exchange, and made my way to the office, not without some difficulty. The clerks were all too busy to notice my arrival. I was not asked to register my name in the hotel book, but did so without invitation. After waiting some little time, however, I succeeded in catching the eye of a clerk, when we held the following conversation together:

"Have you a room for me?"

"Not a room in the house, sir."

"Well, give me a cot, then."

"Not a cot in the house, sir."

"But I am ill, and can go no farther. You may give me a sofa—anything."

"Not a sofa in the house, sir. Nothing in the house, sir."

And the clerk passed on, to say the same thing to another applicant for hospitality—and to another—until he was so tired of refusing, that he did it without pity, or even politeness. I turned on my heel; and, at the same instant, turned on his heel toward me one of the bystanders. It was a small providence, for he was a good Samaritan from New York, who picked me up in my hour of need, and gave me a cot in his empty parlor.

I then learned that I had arrived at the wrong hour in the day. In the great Western hotels, the tide of travel ebbs and flows twice in the twenty-four hours as regularly as the ocean follows the moon. After nine o'clock in the morning, rooms are as easy to be had as any drug in the market; after nine in the evening they can rarely be obtained for money, and never for love. The hospitality of the house ceases at nine P. M. The civility of the clerks is completely exhausted by that time. Travellers arriving later than that are a nuisance to all the officials, from landlord to chambermaid. The cold, inhospitable looks the belated comer gets all round seem to say to him, "Why did you not arrive earlier in the day, sir?" If it would do any good, you might easily account for the lateness of your getting to town, and show that the blame rested on other shoulders than your own; but it will be of no avail. You can have as many apartments as you please to-morrow morning; but to-night you must get your sleep on three chairs, or walking the hall, if you happen to be a somnambulist.

So it is year in and year out. A porter gifted with a strong pair of lungs is kept pretty constantly perambulating the halls of the house, and bawling out, loud enough to waken every sleeper and stun every waker, "All aboard! all aboard! Omnibus ready for the cars!" A person accustomed to the quiet of his own mansion may be annoyed by this; but before he has lived forty days in the hotel, he pays no more attention to them than to the hand organ which nightly grinds its grist of melodies under his windows. Not less embarrassing are the piles of luggage heaped up in the halls and passage ways, against which one is constantly liable to run his nose or bark his shins. And when the trunks are loaded on the backs of hurrying porters, the risk of a collision is still greater; for poor Paddy, with half a ton of trunks to his back, is blind as a bat, and sees nothing but the main chance of the open doorway. The traveller is more in danger of being run down in his hotel than on the river, or the rail. Porters, waiters, guests, all are in quick motion; and one or the other is pretty sure to knock him over. Indeed, the society of a Western hotel is in a constant fiux. The universe, in the Hegelian philosophy, is not more fluid. Every man is either just in from Cincinnati or Chicago, or he is just starting for one of these places. Unless he makes his hundred miles between breakfast and dinner, he counts himself an idler, and talks of growing rusty. A great deal of his business he transacts "aboard the cars," or the steamboats; some of it at the hotels; and all of it on his feet, and ready to "bolt." The dinner table, too, is an exchange for him. Business before soup—it is the first course of the dinner, and the last. Between fish and pudding he will sell a prairie. With every mouthful of bread he will engage to deliver ten thousand bushels of wheat. The "upset price" is knocked hard down on the table with the end of his knife handle; and the bargain is clinched by help of the nut cracker or the sugar tongs. If he sees his next neighbor prefer mutton, he at once offers to sell him sheep by the thousand; if he dines on pork, he will invite him to go into a speculation in hogs. His railroad shares he will dispose of at the price of peanuts; and his State bonds he will give away to any one who will pay his champagne bill, and the piper generally; or rather, he would do so a few years ago.

I was not so ill as to prevent my getting down to the table at mealtime. This was the chief amusement of my day, being as good a high-low comedy as may be seen on any stage, at least west of the Alleghanies. The table groans with good things. Here are the veritable solids, and none of what the Frenchman calls *les choses maigres.* The waiters drop fatness, literally. Your plate is brought to you heaped up with roast beef. Every third man has his pudding. The waiters hand about the iced cream in slices, which suggest the resemblance of small prairies. And, finally, the dinner goes off, like the finale of a display of fireworks, with "Jenny Lind cake," "vanities," "cookeys," "lady fingers," "jelly snips," and "pecans."

The only difficulty is in getting little enough of anything you may call for. Just a bit of a thing—*un morceau*—is an impossibility. A thin cut can't be had. A man, therefore, with a delicate stomach, is entirely out of place here, where the arrangements are all designed for persons who are ready to "go the whole animal." When I came down in the evening, to get a cup of tea and a bite at a biscuit, I never could escape the everlasting "Have a beefsteak, sir?" of the waiters. 'Tis a great country out West, and the men who live in it are feeders to correspond. They want their meat three times a day, as regularly as poor Pat does when he leaves his potato island and arrives in this land of beeves and buffaloes. Even their horses have freer access to the corn crib than negroes do in Virginia. The Western man expects to see plenty around him. Nothing is too good for him. He never stops to count the cost. Corn and wine are his—honey, and the honeycomb. The cattle on a thousand acres are his also. The prairies are white with his flocks; the eye follows the waving grain to the horizon; the buffalo yields him its tongue, the bear its haunches, and the buck his saddle; the wild turkey is brought in from the forests, the canvas-back duck from the bays, and the pinnated grouse from the prairies; the salmon trout is caught at Mackinaw, the whitefish fill the lakes, and oysters "hermetically sealed" arrive by express from the seaboard, every day in their season.

There is plenty and to spare of all things, save of art. The kitchen is indeed no *cuisine*. The cook is not "abroad" in these parts. He is coming, doubtless, in "the good time," but has not yet arrived. Still there is, here and there, a pioneer from Paris, come out to try his 'prentice hand, and "rough it." There was one such in my hotel; but both his dishes and his French were execrable. He daily served up such figures of speech as "Calf's head à la Financire," "Lamb chop santees," and "Macaroni à la

Italienare." These mistakes one might be disposed to attribute to the printer—a "devil" on whom is heaped a multitude of sins not his own; but the dishes themselves forbade it. Evidently these and their printed names were by the same master, and were worthy each of the other. However, 'twas all Greek to the majority of the "customers." The gods on Olympus did not know French, and the Western traveller finds ambrosia in every platter, spite of the misspelling. He goes for the *patés*—finds them good, and doesn't trouble his head about the *patois*. Still there are those—Connecticut men, no doubt, by origin—who will not eat of any dish that has not a plain Old Testament name to it. They admit of but one exception. "I'll trouble you," said such a one at my side, "to pass me that platter of shoat and beans." He felt his native partialities melting in his mouth, and could neither wait his turn nor be withstood. "I'll just thank you, stranger, for that platter," he repeated, in a beseeching tone of voice, which quickly moved my pity, at the same time pointing and beckoning with both hands. After he had "gone the whole hog," he asked the waiter if he had any doughnuts. "Doo-noots?" replied Pat, completely at his wit's end; "I'm a-thinkin' them noots don't grow in this counthry, sir." Upon my word, it was the only thing I ever heard asked for at that table which was not to be had. To console my neighbor, I told him that doughnuts were plentiful in D——, for I had seen them piled up there in tall pyramids, or after the fashion of children's cob houses. Whereupon he informed me that he would stop a day at D—— on his return. I advised him to do so.

But the best part of the dinner remains to be discussed—'tis the waiters. I took more pleasure in these than in anything they brought me. Of all places in this country, I had always supposed that New York was the one for seeing Paddy in his truest and most emerald colors. But 'tis a mistake. He is imported in still more native purity into the West. It is said that the hotel keepers here send out a practised hunter from the plains, who catches Patrick in his wildest state by means of the lasso, and forwards him "express" by way of the St. Lawrence and the lakes; so that he is landed at Chicago without change of cloth or color. Then he is put into cast-off clothes—not a particularly good fit—is instructed to subdue his rebellious locks with pomatum, and is set to serve tables. He pretty soon learns what a beefsteak is, for he eats three a day himself. At the same time he learns, experimentally, the difference between wheat rolls and potatoes. In the course of a week or two he gets pretty familiar with the necessaries of life; and then begins to beat his brains to learn the names of the luxuries of the table. He makes some progress until he gets to the French dishes. These confound him. He don't know French at all, at all. If, at this stage of his novitiate, you call upon him for a *fricassée*, he brings you the *fricandeau;* if you demand a *vol-au-vent*, he runs the whole length of the table for the pigeon pie; if you wish for a *méringue glacée*, he thinks 'tis a plate of ice; and if you order *crême fouettée*, he asks if you will have it boiled. When you decide upon roast beef, his question is, "Done, sir, or not done?" Should you tell him, in selecting turkey, to bring the drumstick, he would inquire if you meant the stick he beats the gong with. His ideas are all as wild as prairie colts.

Still this is Patrick's palmy condition, and best estate as a waiter. For, by the time he has served out his apprenticeship, he is ruined for his trade. It takes a certain number of months for him to get it well into his head that he is in a free country; and this idea, once fully comprehended, is enough to spoil the best waiter that ever came from Ireland. Having a few shillings rattling in his pocket, he realizes the fact that he is his own man. Then he begins to put on airs not in keeping with table waiting and bottle washing. While serving at meals, he hangs carelessly by your chair back, with greasy fingers;

so that every day, after dinner, you have to send your coat to the cleaner's to get the marks of the beast rubbed out of it. He now knows fat from lean, tough from tender, and where the meat is sweetest; but unless you fee him every second or third morning, you will be none the better for his increase of knowledge. He is disposed to be short and crisp, as if belonging himself to the upper crust of society. He laughs behind your back, with Jimmy, at every small practical joke that may be enacted at the tables. If a farmer asks for a bowl of bread and milk for his supper, and then peppers it, first black, then red, he laughs at that. Or if a gentleman, not being able to swallow water without brandy to it, puts a glass of it into his soup, he laughs at that. Every leisure moment he gathers Jimmy and Dick together to chatter with them. Then, if you call him, he is suddenly deaf as an adder. He can neither hear nor see. And when the guests gradually leave the table, and work slackens, I have seen him lounge out on to the balcony, settle himself in an armchair, cock his feet up over the railing, and quietly smoke his cigar.

Patrick is now ready for a strike for higher wages. At the first word of reprimand he will throw up his place. He is too independent to be drilled into line, and always takes the covers off out of time. Look out for him when he comes in with his platters—his very importance will run you down. He is still ignorant, still awkward; but, with ten dollars in his pocket, he is abashed by nothing in heaven or earth; and unless he can have four beefsteaks a day, he threatens to go back to Ireland. The truth is, that the sense of freedom is so strong at the West, it spoils all men for service. Our naturalization laws are annually the ruin of a great many excellent scullions and shoeblacks. Nature struggles hard on their side, but our republican institutions prevail.

The society one meets in a Western hotel consists principally of the gentlemen of the road. I mean the railroad men, so called—road builders and road owners. There are, also, the men of real estate, who deal in prairie and river bottoms. There are grain and lumber merchants. There are speculators of every kind. But all have only one thought in their minds. To buy, sell, and get gain—this is the spirit that pervades this house, and the country. The chances of making fortunes in business or speculation are so great, that everybody throws the dice. Five years hence every man expects to be a nabob. I saw in the West no signs of quiet enjoyment of life as it passes, but only of a haste to get rich. Here are no idlers. The poor—if any such there be—and the wealthy are all equally hard at work. Beyond the Alleghanies the day has no siesta in it. Life is a race, with no chance of repose except beyond the goal. The higher arts which adorn human existence —elegant letters, divine philosophy—these have not yet reached the Mississippi. They are far off. There are neither gods nor graces on the prairies yet. One sees only the sower sowing his seed. No poets inhabit the savannas of Iowa, or the banks of the Yellow Stone. These are the emigrants' homes. Life in the valley of the Mississippi is, in fact, but pioneering, and has a heavy pack to its back. At present, the inhabitants are hewing wood and drawing water—laying the foundations of a civilization which is yet to be, and such as never hath been before. This they are doing with an energy superior to that which built Carthage or Ilium. Though men do not write books there, or paint pictures, there is no lack, in our Western world, of mind. The genius of this new country is necessarily mechanical. Our greatest thinkers are not in the library, nor the capitol, but in the machine shop. The American people is intent on studying, not the beautiful records of a past civilization, not the hieroglyphic monuments of ancient genius, but how best to subdue and till the soil of its boundless territories; how to build roads and ships; how to apply the powers of nature to the work of manufacturing its rich materials into forms of utility and enjoyment. The youth of this country are learning the sciences, not as theories, but with reference to their application to the arts. Our education is no genial culture of letters, but simply learning the use of tools. Even literature is cultivated for its jobs; and the fine arts are followed as a trade. The prayer of this young country is, "Give us this day our daily bread;" and for the other petitions of the Pater Noster it has no time. So must it be for the present. We must be content with little literature, less art, and only nature in perfection. We are to be busy, not happy. For we live for futurity, and are doing the work of two generations yet unborn.

Everything is beautiful in its season. What is now wanted in this country is, that all learned blacksmiths stick to their anvils. No fields of usefulness can be cultivated by them to so great advantage as the floor of their own smithy. In good time, the Western bottom lands will spontaneously grow poets. The American mind will be brought to maturity along the chain of the great lakes, the banks of the Mississippi, the Missouri, and their tributaries in the far Northwest. There, on the rolling plains, will be formed a republic of letters, which, not governed, like that on our seaboard, by the great literary powers of Europe, shall be free indeed. For there character is growing up with a breadth equal to the sweep of the great valleys; dwarfed by no factitious ceremonies or usages, no precedents or written statutes, no old superstition or tyranny. The winds sweep unhindered, from the lakes to the gulf, from the Alleghanies to the Rocky Mountains; and so do the thoughts of the lord of the prairies. He is beholden to no man, being bound neither head nor foot. He is an independent world himself, and speaks his own mind. Some day he will make his own books, as well as his own laws. He will not send to Europe for either pictures or opinions. He will remain on his prairie, and all the arts of the world will come and make obeisance to him, like the sheaves in his fields. He will be the American man, and beside him there will be none else.

Of course, one does not go to the West to study fashions or manners. The guests of a Western hotel would not bear being transported to Almack's without some previous instruction in bowing and scraping, or some important changes of apparel. Foreign critics, travelling in pursuit of the comical, do not fail of finding it here in dress, in conversation, in conduct: for men here show all their idiosyncrasies. There are no disguises. Speech is plump, hearty, aimed at the bull's eye; and without elegant phrase or compliment. On the road, one may meet the good Samaritan, but not Beau Brummell. Anything a Western man can do for you, he will do with all his heart; only he cannot flatter you with unmeaning promises. You shall be welcome at his cabin; but he cannot dispense his hospitality in black coat and white cravat. His work is too serious to be done in patent leathers. He is, in outward appearance, as gnarled as his oaks, but brave, strong, humane, with the oak's great heart and pith. The prairie man is a six-foot animal, broad shouldered and broad foreheaded; better suited to cutting up corn than cutting a figure in a dance, to throwing the bowie knife than to thrumming the guitar. In Europe, a man always betrays a consciousness of the quality of the person in whose presence he is standing. If he face a lord, it is with submission; if a tradesman, with haughtiness; if a servant, with authority; if a beggar, with indifference. At the West, two persons meeting stand over against each other like two door-posts. Neither gives signs of superiority or inferiority. They have no intention of either flattering or imposing upon each other. Words are not wasted. So is the cut of each other's coat a matter of perfect indifference. Probably the man who is "up for Congress" wears the shabbier one of the two. If disposed to make a show at all, the Western gent is more apt to be proud of his horses than his broadcloth. His tread may occasionally have something in it indicative of the lord of the prairie; but he has little or no small nonsense about him. The only exception is, perhaps, a rather large-sized diamond pin in his shirt bosom.

The Western cockney differs considerably from him of New York. He has more of the "ready-made-clothing" appearance about him, and wears his hat drawn closer down over his left eye. Sometimes his cigar is in his buttonhole, and sometimes in his cheek. He chews tobacco. He vibrates between sherry cobblers and mint juleps. His stick is no slight ratan, but a thick hickory or buckeye, and has a handle large enough to allow of its being carried suspended from his shoulder. His watch chain is very heavy—lead inside, and gold out. He is learned in politics, and boasts that a United States senator from his State once put his arm around his neck, and slapped him familiarly between the shoulders. When he was in Washington, he messed with the Western members of the House; and, as Botts did with President Tyler, he slept with them. He knows, personally, all the Western judges and generals in Congress; bets at all the elections; and makes money out of them, let whichever party conquer. He also goes in the steamboats whenever there is to be a race; plays "poker" on board, and lives on the profits. He has a small capital in wild lands, likewise, and owns a few corner lots in Cairo, and other cities laid down in his maps. These he will sell cheap for cash. He affects the man of business, and ignores ladies' society. His evenings are spent at a club house, having the name of "Young America" blazoned on its front in large gilt letters. He dines at the crack hotel of the town; and, having free passes over all railroads, he keeps up his importance in the world by going to and fro, and putting on the airs of a man owning half the Western country.

A family of Germans going by the hotel, one morning, as I sat by the window, struck me as the most remarkable show I had seen in the West. It was, indeed, nothing new or uncommon; it was no pageant. No trumpets were blown to announce the coming of this small detachment of the army general. Probably not a soul in the city noticed the passage of this poor family, save myself. Yet in it was wrapped up the great American fact of the present day—the coming in of European immigrants to take possession of our Western plains. If these States did not have lands for sale at low prices, to attract the desires of the poor and the oppressed in all the earth, they would be of little importance among the nations. For centuries the Swiss have had liberty, but no land; and have been a nullity. But we hold a homestead for every poor man in Europe; and, therefore, gathering his pennies together, he is setting out for America, as the world's land of promise, and the only Eden now extant.

The father strode down the middle of the street. Unaccustomed to the convenience of sidewalks in his own country, he shared the way with the beasts of burden, no less heavily laden than they. His back bent beneath its pack. In it was, probably, the better part of his goods and chattels—at least the materials for a night bivouac by the roadside. By one hand he held his pack, and in the other he carried a large teakettle. His gudewife followed in his tracks, at barely speaking distance behind. A babe at the breast was her only burden. Both looked straight forward, intent only upon putting one foot before the other. In a direct line, but still farther behind, trudged on, with unequal footsteps, and eyes staring on either side, their firstborn son, or one who seemed such. There were well toward a dozen summers glowing in his face. A big tin pail, containing, probably, the day's provisions, and slung to his young shoulders, did not seem to weigh too heavily upon his spirit. He travelled on bravely, and was evidently trained to bear his load. A younger brother brought up, at a few paces' distance, the rear; carrying, astride his neck, one more of the parental hopes. It was the most precious pack in the party, and, judging from the size of the little one's legs, not so very much the lightest. It was a sister, I fancy, that the little fellow was bearing off so gallantly; and very comfortably did she appear to be making the journey.

I watched this single file of marchers Westward until they disappeared at the end of the avenue. They would not stop, or turn aside, save for needful food and shelter, until they had crossed the Missouri. On the rolling prairies beyond, the foot-worn travellers would reach their journey's end, and, throwing their weary limbs upon the flowery grass, would rest in their new home, roofed by the sky of Kansas. Before the frosts of autumn should set in, the log hut would be reared, and their small household gods set up in it. In due season the sod would be turned, the seed cast in, and, later, the harvest would make glad all hearts. Years rolling by, the boys will grow up freemen, and will make the surrounding acres tributary in wheat and corn, as far as the eye can reach. Forgetting their uncouth *patois*, the children will learn the softer Anglo-Saxon accents of liberty, and take their place among their equal fellows in a society where none are bondsmen. The daughters, relieved of the hard necessity of toiling in the fields, will gradually grow up in the delicacy of native American beauty, retaining only the blue eyes and golden hair of their German nativity. In the evening of their days, the brave grandparents will sit in the shadow of vines sprung from seeds piously brought by them from the Neckar or the Rhine; and their sons, and their sons' sons, in the enjoyment of plenty, happiness, and human rights, will remember, with blessings, the original immigrants, and founders of their name.

CHAPTER XIX.

From New Orleans to Havana.

ON returning to New Orleans, I learned that an unusually large number of persons were to sail by the next steamer for Havana, and that all the staterooms had been engaged. What was to be done?—for go I must. The ship's agent could only suggest that I should go on board, and make application for accommodations to the purser, relying upon the rule of the ship, *First come, first served.* Accordingly, to the purser I immediately went. He—a half Spaniard, as I guessed—entered my name as the first applicant for accommodations next in order after the staterooms; whereupon I departed in peace.

"*Queda Usted con Dios,*" said I.

"*Vaya Usted con Dios,*" said he.

Not until after the steamer was well under way

did I give the purser any more trouble. Then I civilly asked for a room.

"The ladies," he replied, "must be accommodated first. I will give your wife a berth in a room with two other ladies; and when the turn of the gentlemen comes, I will see what I can do for you."

The turn of the gentlemen came in the course of the evening; and what did I get? A berth? Not at all. A sofa? Not even that. They had all been previously given out—to the last comers.

"Can you tell me, then, Mr. Purser, what I, the first comer, am to do?"

"You can go to the steward, sir, who will give you a mattress, pillow, and blanket, which you can 'locate' at pleasure in any part of the ship not otherwise occupied."

Now this was not pleasant; more particularly so, considering that I had received from the ship's agent a passage ticket purporting, in consideration of money duly paid, to give me room, berth, and conveyance from the port of New Orleans to that of Havana. Moreover, I had strictly observed the rule laid down by said agent, to make early application for accommodations to the purser on board. In view of these facts, therefore, I resolved that I would have something more satisfactory from the official, or—sink the ship.

My first broadside took effect. The purser at once opened his eyes to see what manner of man I was—a compliment not before paid me—and, having apparently satisfied his curiosity, he straightway referred to his book, wherein it appeared that sofa No. 3, in the ladies' cabin, still remained unoccupied. This he gave me; adding, with civil words, that I would be far more comfortable on that sofa than the unhappy individuals who had been crowded, three deep, into staterooms.

What the purser said proved to be true. At least, I was far more comfortable during the three nights of the voyage than were many of the passengers in my immediate vicinity. These lay about the cabin in all possible places. Some lay on the tables, and some under them. Some slept on trunks, and others on the floor. My next neighbor, whose thin mattress had been stretched upon a couple of large Yankee trunks, bristling all over with tall brass knobs, passed the night in torment; because, as he said, the knobs pierced completely through the mattress, and some distance into him. I believed it, for his breathing was that of a man in an agony. From time to time, in the night, uneasy sleepers might be seen taking up their beds, and walking to different parts of the cabin, with a view to bettering their condition. One poor gentleman, whose bed, for lack of mattress, consisted of seven small pillows, transported them from place to place, tied up in his blanket; but, arrange them in whatever part of the ship he might, the pillows would get out of position in his sleep, and let him down on the floor. One night, when, after unusual pains, he had succeeded, past midnight, in making himself comfortable over a hatchway, judge of his consternation on being shaken out of the first profound sleep it had been his happiness to enjoy on shipboard—say, rather, his indignation on being rudely shaken by the shoulders, and requested to get up, because, forsooth, the hold below was occupied by a waiter, whom, at the hour of four in the morning, it was necessary to let out of his prison, that he might begin his day's work in good season.

"Hope I don't disturb you, sir?" said Patrick to the gentleman, as the former climbed up out of his sub-deck resting place; and adding politely, if familiarly:

"When you is among the Romans, you know, you must do as the Romans does."

The sofa next to mine was, early one evening, taken possession of by a traveller recently returned from California, who, at bedtime, refused to yield it to the rightful occupant. In vain did the latter show his ticket; the former declared that he had paid for his passage, and had good right to sit or lie wherever or whenever he pleased; and, what was more, he refused to be searched on the high seas for the purpose of having this claim verified. He would go to the bottom first. Thereupon, the inoffensive and rather timid passenger, having scrutinized the countenance of the Californian, and finding it exceedingly hirsute, and the nose broken—a sort of half-Socrates, half-alligator physiognomy—sorrowfully went his way, and left his formidable enemy in possession. He did well; for, in the course of the day preceding, the face of this "ugly customer" happening to pass before my eyes, I had, on the instant, made the observation that this traveller had, beyond a doubt, osseous deposits under the *dura mater.* It was a case of chronic suffering from the violence of an ungovernable temper.

The man who waited on me at table, by the way, had a similar ossification, which engendered such a degree of ill nature as would have completely unfitted him for his station, had not his temper been happily modified by an original vein of good humor. As an example of it: one day, the gentleman who sat at the head of the table, a large, pompous citizen from Arkansas, calling to the waiter in an unnecessarily loud voice for a piece of pie, the latter, on handing it to him, said, in a strong, Hibernian accent, and tone scarcely less sonorous:

"Pumpkin pie, sir, by G–d!"

I managed to sleep very comfortably on my sofa; but, having no room, how was I to make my toilet? On going to the barber's for that purpose, I found the door locked; and the barber, in reply to my knocking, cried out that I could not come in, for he "was going to wash himself." However, I succeeded, every morning, in finding a place for ablution; until, at last, I fell in with a couple of gentlemen, friends of the purser, who were in possession of two staterooms, one of which they used for making their toilets in, and where they were so polite as to allow me to make mine. But, well as they were accommodated, one of their berths was so short that the occupant had to lie with his legs either tied up in a knot, or extended out of the porthole. In fact, nobody on board had comfortable quarters, except the officers of the ship, who seemed to regard their passengers somewhat in the light of so many cattle being transported to market. As for the captain, his whole duty appeared to consist, as far as I could observe, in putting on a clean shirt every morning, and carefully refraining from saying anything to anybody. At any rate, the only time I heard him make a remark, was on one occasion, when civilly asked by an innocent youth, evidently travelling for the sake of storing his mind with useful information, what the distance was from New Orleans to Havana, he unfeelingly replied:

"As near as can well be calculated, it is a distance of forty-eight cigars and twelve brandy cocktails."

True, the appearance of the crowd at table might have suggested the idea that the steamer was a second Noah's ark, full of animals; for there was much fast eating on board. Every one had to be in his place the moment the gong sounded, and expeditiously perform the duty of mastication after getting there; otherwise he would find himself put, to all intents and purposes, on short allowance. When, on the first day, attempting to dine methodically, I arrived in due course at the roast beef, the waiter informed me that—to use his own phrase—it was all "paid out." Tenderloin steaks there certainly were to the last in the ship's larder; for I saw the steward and captain's boy eating them at breakfast the morning before our arrival. Somebody, also—probably the purser—must have had fresh eggs, as I heard the hens cackling. But one of my neighbors declared to me, after the very first dinner, that he could eat no more pie; for, on cutting one, he had found a large stick of sugar candy in it, and feared to try another, lest it should be made of candle ends. Nor was it safe, in drinking, to go much beyond the ice water—which, I am happy to say, was both good and abundant. But the claret tasted as though it had been sweetened with sugar of lead, to prevent the acetous fermentation; and I heard the ship's doctor begging brandy of a passenger for his patients, on the ground that that in the storeroom was made of Wilmington whiskey.

But if there was some hurry and confusion in the forward cabin at mealtime, there were sufficiently odd things taking place in the ladies' cabin at all times. At the commencement of the voyage, I heard gentlemen politely requesting ladies to give up staterooms, to which the latter had no good claim beyond that of present possession. One woman, not fancying the upper berth which had fallen to her lot, inasmuch as it would require an inconvenient amount of climbing to get into it, quietly removed the parcels from the middle one, where they had been deposited by the rightful occupant, and filled it, instead, with her own person. When remonstrated with for such an uncivil proceeding, she very coolly gave for answer:

"But I am just returned from California!"

An unanswerable argument. And, moreover, as possession is always nine tenths of the law, so it certainly is quite equal to the entire right to a bed. It would have required half the force of the ship's crew, doubtless, to get that Californian out of the berth of her own choosing; and so, not to make too deplorable a scene, she was allowed to have her own way in it. Furthermore, there was a dashing Southwestern lady on board, who could spit as far as a man. And there was another, so addicted to "dipping"—that is to say, dipping the Althea root in snuff, and then brushing the teeth with it—that her husband was said to have offered her a thousand dollars to relinquish the practice. She had done so for six weeks, but then resumed it. I saw raisins and almonds carried away from table in *moire antique* pockets, and pecan nuts picked to pieces on deck by fingers jewelled heavily. All the Spaniards on board were, if the steward was to be believed, half negroes, whom he would gladly have put at a separate table. There certainly was no lack of traders of the Jewish persuasion; nor of travelling bagmen, who concealed their bags in their trunks and valises. Moses, from the New York Bowery, dressed in genteel broadcloth, a heavy gold chain dangling from his fob, and a diamond twinkling in his shirt bosom, walked the deck with the air of a gallant out on adventures, and smoked his cigars with heels as high in the air as any Christian.

Of course, there were a number of well-bred and well-behaved ladies and gentlemen in this crowd of passengers; though, as everybody knows, it is a severe test of good manners in both man and woman to make a voyage at sea. And this one, certainly, did not fail to furnish illustrations of the truth, that, sometimes, persons who are accustomed to move in the fashionable circles of society will, when removed out of them, both do and say things not quite becoming their station. Then, again, it is plainly true, whether on land or water, that if aspirants for social position would only take as much pains really to be ladies and gentlemen as they do to seem such, they would accomplish their purpose with half the trouble.

CHAPTER XX.

A Havana Hotel.

THREE days of sailing brought me to the ever-faithful island so coveted by our filibusters; and, passing the Moro at sunrise, I entered the beautiful harbor of Havana. As the sun came up over the low hills, covered with forts, or tufted with palms and orange trees, it threw a variegated light over the wide expanse of water, staining it like some great cathedral window. And on this gorgeous mirror lay a multitude of ships of all nations—hulks, spars, and rigging, to the very ensigns, all reflected below. There were among them ships of war, three-deckers, and frigates; also the clipper ships of the Yankees, and the heavy hulls of Old Spain; lateen sail boats, likewise, and the official wherries of the custom house: these latter gracefully moving to the stroke of their ten oars, having a little man in a brass hatband sitting under an awning, and the red and yellow of the royal colors languidly drooping over the stern.

The officer of a Spanish port always proceeds to the discharge of his duties with a considerable degree of deliberation; and so it happened that my first experience of Cuban travel began with an hour or two's waiting. During this time, the ship became gradually surrounded by a fleet of small boats, all offering their services to the stranger for the purpose of conveying him and his luggage to the shore; but all waiting, also, with as much patience as if that were their normal condition. At last, however, came the little great man, with his badges of office, and gave permission to the impatient crowd not only to go on shore, but to do so without any of the formalities insisted on in the mother country, unless it were that of paying the boatmen double the rates which by law they were entitled to. A fee of a couple of dollars carried me comfortably through the custom house; and then a commissioner, a porter, and a cart took myself and effects to my first Havanese hotel.

The old established American houses being full of guests, we were obliged to go to one less known to fame. Even here the landlady received us with the declaration that she had not a vacant room in the house, having just given up to four gentlemen the chamber of her duenna; but she would see, after breakfast, what she could do for us. So we waited another couple of hours. By that time the landlady had concocted the proposition that la Señora should occupy a room in common with two or three other ladies; and el Señor should be quartered in the best corner of the drawing room there was left. This, however, was not promising much for him, inasmuch as the more retired and eligible half of the room was already occupied, and partitioned off by a curtain. As we demurred at any such arrangement, we were again requested to wait until it could be seen what might be done. We accordingly waited. But, at the end of an hour more, our patience was rewarded by the gift of the best room in the house.

It was a spacious chamber, with walls from twenty to thirty feet in height, papered, and much gilded. The floor was laid in marble. The large double doors, three in number, were glazed, and served as windows; there being no other opening excepting one small one situated ten or fifteen feet above the floor. Of furniture there was only too great a supply for comfort; inasmuch as, being the property of the previous occupant, it was every day taken away, piece by piece, by a servant who came at all hours for that purpose. Wardrobes in rosewood, the elegant escritoire, tables inlaid with pearl, gilded chairs, Spanish pictures hanging on the walls, and a great variety of smaller articles, all gradually disappeared and wasted away. In the end, very little was left, save one of the three rocking chairs, a cane sofa, and a bed without a mattress, but spread with white linen edged with lace, and covered with a mosquito net delicate as woven mist, and looped up with blue satin ribbons. The bed had the advantage of being suited to the climate; but its sacking, having been overstretched by the avoirdupois of the previous occupant—a Spanish lady past the age of forty—had finally assumed the form of a hammock.

But, floor and furniture being covered with dust, our first endeavors were directed toward prevailing on the landlady to send us a servant equipped for sweeping. It was long before one came, and he turned out to be a *mozo;* for the boys are chambermaids in this country. At length, the dust removed, we desired to have the necessary materials for washing brought. These came in slow succession, one by one; first the pitchers of water; after a quarter of an hour, the basins; after another quarter, the towels. Last of all appeared the slop pail; it being, apparently, an article hard to be found in the house, and was, in fact, no more than a large tin pan, which evidently had seen service in the kitchen.

Then, finally, we unlocked our trunks; but, alack! the glass doors opening into the drawing room were too imperfectly glazed to furnish the degree of privacy desirable in a dressing room. A too inquisitive eye might easily look through them. So another consultation was held with the landlady respecting the possibility of curtains. At first she gazed at us with a face of amazement, saying the room had always been occupied by Spanish ladies just as it was; but, finally, granted for screen an extra towel. Thereupon we dressed for dinner; for it was time to do so.

After a voyage by sea, we wished, of course, to have the services of a laundress. But nobody in the house, from mistress to maid, could tell us how they were to be obtained. The former declared that ladies were in the habit of sending their linen by steamer to Charleston to be washed! It could, indeed, be sent out of the city; but it would never be brought back again—unless you went for it yourself in a volante. This was sufficiently discouraging; though not enough so to make one lose all confidence in his own wits.

Accordingly, I determined on sallying out of the house in search of a laundress; and, after much inquiry, found an excellent one in Lucy, a black woman living in the *Calle Lamparilla*, who not only washes linen very well, and for reasonable compensation, but is herself a dowager, valued at some twenty or thirty thousand dollars, more or less, besides being largely endowed with the gift of the gab. In order to persuade so independent a washerwoman to lend me her services, I had, of course, to begin with praising everything in Havana. And I began with the plantains.

"Gracious goodness!" broke in Lucy, "nothing so good in dis world as plantains. Fry 'em when dey full ripy. Must have fresh pork fat, Señor. Oh, la! I tell you dey too good for niggers!—ha! ha! ha!"

In a hotel, an inefficient office makes an insubordinate kitchen. So, in ours, the servants were all the time at sixes and sevens; and there existed a chronic row in the household. At best, having their heads turned by the excessive number of guests, the servants could scarcely put two ideas together—not even such simple ones as those of coffee and sugar. Still, the meals provided were more palatable than could have been expected under the circumstances. The bread, as everywhere in Cuba, was excellent. Good oil was better than bad butter would have been; and on fried rice and plantains anybody ought to be able to make a pleasant breakfast. A shadow of doubt, it must be allowed, sometimes rested on the freshness of the eggs; as when, one morning, the waiter, instead of executing his order, came back with the significant declaration, "The eggs won't poach to-day, Señor!" There was a liberal supply of Catalonian wine; though this, to be sure, did not sometimes make its appearance on the table until after everybody had drunk himself full of water. And, finally, the parlor had to serve for dining hall as well as bedroom. The guests were mostly Yankees; and among them, as it happened, were half a dozen newly married couples, who had come to the island for the purpose of enjoying their honeymoon. But a row of more disconsolate brides, as they sat at table the day after my arrival, I had never seen before. They appeared at breakfast with from ten to twenty flea or mosquito bites on necks, arms, and faces; and every one of them looking as though she might have spent the whole night in a fight with these small *diablos*. No doubt they had so passed the time, excepting the hour or two occupied in rubbing the Cuban starch out of their night dresses. Those of them who had rooms on the street, complained that they could not sleep, if for no other reason, on account of the noise made by the watchmen, who all night long kept crying the hours, down to the very halves and quarters. And in the early morning the cries of these worthy guardians of repose were succeeded by the crowing of cocks, the barking of dogs, the creaking of carts, and the chattering of a population which gets out of bed before sunrise. Much as ever did these expectants of matrimonial bliss escape the necessity of making their own beds, and of dusting their chambers. Nor, if they transgressed Cuban etiquette so far as to appear in the streets on foot, did they fail to be most unmercifully stared at. In fact, so many batteries of black eyes were unmasked upon them wherever they showed themselves in public, that they came home pretty well disconcerted, and were even afraid, considering the number of Spanish gentlemen who sat smoking in the drawing room, to stay in the house without their husbands. I heard of India shawls being promised some of them, on their return to the States, if they would not be homesick. And in one case, where such promises of future bliss did not suffice to dissipate present gloom and terror, money was put in the fair one's pockets, and she was sent off to buy Spanish fans and laces. This expedient probably brought relief.

While I think of it—there was another couple of American ladies in Havana at the time of my visit, who were promised by their husbands each a half dozen pineapple dresses, on condition that they would spend six weeks on the island without pouting. So, drying their eyes, they determined to hunt the town for these precious fabrics. They had been told—probably by some gentleman who was a bit of a wag—that the best pineapples were to be had at Sagrado's. And for Sagrado's they accordingly set off.

Now Don Juan de Dios de Escalera de Sagrado was one of the principal bankers of the town, besides being a bachelor of long standing. So, when the two fine ladies from the States, attended by their flunky to act as interpreter, on being shown into the presence of this well-known financier and old Christian—*cristiano viejo*—asked to see his pineapples, he replied, opening his eyes a little wider than usual, that he had no pineapples.

"Oh, yes!" rejoined they; "you surely have pineapples! We were told you had the very best in town."

By this time the banker began to feel a little vexed inwardly, as well as perplexed to imagine what could have brought a couple of fashionable ladies to his bureau on such an errand, at the late hour of five o'clock, when he was just on the point of going to eat his dinner. Therefore, adopting as decided a tone of voice as his politeness would admit of, he said to them:

"Ladies, you are mistaken in the man."

This very explicit declaration brought the two visitors to their senses. Looking each other in the face, and suspecting that something was wrong somewhere, they now turned to the banker with the half assertion, half apology:

"Then it must be some other Sagrado. Please inform us where we can find the shop of the Sagrado who sells pineapples."

"I beg pardon. No man of my name has ever sold pineapples in Havana!" firmly retorted the Don, in an agony of rage, which it took all his high-bred gallantry to suppress.

And, with these words, he gravely bowed the fair intruders out of his bureau—who, for their part, felt, on reaching the bottom of the stairway, as if they had been let down from a considerable elevation.

Having seen about enough of life in this Havanese hotel, I was just on the point of making up my mind to move to a house out of town, when the landlord very opportunely raised the rent on me. As I appeared to be enjoying myself exceedingly, extracting almost as much satisfaction out of everything that went wrong as out of everything that went right, he probably thought that I was anchored in his bedroom for the remainder of the season, and suddenly ran the price of my lodgings up to ten dollars per day. The excuse alleged for this impropriety was, that the room was big enough to hold four persons comfortably. And, moreover, it was declared that such four persons were impatiently waiting to take possession. Mythic personages, I had not a doubt. However, I did not stop to debate the question with him, but told him, at once, that the room was entirely at his disposition—*à la disposicion de Usted.* There was a heavy and sudden fall in the landlord's countenance when I informed him that I should no longer consider his house as my own. But I was inexorable; for who likes to have the rent raised over him? Yet I rather suggested than expressed my congratulations that he should have such a convenient number of candidates in readiness for the premises to be vacated; and also sincerely wished in my heart that these four persons, being Christians, might not all be compelled to sleep in that single bed; still less that any of them should be lodged on the cane sofa, inasmuch as, it having no curtains, they would certainly be devoured by the mosquitos. But I will do the room the justice to say, that, as there were no mats nor rugs on the marble floor, so there were no fleas under them. Not even in the bed were there any fleas; so that we were not obliged, as in Old Spain, to spend half the night, taper in hand, diligently searching for these animalcules; nor did we therefore suffer the least inconvenience from having forgotten to take with us to the ever-faithful isle what little remained of our Italian flea-powder.

The next thing to be done, then, was to get out of the house. But to leave a Cuban hotel against the wishes of the landlord, is like weighing an anchor which has sunk several fathoms deep into the mud. In this instance, Boniface, after due reflection, found himself utterly unable to inform me of any method whereby I could leave his house in season to go, next day, to Matanzas. In the art of speeding the parting guest he seemed a perfect dunce. He did not know whether a porter could be engaged at so late an hour of the evening, it being then seven o'clock; but he would ask the chief boy, or *mozo*. Going out, accordingly, he soon brought in the *mozo*, who, after sitting—or rather standing—upon the question, submitted to him with the gravity of a most learned judge, finally came to the conclusion that he did not know whether, at so late an hour of the evening, a porter could be engaged, or not. The porters generally left town for the country at sundown. Moreover, the landlord was not sure that a volante, though paid over night the price of two dollars and twelve cents for taking me, without baggage, to the railway station the next morning, could be relied upon for keeping his appointment. The *mozo* suggested that, considering that the train was to leave at half past five o'clock, the volante might, very likely, be a few minutes too late. Nor, finally, could either master or man say that, in their opinion, it would be entirely safe to send the trunks off at so early an hour. They might be stolen on the way. Indeed, the *mozo* seemed to think the chances were about three to one that they would be stolen, unless he himself followed the porter.

Here, then, was a small Gordian knot; but one very easily cut by my dismissing both of my advisers, and coming to the conclusion to take lodgings for a few days in the pretty suburb of the Cerro. Thence, it was to be hoped, the departure for Matanzas might be more feasible.

CHAPTER XXI.

My First Volante.

BUT I did not leave the city for the suburbs before having seen and enjoyed it. And among the things first to be enjoyed in Havana is, of course, the volante. The drive I took on the day of my arrival being not for pleasure, but for business, was, indeed, without ceremony, or such parade as one delights in on the Havanese *paseos*. On this occasion I contented myself with ordering the *mozo* to get a carriage from the public square, telling him to take the first and best one he should find.

"How much is it the pleasure of the Señor to give for the hour?" inquired the boy, palmleaf in hand.

"What is the legal fee?" I asked, in reply.

"Fifty cents, Señor; but they ask more."

"Very well; I will give a dollar."

The boy went away, and, returning, said there

was a negro in boots at the door; but he would not go for a dollar. Thereupon word was sent to him that he might depart in peace—*que el vaya con Dios;* and the boy was directed to find another charioteer, who would be contented with double the fee allowed by law.

This time he came back bringing with him a most sorry-looking black boy in slippers. His volante would answer the purpose; and so would his horse, albeit the animal's tail was braided, and tied up over his back to the saddle; but the fellow's coat was rather the worse for wear, and was neither yellow nor scarlet, but of a dull middle tint, produced by long exposure to the rays of the sun; and his feet were in slippers, without stockings. I observed, however, that he possessed a pair of well-developed heels, stoutly shod with spurs, besides having a tough thong in his hand capable of doing good service. And so, without stopping to reflect upon the consequences, I pleased myself with the idea of making a dash through the town in the vehicle of this comically accoutred Jehu.

This I accordingly did. The fellow drove pell-mell through the narrow streets, running, at the very first corner, into an ox cart. But this gave an opportunity for observing the fine bullocks which were harnessed by the head to the tongue of the vehicle, having broadly branching horns, large, dark eyes, and the beautiful dun color of the oxen of Italy. Getting extricated from the cart, my driver cracked his whip smartly around the haunches of his tough little steed; and, at the same time, made his bow to a big negress that went by, holding her petticoat up, and puffing away at an enormous cigar, which she grasped between her ivory as she grinned. But if my man tore through the streets and lanes at the top of his bent, he had, nevertheless, to turn the corners gently, inasmuch as both horse and rider were several yards in advance of the carriage. Once on the way, the fellow was so unlucky as to overtake a funeral procession; and, his horse being at the time pretty well blown, he seemed to be very willing to accept the excuse for bringing down the animal's speed to a walk; and so, for a short distance, we fell into line, as if we were the hindmost weepers, and constituted the very cue of the mourning.

On this drive, my attention happening to be particularly attracted to the colored part of the population, I observed that they were decidedly superior in physical structure to the blacks of our Southern States. I saw many tall men and strapping negresses. Several of the latter had their arms set off with bracelets washed in gold, and their fingers with enormous rings of similar material. Others wore showy coral earrings, besides stones more or less precious; while nearly all were elaborately tatooed *à la mode Africaine.* In addition to this finery, the head was generally wound about with gaudy handkerchiefs; but they sported no crinoline of any kind beyond a single loose gown. A cigar, however, long drawn and portly, graced the lips of the principal wenches, who knew how to carry it cocked up as jauntily as any hidalgo, and were also expert in the art of holding it between their teeth through all their chattering, grinning, and even ha-ha-ing. Several neatly dressed and respectable-looking dames of color, being apparently of the higher class of house servants, I met airing themselves in volantes, and looking down upon the world in the streets from a point of elevation not a whit lower than was my own. Indeed, if there be any truth in Don Jose Francisco y Rodriguez, Oficial de la Real Hacienda, these slaves were as well coached as the most powerful potentate could be. "Pues," says this Havanese Ford, in his learned guide book, "puesto uno de estos carruages en el paseo, en nada se diferencia del mas fuerte potentado, tanto in librea como en adornos; y lo que es mas, lo módico de sus precios."* One or two colored gentlemen, also, I

* Translation: "Since, in one of these carriages on the *paseo*, one does not differ from the most powerful potentate, whether in livery or trappings; and, what is more, the price is moderate."

passed in the course of my drive, dressed so completely according to the latest fashions, and demeaning themselves with such perfect propriety, that I was at no loss to recognize in them the free negro, and possessor of a handsome little fortune.

In good time, my postilion, *sans* toggery, brought me safely back to the hotel. I was thankful for it—unusually so—because, in twice crossing a railroad, the thought occurred to me that, the shafts of the carriage being of such a ridiculous length, the train might smash me long after my man and horse had got over the track, and were entirely out of danger.

CHAPTER XXII.

Dolce Far Niente.

THERE is a peculiar, indescribable charm in life on this island. The air possesses an extraordinary degree of vitality, which invigorates the human system, and makes all the wheels of life move with less friction, and more regularity. Though a warm climate, one feels braced by it. Happy, he knows scarcely why, the stranger finds that he requires but few resources for his entertainment. To sit in the shade of the palm trees, to lean over a balcony which faces the street, to recline in an easy chair in rooms with floors of marble, high ceilings, and doors and windows standing wide open, is as pleasant amusement as one need wish for. It is as good as a play in other countries, to look down into any Cuban courtyard, where the business of a great household is being conducted; as, for example, into that of my Havana hotel, in one corner of which a small wine-merchant stored his bottles and boxes; while on a table, in another, half a dozen cross-legged tailors plied their needles in mending old clothes. The streets of the town abound in odd, comical sights; and the quays are an ever-interesting spectacle, where one witnesses the lading and the unlading of the ships of all nations. All men so enjoy life in this tropical city, that they rise early in the morning, and go to their work, or their pleasure, in the cool of the day. For every early morning, when the air is fresh and exhilarating, is like a small cup of the elixir of life. The evenings, likewise, are serene, effulgent with stars, or full of moonlight. Indeed, in this Eden, as in that one originally prepared for the enjoyment of man, it is the evening and the morning which make the day. At noon, when the sun has half done his task, there is a short pause in the life both of man and beast. Business rests for an hour after its fatigue; pleasure takes its siesta; and the hum of the great, noisy city is scarcely audible. But the brief noontide past, all is astir again until the time of the going down of the sun. The dinner is by no means a great event in the Spaniard's day; it being a frugal repast, made cheerful by only a slight draught of wine. The stranger is not asked to share the simple meal; but is entertained, if at all, with a cigar, or a cup of chocolate, or even a glass of orange water. At evening, however, the Habañero is capable of performing many kind offices for you; such as sending his volante for you to take a drive on the *paseo;* bidding you to the *tertulia;* offering you a seat in his box at the opera; accompanying you to the *plaza* to hear the music, to Domenica's to eat ices, and to the Captain-General's when the latter gives a ball or fandango. So easy is it to entertain and be entertained in this Gan Eden.

But, strange as it may seem, it is no easy matter for most Yankees who visit the island to fall into this simple, natural way of living. Immediately after my arrival, the observation was forced on me, that the greater part of the Americans staying at the hotels were busy in inquiring how they should be able to get away from the country which they had come to visit. It was truly a hard lesson for them to learn the *dolce far niente.* Having hastily seen everything in Havana that could be seen hastily, they, at the end of two or three days, knew not what to do with themselves, unless it were to watch the coming and going of the American steamers, to go hither and thither in search of American newspapers, to talk over and over again among themselves the story of their voyage to the island, to discuss the question of routes, the hours of the trains on the railroad, and the days of departure of the coast-going steamers. They smoked their cigars with a certain degree of impatience, and were too soon at the end of them. They were in perpetual motion, driving, walking, boating; and found their seats uneasy, even though they were placed beneath palm trees and the stars of the tropics.

A portion of this restlessness was owing, no doubt, to the very poor accommodations afforded by the public inns, at that season overrun with guests. To this cause, especially, was to be attributed the discontent of the fair sex; for the landladies unfeelingly separated those whom God had joined together, not even paying the slightest regard to the circumstance that some of them were newly married. Hence it happened that most of the American visitors were kept pretty busily employed during the winter, first in finding lodgings, and afterward in changing them. They were to be met with every day in hot pursuit of cool apartments. They were constantly looking for clean rooms, clean beds, clean tablecloths—and, alas! finding none. It was one perpetual round, a vicious circle, from the fryingpan into the fire, and back from the fire into the frying-pan; their chief consolation, meanwhile, being to compare the different degrees of elevation at which they found the thermometer standing in these two different situations.

It may, indeed, be a little too much to expect that men should be perfectly happy when so unsatisfactorily lodged; still, no one who knows anything about Spanish countries ever goes to them for the sake of the pleasure to be derived from sleeping in their beds. Every traveller should make up his mind not to find fault with Spanish sacking because it is not a mattress; and, especially, never to pick quarrels with the fleas. All that he can reasonably look for, is a couch with a mosquito net, windows without glass, doors without locks or latches, water enough to bathe the end of the nose and the tips of the fingers, and a towel just big enough to wipe them dry. Whatever he may find over and above this, is so much good luck, to be accepted with thankfulness, and paid for with extra *pesetas.* In none of the dominions of Her Most Catholic Majesty can the traveller expect to find the roast beef juicy; and he must visit them with his mind made up to eat *tortillas.* Cheerfully should he accept oil for butter, and a stone for cheese. But, having good bread and chocolate, a plenty of eggs, chickens, rice, fried plantains, and sweet oranges, surely any man of a sound mind and stomach may be content. What is lacking in some of his comforts, will be more than made good by the air fresh from heaven which he breathes, by the sun shining by day and by the moon and stars shining by night. In case of a "norther," finally, he can sufficiently comfort himself by simply lighting his *cabaños.*

That day, certainly, may well be called a happy one, which is brought to a close in the *Plaza de Armas.* You go there between the hours of eight and nine to listen to the music of the band—one of the largest and best in America—which plays nightly before the palace of the Captain-General. Dressed in fine linen, you sit in perfect comfort of body in the open air, with nothing between you and the stars but palm leaves. The air is perfectly pure, save that it may have in it the scent of flowers; for it is in the midst of a garden, beautiful with tropical plants and shrubs, that you take your seat to listen to the sweet music of overtures, symphonies, and waltzes. If, leaving your chair, you stroll through the grounds, the perfume changes from rose to violet, from orange blossoms to the sweet-scented shrub, from heliotropes to geraniums, pinks, and mignonette. The gaslights show the various hues of the flowers, and are reflected from the polished surface of innumerable green leaves. Even without the gas you can mark the flashing of the Spanish eye as you pass along the ranks of the promenaders, and distinguish well enough the features of the fair Creoles by the light of their smiles. If tired of the beautiful promenade between these hedges of rose and orange, and beneath the graceful palmtops which seem to reach the sky, you can take a volante, and, with a friend by your side, sit chatting in its easy seat during the intervals of music; and when, at last, you have listened to the strains of the final march, until they are lost in the distant streets, as the band retires to its barracks, you can drive to Domenica's, which is hard by, and taste an ice.

Certainly, you don't mind being cheated out of sixpence. For the waiter, seeing, at first look, that you wear the American whisker under your chin, or have English shoes on, will Jew you to that extent; and there is no help for it. But the joke of paying sixpence black mail to the Domenica you enjoy no less than the ice. It is, in fact, quite as good. And, generally, in Cuba, any person for whose services you have occasion will expect from sixpence to half an ounce for so much as looking at you. You cannot begin to turn around without its costing you a piece of money. To do it with any flourish of the hand, as much as to say, Here am I, a man of consequence when at home in the States, will cost you a gold piece. It may also be a useful piece of information for somebody, if I add that there is one occasion, especially, when a well-filled purse is indispensable to the stranger in Havana; and that is, when he goes shopping with his wife. She wants, of course, to buy a few articles—the *spécialités.* But fans, my dear sir, are a hundred dollars apiece; that is to say, the best talking ones. An article less chatty you may get for fifty, or a very stupid one for twenty-five even. But a dollar fan is as dumb as a mute at South Boston. Pray don't think your wife extravagant if she want a couple dozen of these eloquent, airy nothings. You know that for your own best *cabaños* you paid the enormous price of two hundred and eighty dollars per thousand. Did you not give three hundred dollars for a dozen of embroidered shirts? Surely, then, you cannot think it a piece of extravagance in your better and more prudent half to buy tablecloths at twelve dollars each, and towels at fifteen per dozen. The muslins, to be sure, are so lovely that they are cheap at any price; so are the pineapples, the grenadines, and, especially, the laces. Guava jelly, too, is cheap and good; and you cannot have too much of it. Buy fifty dollars' worth.

It is, doubtless, very true that no man should ever count the cost of his *dolce far niente.* Still, let me tell you, that if, some fine day—which is almost any day in the year—you say, on removing the mosquito net in the morning, This day I will order horses for an excursion into the country; I will go to Señor Don Fulano's sugar estate, and spend a week with him—let me tell you that it is necessary to put much money in your purse. You will want it to give to the robbers. For they will waylay you, and, in case of not finding in your pockets a number of gold pieces corresponding to the dignity of your personal appearance, they will rap you over the head soundly for travelling with less money than becomes your station. Or, being armed with pen, ink, and paper, as the gentlemen of the road always are in Cuba, they will make you draw a check for five thousand dollars—it may be ten—and lock you up in a cave for safe keeping until your banker shall place that sum at their disposal. No Creole of distinction ever travels about the island light-pocketed; and, in case of meeting disagreeable compatriots on the road, he relies for safety much more on purse than pistols; the latter being worn merely for show, and as a sign of personal consequence, although required by law to be of a length not shorter than fourteen inches.

But, for my part, I was never robbed in Cuba, except in the hotels, and offices of the Government. In all my travels about the island, in fact, I never met a *montero* who had so much the look of a cut-purse as the one who was seated, one day, by my side at a *table d'hôte* in Havana. He was a stalwart, swarthy native, with mustaches as long as Louis Napoleon's, and spurs as long as his mustaches, but with a jacket cut so short as scarcely to come down to the small of his back. I know not by what ill luck I was placed next to him at table; but, as misery often has strange bedfellows, so a gentleman at the *mesa redonda* in Cuba is liable to find himself at the side of *monteros*, German Jews, and bagmen. Having the appetite of seven men in one, my fellow had no sooner taken his seat, than he had emptied every dish within reach; and, while still eagerly occupied in gobbling them down, tapping me gently on the arm—for his mouth was too full for speech—he pointed significantly with his knife to a dish of very nice fried plantains, which had been placed before me. He wanted some of them. But no one waiter being adequate to the supply of all his wants, he made application directly to me, and, with an expression of face which plainly said, That plate of fried plantains, or your life, Señor! I acknowledge the amiable weakness of having preferred resigning the plantains rather than my existence, it being at that time particularly sweet; and I had, besides, an engagement for the evening at the Plaza. So I handed the dish to the barbarian, and held on to my lease of life.

CHAPTER XXIII.

The Paseo Tacon.

IT is the aspiration of every lady in Havana to have her volante. And well it may be; for the etiquette of the town forbids her setting foot in the street. She is scarcely permitted to walk even to church. The streets being narrow, and the sidewalks, where there are any, having width enough only to allow a single person to pass, it can well be understood that a lady, in attempting to walk in such a city, would be exposed to being jostled, or otherwise incommoded. Moreover, she could not walk far without soiling her dress in the abundant mud or dust. Nor could she well escape being stared at, and, very likely, made the subject of impertinent remark. The volante, therefore, is both necessity and luxury for her. She must have it in order to go to church, to go a-shopping, to take an airing, to make visits; and, without it, is little better than a prisoner in her own house. It costs about a thousand a year to keep a volante with two horses; and a Spanish lady will forego almost any luxury, except fans, in order to have this amount annually to spend on a carriage.

It is indispensable that the volante be drawn by two horses, or rather mules, at half tandem. The mules, also, must have their harness well washed in silver; they must have tag and tassel; and, especially, must have their tails braided, and tied up with gay cords and ribbons over their backs to the saddle. There must be, furthermore, a negro on the back of the leading mule; and he must have, besides his palmetto hat, a laced and braided jacket, be it green, yellow, scarlet, purple, or sky blue. It is proper that he should wear leathern breeches. Jack boots are as indispensable as the indispensables themselves; while his heels must be spurred, as near as may be, like Don Quixote's. The volante itself should be more or less silvered over, and painted to correspond with the postilion's jacket. Then, when the forward mule has been trained to go on a canter, and the shaft mule on a trot, the Cuban lady has all that heart can wish for in the matter of a carriage.

The Yankee in Havana, who, wishing to spread the feathers of his American eagle a little, orders such a turnout from a livery stable, will be charged half an ounce for his afternoon's airing. It is as necessary for him to have doubloons in his pocket when he drives to the *paseo*, as it is for Queen Isabella when she goes in state through the streets of Madrid, scattering gold. I did this thing the first holiday afternoon after my arrival, driving more especially over the Paseo Tacon. All the world and his wife were there. Hundreds of volantes passed and repassed on a walk, from one end of the long promenade to the other; their great number preventing them from moving any faster. Bordered on either side by tall trees ever in leaf, the road runs between flower gardens and green fields, and commands a view of the city, the adjacent hills, and the sea. At the hour of sunset the prospect is truly beautiful, when the palms are seen on the western hills gracefully grouped together against a sky of gold and purple. Recently, a few four-wheeled carriages have been introduced by hidalgos anxious to make themselves conspicuous by innovating upon the customs of their country. But the volantes far outnumbered all other vehicles on the *paseo*. Most of them were occupied by two or three ladies, their crinoline being protruded as much as possible on either side, and giving to the carriage the appearance of being winged with gay plumage. It is a fashion which has no inconvenience in the usually still weather of Havana, when the evening breeze is scarcely strong enough to stir muslin; but is sufficiently awkward in a "norther." This wind, luckily an infrequent visitor, by bringing confusion into the ladies' dresses, and leaving the fair wearers not a shadow of an excuse for fanning themselves, puts an end at once to all pleasure-driving on the *paseos.* At all other times, the promenading lasts not only until the day fades out of the west, but is industriously continued by gaslight.

When taking this drive, the ladies have nothing on their heads, save, perhaps, a veil, a wreath of flowers, or a coronet of diamonds; and nothing on their necks or arms. Nor do they conceal the beauty of their hands, even, and the brilliancy of their rings, by putting on gloves. The thinnest and tiniest of white satin slippers cover the feet. Two ladies occupying the same volante always select dresses which will make a handsome contrast of colors. If one skirt be pink, the other will be green. If one be straw color, the other will be lilac. The whole promenade glows with the high-tinted silks and muslins. Indeed, what with the ladies' dresses and the postilions' jackets, the gayly painted carriages, the well-groomed mules and their glittering trappings, the scene is a shifting tapestry of all colors, gorgeous as the processions of princes. It is a vain show, no doubt, but one which gives supreme delight to lovers of pleasure who live so near the sun. The tropical day has no entertainment half so much prized. These gentlemen would sooner go without their dinner, and these ladies without their sweetmeats, than miss the afternoon parade. Nor is it, in fact, the monotonous scene which foreign, uninitiated eyes may find it. That fair Señora who drives to and fro on the *paseo* by the hour, is enjoying a varied entertainment. Far from being an idle, listless spectator of the scene, she is diligently exercising her eyes on every passing dame and cavalier; she is exercising her pretty little hand in constantly opening and shutting her gayly painted *abanico;* and with that graceful instrument, though she do not part her lips except to smile, she is talking quite as fast as her tongue itself could go. She can speak few foreign languages; but she knows thoroughly the language of the fan. She can both confess and accuse, rave or sigh with it. She kisses you with it; she sends you an invitation by it; and she tells you whether to come that evening to the opera, to the *plaza*, to Domenica's, or to her own house. Thus she holds pleasant discourse with friends and acquaintances, who, from carriage or saddle, reply with bows and smiles, and all those movements of the eyes which Spaniards are adepts in. In this way, the *paseo*, instead of being a monotonous, tiresome parade, becomes as chatty as the drawing room, as amusing as a play, and I know not how much preferable to reading the Havana newspapers.

Unfortunately, there is not connected with the *paseo*, as in many of the towns of Old Spain, any promenade for pedestrians, where gentlemen and ladies, alighting from their carriages, can stroll for a half hour through grounds tastefully decorated with shrubbery and flowers; where friends can pay the calls of the day, and fair ones hold their temporary court *sans cérémonie.* But, the Paseo Tacon being situated at the foot of a hill which is crowned by the Castello del Principe, the afternoon drive may conveniently be varied by climbing the tempting summit. There, at the hour of sunset, is presented, on one side, a view of the purple sea; on the other, of the cream-colored city, now slightly tinged with the hue of roses; and, beyond the walls, of far-reaching green plains, dotted with groups of palm trees. Spires, and domes, and towers burn in the last rays of the gorgeous tropical sunset; while the hilltops of the distant horizon glow with the reflected light of the clouds in which they lose themselves.

CHAPTER XXIV.

Church and Opera.

I AM sorry to be obliged to represent the Cubans as not very diligent churchgoers. In the mother country, the Spaniards are much more exemplary in the performance of the duty of attending mass and vespers; often filling not only all the seats, but even the aisles of their churches. But, on the island, the sacred edifices contained, whenever I visited them, but a paltry handful of worshippers, and always presented on the marble floors abundant space for the servants to spread the broad carpets and cushions of their mistresses. Generally, the congregations consisted one half of Africans, who are not here compelled to pray in a corner, as in our Northern churches; but who, on the contrary, often occupy the very foremost places before the altars. Always well dressed, the blacks sometimes come to church in great state even. One strapping wench I remember to have seen in a chapel, making herself conspicuous, directly in front of the high altar, on a cushion which had been brought to her for that purpose by a most respectful black boy. Being dressed in a fine pineapple, a lace mantilla, and embroidered skirt, wherein she seemed to take as much delight as if it had been bought off the altar, she sat there apparently enjoying the unction of extreme comfort and self-satisfaction. Her fan, which was opened and shut at the end of each ave and pater with all the air of a fashionable belle, was about as gay as any Señora's at opera or *paseo*. There appeared to be only one little mistake about her—her fashionable hoop had been put on backside foremost.

It was in the freshness of the early morning, and before the rays of the sun had become potent enough to require the protection of an umbrella, when I went, for the first time, to the cathedral. At that hour, the quiet of the place was not much disturbed by worshippers; and it was pleasant to stroll through the different parts of this collection of venerable edifices, hearing the music of the chant in the remotest courts, and the echoes of the organ repeated along all the corridors. In some of these inner courtyards tall trees were growing, and water was trickling from ancient fountains; while here and there were to be seen a few plants and flowers. In the course of my walk through the buildings, I observed some priests praying, some receiving confessions, some promenading and chatting, and others eating and smoking. But what interested me most was, not the sight of the somewhat neglected courtyards, nor the deep voices of the priestly choir, which reverberated so far through the aisles and cloisters, but the spot where lie enshrined the ashes of the discoverer of America. Alas! that so many heroic qualities of character should lie buried there under the stones, and so few be found living and breathing on this island!

The churches, it may be added, opened here every morning and evening to all persons who may be disposed to come in for the purpose of offering up their prayers, are much more accessible than in our Protestant States, where the sacred doors remain closed six days out of seven, and where, even then, the congregation is shut up in pews, located according to the color of the skin, and the monetary value of the worshippers.

But the opera in Havana, on the other hand, is far more difficult of access than that in New York. In the season of the Carnival, for example, a box—and you cannot take a lady to any other part of the house—will cost you fifty dollars. Do you think it paying too much for the privilege of seeing a *prima donna asoluta?* Rather consider yourself a fortunate man that the price is not double that sum. Indeed, it is more probable that, on a grand gala night, you will not be able to get a box for either love or money. For every pretty Señora and Señorita in Havana will be dying to go, and all the best places will have been engaged weeks beforehand. The Havanese mind seems to be smitten with a perfect rage for the opera. This is the grand and fashionable entertainment—the most expensive luxury of the town. The gentlemen all assist at the spectacle in dress coats and embroidered shirts, with stars and ribbons in their buttonholes, hats brushed to a hair and mustaches waxed up to their eyes. The ladies, of course, are present in all their crinoline, but with dresses quite ready to fall off their shoulders, and laced about the waist within an inch of their lives. Every lady has her fan; every lady is flounced. All have their hair done over a cushion, and all have their faces done in eggshell, which they call *cascarilla.* The long line of boxes flashes with jewelry, like the blazing mouths of a whole park of artillery. For there are diamonds on the brows of every lady who has a pretty forehead, diamonds on all the tapering fingers, diamonds on all the round arms, diamonds on the necks which are brunette, and pearls on the blonde ones. The boxes are so arranged that the toilets are seen from top to toe. Not a head, not a neck, not a waist, arm, finger, foot, but what is visible from every part of the house. The Havanese wish to see and be seen whenever they go to hear music; and, much as they pay the piper, they pay the jeweller and the dressmaker more.

The season I was in Havana, the *élite* of the city were divided into two hostile camps, fighting, the one for Garcia and the other for Gazzaniga; and making the contest second only to the never-to-be-forgotten one carried on a few years ago in New York between the partisans of Alboni and of Sontag. It was a war of the roses; for the victory was decided by the greater number of bouquets with which the stage was strewn from one end of the play to the other.

Garcia, I believe, won the greater triumph in a contest wherein neither champion suffered defeat. Her appearance on the stage, the evening of her farewell benefit, was the signal for filling the air with miniature balloons and pigeons, and showers of bouquets, to which were attached printed slips of complimentary verses. No sooner had the first act ended, than the prima donna was again showered with flowers. After the second, she was presented with a gold bracelet. After the third, her brows were crowned with a wreath of diamonds, all supposed to be genuine; and when, at the conclusion of the opera, the curtain was about to fall, lo! Garcia appeared surrounded with the dazzling brilliancy of Bengal lights. This *furore* cost the Havanese a handsome little sum, variously estimated by the enthusiasm of the fair donna's admirers at from five to twenty thousand dollars.

So mad, every time Carnival week comes round, do these lovers of pleasure run over some second-rate warbler on the stage. Oppressed mortals, they have no Congress sitting in Havana to inspire them with a nobler, a political frenzy. They have no Tammany or Fanueil Hall wherein to let off their pent-up passion. No grand senate chamber furnishes them, from time to time, with the spectacle of the representatives of the nation caned in their seats, or seizing each other by the coat collar. They have, instead, only either the fight of bulls, or this fight between the followers of two rival prima donnas. Well, let them, for the present, rave, and throw up their hats when a Garcia or a Gazzaniga splits her throat to please them; for it is, no doubt, but a short time which will be vouchsafed them wherein to listen to dulcet music, as if it were the *summum bonum* of existence. After the island is annexed, we will send them a supply of political orators, who, making their sweet voices heard loud above the trilling and warbling Melopomenes of the stage, shall teach them the higher art of the stump speech, and how to talk to Buncombe. Happy day, when they shall prefer the platform of rough boards to the boards of Terpsichore; when they shall forsake bull fighting and cock fighting for a free fight at the polls; and when, after dinner, instead of finding entertainment in the vanity of a volante, or coffee at Domenica's, they shall sit out the evening hours in their "Pewter Mugs," gravely discussing, over doctored whiskey, the wholesome doctrine of universal suffrage, and the principles of the year '98, immortal in Virginia.

CHAPTER XXV.

Oranges and the Quays.

IN different countries the wise traveller learns a different lesson. Whoever visits Italy, for example, finds that his eye is trained to detect and appreciate the beautiful. For, besides the treasures of art, all the forms of nature wear there an unusual grace, and present an inimitable harmony of coloring. In nature, art, and man, lives everywhere and reigns paramount the spirit of beauty. By this is the thoughtful tourist perpetually delighted and instructed; not caring to find the Northern idea of utility developed in such a country; not wishing to see its lazzaroni shut up in steam factories; nor even its *improvvisatori* and ballad singers transformed into demagogues and expounders of political constitutions. Enough for him that there is one country in the world which enkindles in all persons of genial minds and hearts a warmer love of beautiful art and letters; so that, returning to their own homes, humble though they be, they are able to discover in them a thousand charms and graces never seen before.

But whoever goes to Cuba has quite another lesson set before him. He learns how to eat oranges! And what would that youth at the New England tea-drinking not give to know how to cut the orange which he wishes to offer to the maid for whose tender sake his cheeks are turned to purple, and his knees tremble under him! He does not know how to proceed. Shall he peel it for her? Shall he offer it to her cut into quarters?

Now I propose to inform this bashful young man how the Cubans perform this feat; and surely they ought to be considered experts. First, then, they pare the fruit; taking great pains that the knife pass just beneath the outer rind in such a way as to remove the yellow and leave the white part of it. This is important, because, if the blade anywhere runs so deep as to touch the pulp, the juice will trickle through the wound when the orange is eaten, and so will spot the lady's fine brocade, or calico. The orange, peeled as aforesaid, is cut through the centre into halves, each forming a perfect cup for containing the precious liquid. And then all that remains to be done with the two halves is, to eat them. If the nose be a trifle too much hooked, or run out to a point unusually long, it may be a little inconvenient to drink the juice after this fashion; so that, in cutting an orange for a lady with such a nasal member, it might be questionable whether some better way of doing it could not be hit upon. Every rule will have its exceptions; and every man must rely on his wits in emergencies.

Who does not love these delicious golden rounds? And is it not a piece of good luck, that this is one of the few kinds of food which cannot be adulterated? Down in Connecticut there may be men clever enough to whittle out a wooden nutmeg which shall pass in Virginia, and the South, for a merchantable article. But what Yankee ever yet went about the country peddling artificial oranges? There be mock oranges in nature; but this is a trick of hers whereby nobody is deceived. So there are different varieties of sweet oranges; as, in the firmament, the stars differ from each other in glory. The perfect fruit is that, whether grown on the south side of Cuba, or in the Algerine valley of Blidah, which you yourself pick up beneath the tree where it has been lying all night with the dew on it—which you pick up before the first ray of the rising sun gilds its rind. Then its juices are cool, and as much better than after they have been fermented, from exposure to a tropical sun in the streets and shops of the city, as champagne is better when served cold from the ice than lukewarm from the sideboard. When you are in Cuba, get early up, and, in the freshness of the morning, fill your basket with oranges from under the oldest trees, and eat them after the termination of the morning's walk or drive. Cuban servants will pare them neatly for you; but, if not too indolent, you can do it yourself. A half a dozen is not too many to eat; particularly if, at breakfast and dinner, you mix Catalan wine with your water.

Who, indeed, does not love oranges? The father returning from town makes his children happy, if, on searching his pockets, they find this sweet fruit of the tropics there. Even the baby plays delighted with one of them, as with a ball. The schoolgirl goes on her way with a brighter face and a gayer song, for having a big Havana in her satchel; and old age, likewise, smacks its shrivelled lips after tasting these sweet juices. How ornamental their golden globes are on the dinner table; and how welcome whenever there is a feast and frolicking! All over the North, the peddler hawks them from village to village; in the shop windows of both town and country, the eyes of passers by, young or old, greet them with pleasure; while at the bedside of sickness their juice is among the most grateful of the drinks prescribed by the physician—a solace to the parched mouth of humanity throughout the world.

The orange markets are everywhere in Havana. This fruit, which all men buy and eat, is cried about the streets, having been brought into town on mule and donkey back. It is sold in all the vegetable markets, where it is displayed in heaps and baskets; and may also be bought by the boat-load, or the single one, along all the principal quays. These latter are not, perhaps, the most eligible places for selecting choice fruit; but one is more entertained there by the graver movement of men and affairs, than by the huckstering and haggling of the other markets.

Whoever would gladly see an example of toil alleviated by merriment, should by all means go to the quays of Havana, and look at the Africans—pure specimens of the race grown in its native land, black as charcoal, strong limbed, and tattooed. Here all the work is done by them, sprinkled only with a few Chinese and Spaniards. With what hilarity and jesting they roll out the hogsheads of molasses! with what ease they transport on their heads the bricks, and boxes of sugar! They are but half clad, wearing no shirt or jacket; and you see the fine play of their muscles while they are busy at their tasks. There is much work to be done on the quays, but still more laborers to do it; so that nearly a third of them are unemployed, and cracking jokes with those who have something to do. Of the former, some stand chatting in groups; some, smoking their cigars, sit about on bales of cotton and boxes of sugar; while others, supine, or flat on their breasts, lie sleeping in the sun. They are strong fellows, and willing enough to exert their powers on the slightest pinch of necessity; but it is amusing to see how many of them it will take to pull a boat up to the pier, when there happens to be plenty of them at hand, each one putting forth the least possible modicum of strength, and all making a jest of the effort. To unload a barge of bricks, each parcel of four must pass through the hands of as many different negroes. The first one picks them up and hands them to the second, who tosses them to the third standing in the prow, and he to the fourth standing on the quay. Indeed, there are two more—one to bear them across the quay on his head or his shoulder, and the other to receive them at the cart. The division of labor seems to lighten it; the companionship in toil makes all work with a will. One half of these black men may be estimated to be constantly on the grin, and the other half to have cigars in their teeth. What a horse-laugh that wide-mouthed fellow on the topmost cotton bale ejects from his throat! and did you ever before see two such cannibalistic rows of ivory? He has just pulled the wool over some brother nigger's eyes, and gone into convulsions about it.

These Africans have well-developed chests, and, in most cases, handsomely turned arms; but their limbs are always deficient in symmetry. In the whole crowd you will not be able to find a single form which is, throughout, well proportioned. Either their bodies are too long for their legs, or their legs are too long for their bodies. An Apollo Belvidere is not to be sought for here. They have good height, however, and generally dwarf their Spanish and Chinese associates. Of these last-mentioned laborers, the former are a tolerably merry set, and even more noisy than the negroes; but disputatious, also, and of a blood that mounts more quickly into passion. But the Chinese, with his slender legs and thin body, appears not to be so happy at this heavy work of the quays; has rather a homesick look, and sometimes wears a visage not a little sulky. Still he has brighter eyes and more brains than the African, and will finally succeed in domesticating himself in our tropics; although, for the first few years after cutting off his pigtail, he naturally feels a little uncomfortable, and does not quite know how to make himself at home without his pet appendage.

CHAPTER XXVI.

The Cerro.

I WAS very comfortably lodged, for a few days, in one of the hotels in the Cerro. This suburb consists mainly of a single street some three miles in length, the half of it nearest the town being occupied by shops and the homes of shopkeepers, and the other half by the villas and chateaux belonging to the wealthy merchants of the city, and official personages of distinction. The most of these stand directly upon the street, though a few are situated at a little distance from it, in the midst of groves and gardens. In passing along this more rural part of the Cerro, one gets a view of beautiful green lawns, of pretty collections of flowers, of tropical shrubbery growing in the greatest luxuriance, and of palms towering over all, no less gracefully than proudly, toward the sky. The mansions are gay with bright colors, the white being everywhere striped with pink, sky blue, and apple green. At evening, also, nothing of the kind can be more charming than a drive through this portion of the Cerro; for the houses—the piazzas included—are all brilliantly lighted with gas, and have their doors and windows thrown wide open. The passer by, looking directly through the halls, sees pretty vistas beyond leading to orange gardens, or terminated by vases of bright-colored flowers. He also sees the members of the family gathered in groups on the piazza, or arranged, according to age and sex, in two formal rows of rocking chairs. There they sit, the ladies opposite the gentlemen, and rock themselves the whole evening through. The Spanish fans make a pleasant breeze when none blows in at open doors and windows; the flowers diffuse through the rooms a sweet perfume; the blaze of gas makes every countenance visible, even from the street; exhibits all the toilets, and every article of the furniture, the volante which stands in a corner of the hall included. You hear, as you pass, the song, and see the dance. You hear, also, the mellifluous hum of the soft Spanish voices, and their musical, ringing laugh; and you see even the fingering of the piano, and the thrumming of the strings of the blue-ribboned guitar. Charmed with the sight, you exclaim, "How social this is!" And, as you see the guests coming and going, you can hardly restrain the desire to enter these hospitably open doors yourself, and make your bow to such fair company.

Hard by the Cerro stands a fine old chateau, approached by an avenue of palms full half a mile in length. As the sunny day draws to a close, it is a pleasant promenade from the hotel to pass between these graceful rows of sentinels into the grounds and gardens of the chateau. You may even be asked into the house by the gracious and hospitable inmates. And if, by any chance, an acquaintance thus begun should lead to intimacy, I will not say that a dinner party may be given you; but it is possible that the polite hostess may invite you, if a lady, to join her, some morning, in the bath.

Nor, in this hot climate, is such a favor to be lightly esteemed. For the bath is one of the greatest of Cuban luxuries. The bath house is often built in the midst of a flower garden, and looks like a summer bower. The descent is by marble steps into a basin of clear spring water of a temperature so grateful that an hour passes only too quickly there. At the end of it, female slaves stand ready with snow-white napkins to make the toilets; and, afterward, the bathers, lounging on couches, are served with fruits and iced drinks. Conversation, embroidery, books, follow; or, it may be, the siesta. And thus, ere one is aware, is passed an entire morning.

A pleasant drive, just off the Cerro, invites the stranger to a place of some little resort, called the Bishop's Garden. But, unfortunately, the pleasant days when the good bishop lived here are long since gone; and now, all that remains is an old palace abandoned to decay, fish ponds in which there are no fish, flower gardens wherein there are no flowers, and walks, half overgrown with grass, leading through grounds in which neglect is making graceful mockery of all previous labor and painstaking. It is a pity, indeed, that such a fine old palace should be given over to the bats and the lizards; and that the visitor to this naturally beautiful spot should see no signs of work anywhere, except the constant working of the luxuriant tropical vegetation. Here are magnificent groves and clusters of trees, containing the palm, the ceiba, the beech, the mango, the mamey, and the sapote; while up many a stem is seen climbing the ivy, or the vine, or the Indian fig, and other parasites whose name is legion. The scene, in spite of the large, pink-colored water roses which lie floating on the artificial waters, is a little less gay than harmonizes well with the mood of mind in which one takes his afternoon stroll in the tropics. However, the way homeward by the Paseo Tacon will sufficiently exalt the spirits again; for, along the line of the western horizon, glowing at sunset with that beautiful tint of pink which one sees in sea shells, there stand, in bold relief, palm trees grouped together as gracefully as the Three Sisters, or the Muses, in old Greek art. And, haply, when the traveller, returned to his home in the North, and sitting muffled, on winter nights, by the fireside, thinks of the sunny afternoons when he rambled through the green suburbs of the Havana, he will see the blazing logs converted by his dreamy eyes into those same groups of dark palm trees, standing amid the pink-colored sea shells of the Caribbean.

CHAPTER XXVII.

Excursions.

WHAT excursions into the country ought I to make from Havana? asks the Yankee, who expects to see everything, and counts the very best of it not too good for him.

This question you will very likely ask of your banker, to whom you bring a letter of credit; and, in consideration of the three and one quarter per cent. which he charges for the trouble of counting out your ounces, he is willing to answer a few questions. He may not do anything more for you; but a few questions he expects to answer every man who comes from the States. Perhaps, when the rate of exchange goes against him, and he cannot have the face to deduct from your money more than one or two per centum, he will be a little more laconic; but the chances are ten to one that you will arrive at a period of what he will term a small financial crisis, when, of course, money is very dear, and you will not object to paying a handsome premium for it.

Take care, by the way, if you ask the banker's clerk to give you small money, that he do not shrug his shoulders. For it is a first principle with the Cuban to take all the silver he can get, and give as little. And when you do succeed in extracting it from him, I would not like to insure you against there being some light-weight pieces among it. Your twenty-five-cent coins may not turn out to be of the value of more than twenty; and you must not presume that any native will take them for more than they weigh in the scales. He knows their avoirdu pois the instant they touch his palm. "Five cents more, if you please, Señor," says he, promptly. Indeed, I remember, in one instance, when making a negotiation with a Habañero of the value of a single sixpence, that I was obliged to produce no less than four of these coins before finding one that came up to his very nice notion of what was standard value. Still, as few strangers speak the language of the country, they ought to bear in mind how much trouble they give everybody with whom they have dealings, from the banker down to the orange merchant, and be ready to pay a shilling or so in the dollar, for the privilege of talking incomprehensible Spanish, looking out of curiosity at twice as many things in

12*

the shops as they purchase, stopping people to inquire their way about town, and blundering generally. Then, too, the amusement of seeing so much close reckoning in a country lying so far removed from the North Pole, ought to be considered as worth something.

Well—your banker advises you to go to Guanabacoa; says it is the most agreeable excursion to be made out of Havana—in fact, about the only one, unless you choose to go to San Antonio and get a fish breakfast. Accordingly, little choice being left, you decide in favor of Guanabacoa. Go, as I did, in the cool of the afternoon, and just as the clouds of sunset are lying, one above the other, parallel with the horizon, and showing narrow spaces of sky between, crimson, and gold-colored; as though the red and yellow of the Spanish ensign had been hoisted athwart the heavens. Your satisfaction in taking this excursion, be it more or less, begins with a drive in a volante from your hotel to the harbor. Thence you are carried on your way a half a mile across the harbor in a ferry boat. Next, entering a very neat and strongly built station house, filled with comfortable railway carriages, you take a place in one of them, and are borne by the train through a beautiful country of rolling hills crested with palm trees; through fields green in winter, and pastured by cows and oxen; between hedges of cactus, and a great variety of beautifully flowering plants of the tropics; within sight, during most of the time, of the blue waters of the harbor, past villas gayly striped with blue and green, and surrounded with orange groves and banana orchards, and thickets of tall oleander. The journey lasts just eight minutes. Indeed, at the end of seven, the shriek of the engine, announcing the approach of the train to the town, surprises you in the very midst of your enjoyment of the lovely prospect. But the road ends at Guanabacoa; and you must immediately leave the train, or be carried back, in eight minutes more, to Havana.

It was my good fortune to make this excursion on a saint's day; and, on turning the first corner of a street, to stumble upon a procession of the Holy Virgin, arrayed in all her artificial flowers, gold lace, and brocade. But, to tell the truth, it was a third-rate procession of a third-rate town, consisting of not more than a dozen Spaniards, and as many negroes, the latter being scarcely blacker than the former. Three or four greasy candle-bearers headed the procession; a few boys followed, bearing waiters of bread and cakes; then came one solitary priest, but a portly one, swinging a censer of incense; and, after him, was borne high in air, on the shoulders of half a dozen negroes, the Blessed Virgin herself.

But, unfortunately, the foremost of the bearers happened to be considerably taller than the hindmost; so that the Madonna stood with her head thrown back even farther than became the Queen of Heaven. Indeed, her position looked decidedly ticklish; and the whole affair went so askew, that the porters, whose shoulders were becoming uneasy from the unequal pressure, came to a halt for the purpose of getting the tall blacks and the short blacks rightly distributed under the burden. But they seemed too stupid to know how to do it; and the Virgin, finally, had to go up the steeply ascending street in a position which would have broken her back had she been mortal.

A few steps farther on, I met a girl bearing a basket of natural flowers, which took the color entirely out of the artificial ones of the Virgin. The brilliancy of the scarlets was second only to that of the sun between the tropics; the blues were as deep as that of the Caribbean; the purples vied with the clouds of the sunset then glowing in the west; and the roses—white, red, and yellow—were fair enough to be wreathed in the hair of the maids of Andalusia. I admired the flowers so much, that, at parting, the damsel, in polite Spanish phrase, placed the basket at the disposition of the stranger—though not expecting, of course, that he would accept it. But it was a beautiful vision, this of the flowers and the maiden, which harmonized well with the blushes of the sunset; and for some little distance behind, the basket, as it was carried along, left a sweet scent floating in the twilight air.

It was pleasant to step for a moment into the principal church of the town, as the priests were extinguishing the last tapers, and the gloom of the ancient edifice was becoming still more deepened by the falling shadows of the evening. The plaza—for every Spanish town has one—though too small for palms, was well filled with flowering shrubs; while a couple of pretty gardens at the end of the principal street, with their stiff, large cactus trees and towering pines, heightened the pleasure of the promenade.

And so ended my sight-seeing in Guanabacoa.

The light of the new moon shining out of the still pink and purple west guided me on my way homeward; and as I recrossed the beautiful harbor of Havana, the gliding of every prow, the dipping of every oar, and even the ripples which the soft south wind raised upon a portion of the surface of the harbor, made the waters all around flash with phosphorescent light, as brightly as the stars overhead, and the crescent moon. The large clippers, and the ships of war from Spain, were casting shadows blacker even than themselves over the harbor; while along the line of the quays the lights of the city sent streams of flame, trembling and dancing, far out across the water.

On my excursion to San Antonio, the incident which gave me, perhaps, most pleasure, and may best be worth mentioning, was the meeting with a party of four young bloods—*partie carrée*—who, wishing to see the island, had been sent out by a Spanish friend of theirs to spend the day at this small bathing place. Making the journey in the freshness of the morning, they reached the town with appetites exceedingly sharp set. Summoning at once, therefore, the landlord of the inn at which they had alighted, they inquired if he could give them a *déjeuner à la fourchette.*

"Certainly," replied mine host, with the look of a man who was ready for all emergencies; "and with what may it please the gentlemen to be served?"

"Have you fish?" inquired the spokesman of the party.

The landlord, his eyes sparkling, instantly collected the fingers of his right hand to a point, and, bringing the same gracefully to his lips, removed them with an audible kiss, saying:

"The gentlemen shall be served with red snappers—the best fish in the kingdom of the two Spains."

"Good. And have you any beefsteaks?"

Another kiss, even more resonant than the former, was the reply; while, at the same time, the portly innkeeper's eyes ran over with smiles, and his mouth, watering, ran over with saliva.

But to serve a repast so magnificent, required a little time. The Señores must give a half hour for it—which, on this island, means an hour and a half. Accordingly, the young gents, in order to kill the time, sallied forth in their volantes to see the country, which, at that hour of the day, was pretty brilliantly illuminated by the sun. But, bidding defiance to heat and dust, they overran no less than three plantations, seeing sugar, coffee, and cotton fields, and got back to breakfast before the waiters had fully done rubbing themselves in garlic, preparatory to bringing in the dishes.

So these tyros of travel sitting down to their fork breakfast, the platter of fish was brought in and set before them, with an air, on the part of the chief waiter, which seemed to say:

"Señores, it is good enough for the king."

The Señores were hungry, and looked at the dish with longing eyes; but what did they behold? By the faith of San Antonio Abad, they saw four fish heads—four enormous fish heads; and each a head without a tail, much less a body; but, altogether, having eight big, glaring eyes, wide open, and all staring at these foreign gentlemen! The gentlemen stared in return with their eyeglasses. But it was of no use; the fish heads with the naked eyes outstared them. And so, after parley and objurgation, the eaters, completely discomfited, ordered the waiters to remove out of their sight the heads of the eaten.

But now came the turn for the waiters to open their eyes a little. The Señores not eat fish heads! They stood still in their places, absolutely petrified in the face, and their feet as good as glued to the floor with amazement. Not eat the heads of the red snapper! It was some seconds before they could recover presence of mind sufficient to obey orders. But as they finally did so, their countenances changed. To surprise succeeded the expression of contempt. Surely, they thought, these *caballeros* from the States were, at home, no better than flunkys. And one of the *mozos*, who was a black boy, in taking the platter out of the room, was overheard to say to his fellows, with a significant pointing of his thumb over his shoulder:

"Fish heads too good for 'em!'

The foreign gents then awaited, in mingled indignation and dismay, the serving of the steaks. On their appearance, however, the party took courage, seeing that this dish had, at least, no eyes wherewith to stare them out of countenance. The steaks had, on the contrary, a decidedly gentle and inoffensive expression, being cow's meat—the meat of cows no longer suited, by reason of age, to the purposes of the dairy. They had, in fact, been jerked beef when already on the hoof; and now, though done in oil and onions, were not susceptible of mastication except between the molars of a native.

But the leading gent of the party ventured so far as to attempt to swallow one of the morsels; while the others, less rash, paused to see the result. They not only held back, but they almost held their breath during the performance of the experiment. And well they might; for the face of the adventurous young man became, in the act of swallowing, first red and then purple. In fact, he was on the point of —suffocating—not, of course, from the steak, but from indignation, and gasped out:

"Help! unbutton my waistcoat!"

Finally, they all made their breakfast on bread soaked in wine and water. For on good Spanish bread, as I have elsewhere had occasion to observe, nobody need starve; and so the young men all departed, leaning on this staff of life, and obliged to content themselves with the simple pleasure of paying their bill, which amounted to three dollars for each person. As usually happens in this country, the landlord had decidedly the best of it; he being left in possession of the steaks and fish heads. He had, in fact, taken in twelve dollars, and also saved his bacon.

CHAPTER XXVIII.

A Cuban Steamer.

I WENT to Matanzas by the steamer, going on board at a late hour in the evening. Spanish friends had told me that this was the least disagreeable way of making the journey; though they dropped the hint that some of the vessels, being old ones, were not quite trustworthy in a norther; and, indeed, that none of them would put to sea while the wind was blowing from that bad quarter whence comes so much discomfort to the Cubans—cold, hurricanes, and filibusters. But, at the hour of my setting off, only the softest zephyrs were fanning the evening sea; while overhead was spread a canopy of lustrous stars, pink colored, and green, and silver. All these hosts of heaven seemed to be set in motion by the movement of the steamer down the harbor, accompanying and guarding us, like myriads of the angels of God.

Thus divinely and gorgeously attended, we left behind the city with its thousand lights, the Moro with its fire beacons, the harbor flashing with phosphorescent ripples; and passed at once out upon the ocean, to find it more softly but scarcely less beautifully illumined by the light of the tropical moon. Like a cork in the water, the little steamer rose and sank with the heaving of the great ocean's breast. But no storm winds that night were abroad on the deep; and the dark island lay sleeping in the embrace of the moonlit sea as peacefully as, in the wakeful mother's arms, the infant.

But what a Babel is the cabin of this Cuban coasting steamer! Two or three different languages are being spoken, the Spanish scarcely predominating over the English; and everybody is speaking at once. In the gentlemen's cabin there is an equally great confusion of postures, the passengers having assumed all possible attitudes—standing, sitting, reclining, lying. All, too, are smoking—even those who are asleep. At least, a number have gone to bed with unlighted cigars in their mouths, after tired nature has refused to smoke any longer.

The scent of the tobacco must, of course, reach the ladies' cabin, which is separated only by an ill-shutting door from that of the gentlemen. But do not suppose that the fair Señoras are annoyed by it.

On the contrary, two out of the three Cuban ladies who occupied the narrow quarters, lay in their berths smoking through half the night, and spitting, too, on the floor, wholly regardless of the direction. The third seemed less addicted to the use of the weed; still even she could not muster strength enough to arise next morning without the help of a cigarito. First having rolled it with the very prettiest of tapering fingers, she lighted it by the cigar of the man-maid who, during the greater part of the night, had been in and out of the room, apparently for no other purpose than to keep the Señoras' cigars going. In fact, the three smoked, spat, jabbered, giggled, and ha-ha-ed until long past midnight. But they jested not more freely with each other than with the man in waiting, whenever he came to rekindle their fires; though pretending, at the same time, to be dreadfully distressed at his presence. And yet the trio were, as the world goes, genteel ladies, having a good standing in the best society of Havana, and were dressed in rich silks, fine laces, and petticoats six inches deep in embroidery.

It was a piece of good fortune that the hours of this night were short ones; though it must be confessed that three o'clock is an early hour for rising, even in a Spanish country. But at that time of night the steamer's whistle blew a blast loud enough to awaken passengers the most grievously afflicted with deafness; and in a few minutes we were all aboard the small boats which had surrounded the ship, each one with its lantern. It was a good mile to shore; but the horns of the moon also contributed to make our water path sufficiently visible.

The boatman, arrived at the landing, looked sharp at my *pesetas*, holding them up to his lantern; but, finding them sufficiently heavy, he passed me and my baggage on to a negro who was standing, half asleep, over a wheelbarrow. The negro, when aroused from his nap, placed the trunks on his vehicle, and civilly invited me to follow on foot. There being no other way of going, on foot I went. And a sufficiently dismal walk it was; for, in proceeding through the long, dark streets, I found a plenty of dust, together with a great deficiency of gas; so that it was not until after much fumbling and stumbling that I reached the hotel.

At that early hour the heavy door was barred equally against travellers and robbers. I bade the negro knock; but he did so in vain. I bade him knock once more—thrice—four times; but it was not until he did so with his shoe heels that I heard the low sound of footsteps within.

"Who's there?" asked the voice of an African, manifestly half asleep.

"Travellers, and men of peace," was the reply.

Thereupon the porter went away, apparently to some remote part of the house, to get a light; came back again for I know not what purpose, and then once more went away, probably to ask permission of the landlord to admit the outsiders. It was granted and the ponderous door on rusty hinges opened to receive me. I was ushered into the drawing room; and there the negro would have left me to pass the remainder of the night, had I not bidden him call his master, and make ready an apartment. Very submissively but drowsily the porter did his errand; and, returning, went to bed again. At the end of a quarter of an hour, no landlord being forthcoming, I went again for Sambo, otherwise called Crescenzia, who very obediently, and as if fully expecting to do so, got up a second time, and was soon heard in an adjoining room calling the landlord by name, and vigorously shaking him. The latter, sufficiently awake to talk intelligibly, promised to get up and make provision for the newly arrived guests. So Crescenzia once more went to his couch, and I once more began my vigils. Another quarter of an hour I watched for the coming of the master of the house; but, instead of approaching footfalls, I could hear nothing except the stentorian snoring of half a dozen sleepers. Thereupon, summoning Crescenzia for the third time, I insisted on going with him to the bedside of the somnolent landlord. Most cheerfully the fellow complied with my order; and, arrived there, he seized the man by the shoulders, and shook the sleep out of him by main force; while I stood by, holding a candle, and seeing that the operation was thoroughly well done. Of course, the *amo de casa* had to open his eyes; he yawned, stroked his beard, stretched himself, and, rising in his bed, made me as polite a bow as he well could, while repressing another yawn by covering his mouth with the palm of his hand. He now began, as I supposed he would, with expressing his regret that he had no room in his house unoccupied. Next, having by this time got his feet out of bed, he said—what I equally expected to hear—that he would be able to place an apartment at my disposal in the course of the day. It was the old story. But, finally, by dint of encouraging him by my regrets at having disturbed him at so unseasonable an hour of the night, as well as by professions of respect for himself and the excellent house over which he presided, I succeeded in getting him to say, as he drew on his pantaloons, that he would order a cot to be made up in the parlor, where I could sleep undisturbed until six o'clock.

The cot spread, I immediately fell so soundly

asleep as not to hear the waiter when he came, at half past five, to bring me coffee, in accordance with the Spanish custom of drinking it in bed, preparatory to rising with the lark. However, there are no larks, I believe, in this country; and one cannot say here, with the accomplished author of "Thorndale":

> "Rise with the lark; your motions shall obtain
> Grace, be their composition what it may,
> If but with hers performed."

But there are fighting cocks; and I slept through the crowing of no less than seventy of them in the pit, or rather yard, next door. They had begun their defiant chanticleering not long after my arrival, giving tongue in full chorus, the entire roost of them; and fiercer or more lusty crowers, surely, never were collected together next door to a hotel. Think how many ill-sounding words must have been uttered over these heralds of the dawn by the nervous invalids wont to come every winter to this island in pursuit of health, and to this lodging house in expectation of sleep. Alas! to them this pit full of cocks must have been of the nature of the pit Tartarean. However, it was an occupation rather amusing than otherwise for me, while waiting for a place to lay my head on, to listen to the rivalry which was going on between the snoring sleepers in an adjoining room, and these crowers in the adjoining premises—it being a concert peculiarly Spanish.

Matanzas, I may here add, is a pretty town, lying with its back against the hills, and its front toward the sea, which here forms a spacious and convenient harbor. The town is built a certain distance down on either side of the water, in the form of a horseshoe. At one extremity lies the *paseo*, commanding a view of the shipping; and on the other side runs along the line of shore a pleasant beach, abounding in shells, and much frequented as a pleasure drive. Hither the lover of fair sea views goes to see the sun descend behind the hills, and also to see it rise in the morning out of the ocean. The *paseo* is a short one; but the *plaza* is larger than that at Havana, and well filled with flowers. On this square are many fine houses, built of one story, but, in some cases, extending from street to street, and having a courtyard in their centre, with suites of rooms around it. The drawing room is always on the street, as well as the hall of entrance, in one or the other of which stands the volante; for the volante is kept in Cuba almost as much to be seen as to be used. The bedrooms are situated in the rear, and those occupied by the ladies have windows furnished with iron gratings, and no doors opening externally. In these chambers the pitchers and basins may be of silver; while in some boudoir, or place equally conspicuous, will be displayed the family knives, and forks, and spoons. The furniture, however, is generally very plain, it being liable to be eaten up by insects, and to be injured by the intense heat of summer. The floors are laid in tiles or marble, making the rooms look cool and comfortable in spite of the ominous mosquito nets. The walls are mostly white, or stained with little show of art; though a few of the best houses contain frescoed ceilings, and even such luxuries as a swimming bath, a gymnasium, and a small theatre. But the principal luxury generally aimed at in building these houses is a sufficiency of cool air; so that the rooms are large and lofty, and incapable of being heated artificially. Indeed, there are no such things as either stoves or fireplaces, excepting in the kitchen. This room, by the way, though not enjoying a reputation for neatness, is nevertheless, in private houses, often kept thoroughly swept and scrubbed, and looking every whit as clean as the drawing room.

CHAPTER XXIX.

Fighting Cocks.

BEFORE falling asleep on the morning of my arrival at the hotel, I resolved that it should be one of the first duties of the day to visit the cock-yard whence emanated the extraordinary chanticleering mentioned in the preceding chapter. Before seeing the bay of Matanzas, or the *paseo*, or the sea beach, or the valley of the Yumori, I would pay a visit to these cocks, and compliment the Don who owned them on their remarkable capacity of wind-pipe.

In fact, I did so before breakfast, and hat in hand. It was then past nine o'clock, but the seventy had not entirely finished heralding the morn. Some of them, indeed, seemed to be crowing over each other; and the principal group, immediately on my entrance, all went off in a blast apparently to do me honor. But my looks entreated silence. I wished to express without delay to the Don, who stood before me in a rusty dress coat, and head tied up in a black silk nightcap, my admiration of his crowers. And when silence had been obtained, I at once spread myself out into an immense circle of amplification upon the great public advantage there must be to the town in having its inhabitants—men, women, and children—all waked up betimes in the morning; a period of the day so beautiful in these tropical countries, and so favorable everywhere to moral impressions. The Don bowed his satisfaction; and, in a strain even more eulogistic, set forth the honor I had done him, and his cocks, by this visit.

He then ordered the negroes in attendance to show their best birds; and very noble, full-fledged, and high-stepping fellows they were. Head and tail, they were of the brightest crimson. They were also duly plucked on the back; had their spurs on, and stood as proudly erect on their legs as formerly did the cock immortalized by Plato. Nor, like so many young beaux in eyeglasses, would one suffer another to look at him without instantly replying with a challenge to mortal combat. And when I praised their haughty tread, and boiling, tropical rage, the thin little Don, bowing almost to the ground, unhesitatingly put the entire roost at my disposition—*a su disposicion de Usted.*

What if I had taken him at his word! For the man prized each cock at I dare not say how many ounces. Here was, in fact, a considerable fortune carefully invested in roosters, as well as a still greater one in anticipation from the doubloons they would win in the ring.

"This bird," said he, proudly pointing to one tied near a small hill of earth, "this fellow has killed three competitors; that one yonder, four—all reckoned among the best fighters on the island."

"Next Sunday," he continued, "they will win for me a pile of ounces."

And he made a significant gesture with his hand to show how high the pile would rise—himself, meanwhile, strutting with as conquering an air as if he had been one of his own cocks; his little black eyes flashing with the rage of combat, and his unconscious hands almost tearing his nightcap to tatters. So hot was his Castilian blood; and so intensely was felt, by anticipation, the ire of the day of battle, and of the pit stained with blood.

No doubt, on the following Sunday, the cockpit was crowded to its utmost capacity. At least that at Havana was, the day I saw it; and it was one capable of holding a thousand persons. Built with an open but solid framework, only sufficiently covered to protect it from sun and rain, the seats were arranged story above story, and were all filled with Creoles, mostly of the middle class of society. I could almost imagine this tower ready to fall to the ground like that of Babel; for speech was here confounded in the multitude of voices. The moment the cocks had been weighed and set in the ring, they began to pitch into each other; and, at that moment, began also the tumultuous vociferation of the betting. Hundreds of men, half infuriated from sympathy with the madness of the fighting in the pit, were crying to each other from one part of the building to the other, every man pointing to his bird with furious gesticulation, and shouting at the top of his voice, "A dollar on the red!" "An ounce on the white!" And as, in the progress of the spurring and pecking, the red or the white get the nose-bleed, or lose an eye, or are knocked over, the betters cry out to each other, "Two ounces to one on the red!" "Two ounces to one on the white!" Every time the bill draws blood, or there is a hit of the spurs, the discord of the voices rises higher; and then, when one of the cocks seems to give indications of having had quite enough of the fight, it lulls again. This lasts until one of the two combatants falls lifeless to the ground. Then, for a few minutes, there is comparative silence, interrupted only by the jingling of the gold and silver passing from hand to hand.

For, wherever there is cock-fighting, there is betting; pockets are emptied of small gains; and doubloons, too, are tossed about with the *duros.*

But can anything be either more absurd or hard-hearted, than this enthusiasm of men over the paltry rage of a couple of roosters! And no wonder that, in countries where such amusements prevail, the national face is so little expressive of sensibility and delicate emotion.

CHAPTER XXX.

A Matanzas Fonda.

BY half past nine o'clock I had returned from the cockyard to the Fonda, and was ready for breakfast. And an excellent Spanish breakfast it proved to be, with Catalan wine, which, in these tropics, I drank with greater relish than formerly in Catalonia. But the *chef-d'œuvre* of the meal was, I will not say, the beefsteak pie, so much relished by the Cubans, but the *tortilla con seso.* This is a very famous dish. You may not relish the idea of a brain omelette, but you will be a happy man the day you taste its reality. I could tell you how to make it, if it would be of any use. And, indeed, not to leave your curiosity unsatisfied, know that there must be a small cup of boiled *seso;* nor be disturbed at the thought of adding half the quantity of chopped onions. A delicate flavor of parsley also, must per vade it. It must be hot with pepper. And when you know that four eggs are to be added, you know all that can well be told about it. Then, if you do not succeed to your mind in making it, take a trip to Matanzas some day, and get permission to see it done by the cook of the *fonda*.

But there is one thing I cannot explain to you at all; and that is, why *prima donnas* should expose themselves at the public breakfast tables without their faces being painted. It causes such a perfect disenchantment, that no one who has beheld them under such circumstances in the morning, can possibly get up the illusion requisite for enjoying the entertainment of the stage in the evening. It also might puzzle me to tell why American ladies should come to breakfast in dresses *décolletées*. So much dressing at this early hour was certainly very ill-suited to the apartment in which the meal was served, it being no other than the hall of entrance, with its *porte cochère*, and opening, without any door, on the inner courtyard. Nor was the drawing room itself much better adapted to the exhibition of over-elegant toilets; for there the gentlemen smoked their cigars in the presence of the ladies; and there suddenly appeared, one morning, in the midst of the assembled company, the landlord's horse, who proceeded through the room as quietly as if he had been a guest of the house, and quite as unconcerned at the remarks which were made about him. He was on his way to the stable, the door of which he seemed perfectly well able to distinguish from the others standing open in its vicinity. He even knew enough to stop before a clothes line stretched across the court; standing there until the wet linen had been lifted for him to pass under. Truly a very sagacious brute, and well-behaved!

My room was on the first floor, as were all others, and so convenient of access that, on entering it, I could but recall to mind the case of the stout lady from Cuba, who, being so unfortunate as to have an apartment in the fifth story of one of the hotels in New York, resorted to the trick of fainting every time she came in from the street, in order that she might be carried up stairs by the waiters. The *ruse* answered very well for a time; until, one day, Patrick and James vowed that they would be blistered before they would carry the lady up any more, unless they had each a quarter for it. Whereupon the lady ceased fainting.

My room opened on the inner court, by a door large enough to admit two horses abreast; and of the same size was the window, which had heavy wooden shutters inside, and a still more heavy iron grating without. There being no glass, the passer-by looked through the open grating upon the occupants of the apartment, very much as, in a menagerie, he would take a peep at the lions. There, at half past five o'clock in the morning, appeared the venerable black woman who brought me coffee, and peeled oranges; and so black, withal, was she, as almost to put out the breaking light of the dawn, bringing back Erebus and the old night. Certainly she would have done it, but for the lighted end of her cigar, and the white of her eyes. There is, in fact, no such thing as privacy in a Cuban *fonda*. The partitions between the rooms extend only two thirds of the way up to the ceiling; so that all conversation not carried on in an undertone is necessarily overheard by your nearest neighbors. If, in their sleep, any of them happen to have the nightmare, you are sure to know it; while every word Mrs. Caudle says to Mr. Caudle goes through half the house, and terrifies all the husbands.

Nor was I the sole occupant of my apartment. For in one corner, between the rafters—all of which were uncovered—a couple of very loquacious bats had built their nest. And, though quiet through the day, they kept up, at night, a perpetual chattering. Judging from the noise, one would have said there was a large family of bat-children in the nest. They certainly had a great deal to say for themselves; but, for my part, I never spoke to them, nor in any way gave them to understand that I was aware of their presence; so that, in fact, the two families—mine and theirs—though living in the same apartment, took as little notice of each other as might have done any two parties of Englishmen thrown together by chance on their travels. The beams of the roof had been left bare for the sake of better ventilation; as, for the sake of the additional coolness, the floor had been laid in cement. The walls also were of a cold color, being whitewashed. The couches had no mattresses, and did not look at all hot, like, for example, the feather beds of the Teutonic nations. On two slender tripods stood two very small white basins. There was one pine table, and on it a toilet glass twelve inches by eighteen. A row of nails driven into the wall answered the purpose of a wardrobe, and had probably been driven there by some travelling Yankee, who had the wit to invent this species of clothespress. There was no carpet on the floor; but before the two beds lay two rugs, luckily of a pattern so small as to preclude the idea that the fleas of the house could possibly think of having a wake or mass meeting under them. Such were the quarters wherein I passed a week most happily, if not comfortably; and to the credit of the Cuban family in the ceiling, be it repeated, that, during all this time, they picked no quarrel with me.

The nails which the sagacious Yankee had driven into the wall of my room answered still another excellent purpose; for thereupon, every morning, was hung the day's supply of fruit. A big basket held the oranges; the bananas were suspended by their branches, and the pines were tied up by strings; but the cocoanuts were more conveniently heaped in a corner. With all this abundance of sweet stores, and a bottle of Catalan wine, I pleased myself with the thought that I could easily endure a famine, or a siege of twenty-four hours' duration; and, certainly, the plank door, as well as the iron gratings of the windows, would have held out that length of time against any reasonable number of beggars or bandits.

CHAPTER XXXI.

The Cumbre.

IF you happen, toward evening, to be standing in the doorway of your *fonda* at Matanzas, and see a very good-looking negro drive up, with a couple of stout horses and a tolerably neat volante, do not think of engaging him for an excursion, next morning, to the valley of the Yumori. He will ask eight dollars and a half for about three hours' service. He will agree to go even for six—I dare say for five; but the trouble is, that he will not come to fulfil the engagement at either price. Should you appoint the hour of sunrise for the setting off—the time of day when the *nosotros* and genuine Spanish Christians usually begin their journeys—you will have the satisfaction of getting up early, and waiting all the morning for a black man; but he will not come. He will not come—and this is the key to this small mystery—unless ordered by your landlord, who shares with him the fee.

Accordingly, I ordered my volante in the regular way, through mine host. I desired it to come at five o'clock, and it arrived at six; which was very good luck, considering the dilatory habits of the gentry of the whip in Matanzas. And how pleasant it is to set off on an expedition to the country in the freshness of the Southern morning! In fine style the tandem took us through the streets, already astir with industry; and as we crossed the bridge, the bay was flooded with the amber light of sunrise. The shipping lay partially enveloped in a mist, which was like dust of gold; while the ripples on the water, just awaking from their night's slumbers, resembled a wide expanse of gilded fretwork. We gazed with delight at the fair, artistic scene, as we passed on along the *paseo;* and, after reaching the hillside beyond the town, turning around, we gazed again; for it was, indeed, a genuine Claude, and no copy.

Ah, how fresh, how still was that morning air! how blue the sky overhead, and white the thin, fleecy clouds that floated in it, as the volante wound its way up the gentle acclivities of the Cumbre! The heavy dews of the night, which had been brought down by the land wind to this margin of shore, lay in drops in the hollow of every leaf, and hung from every blade of grass and projecting point of vegetation. We climbed up the road of rocks, between flowering hedges and thickets draped with morning glories delicately pink-tinted. The fields on either side were crowded with a rank growth of strange plants and shrubs, mingled with flowers of such gorgeous beauty as is becoming on an island lying so directly in the eye of the sun.

It was a region of country much neglected by the owners of the soil, but wherein nature wrought with irrepressible power, and with a satisfaction apparently none the less deeply felt by herself for not being noticed by the eye of man. At all the villas by the wayside, including those which stood unoccupied, and with broken gates, we saw groves of crimson oleanders, here endowed with fragrance. For long distances by the roadside there were magnificent rows of aloes, at this season just out of flower; the very stone walls were tipped with cactus, or hung with jessamines; and scarcely a bank or patch of grass was anywhere to be seen of which the flowers did not make a fair enamel. Here and there we passed under specks of shade, cast by palms, and pines, and wild oranges. Cattle, also, we saw browsing in the pastures, and striped-faced goats nibbling by the roadside, and flocks of sheep on the distant hilltops.

As we mounted the upper heights, the air became still purer than below. To the golden haze of the morning succeeded the more brilliant light of the sun, shining in full splendor, without a cloud. The blue waters of the bay lay far beneath us; while the ocean, whitened by many coming and going sails, stretched away beyond reach of the eye. Alas! what lacked the heights of the Cumbre, surmounted by graceful palm trees, and blooming with flowers just washed in the dews of the morning—what lacked this view of mountain, and plain, and shore; of city, and harbor, and the sea? Only the nightingales of the Pyrenees and Sorrento!

Perhaps, however, there is one more thing to be desired on these beautiful mountain tops; and that is, better roads whereby to reach them. As it was, we came by a mere cart track, so full of rocks and stones, and all manner of holes, that none but well-trained animals could pick their way through them; while no carriages with wheels less large and cumbrous than those of the volante would escape a breakdown. Nevertheless, in this buoyant air one can hardly experience the sensation of fatigue, and instantly forgets the toil of the ascent the moment the height is gained, from which he looks down upon the valley of the Yumori.

In the neighborhood of Matanzas there is, truly,

no second sight to be seen after it; and whoever, on beholding the bay of Naples, failed to be overtaken by the wish to close his eyes on all sublunary scenes, may possibly feel that he has reached his final climax when once he has seen the Yumori. Its features are well known to those who are familiar with printed descriptions of this island; for it is the lifelong boast of all travellers who have ever seen it. Every tourist will tell you that it is like the happy valley of Rasselas, prince of Abyssinia; and you will do well to believe him. For, imagine yourself standing on the summits of the Cumbre, and looking down into a valley encircled by mountains, as if it had formerly been the bottom of a great lake. Around its entire edge it is filled with softly rounded hills, sloping gently toward its centre, which consists of a comparatively level plain. And on the tops and sides of all these gracefully rolling hills, as well as at intervals throughout the plain, imagine innumerable palm trees, white stemmed and green topped, standing either alone, or gathered in open groups. They form the drapery of the landscape, which, when I saw it, was more beautiful from being, in the remote distance, partially veiled by the still lingering mists of the morning. How lovely not only these dark palms, like the cattle on a thousand hills, but how soft and fair the green of the sugar plant which covered the greater part of the vales and hillsides! Even those declivities the soil of which had been recently turned by the plough, being of a rich brown or chocolate color, heightened the beauty of the mosaic landscape; while the few hills which were not under cultivation, but overgrown with wild shrubbery, displayed the purple tints of English moors, or of the heaths of Scotland. We lingered long in the presence of this great beauty of nature, and declared, as we drove along the mountain's brow, overlooking it, that this was a happy valley, whether or not that of Rasselas. And, far below, we descried on one of these rounded hilltops a snug little villa, with its gardens and palm groves, which we affirmed should henceforth be numbered among our *chateaux en Espagne.* Two or three other villas, at which we stopped on our way, were also pretty; and at one of them we were hospitably entertained with such oranges as no prince of Abyssinia ever tasted; with cigars which were the very topmost leaf and flower of all tobacco; and with a glass of whiskey that was as the dew of the mountain, even of this bread mountain, called *Pan de Matanzas.* We here saw coffee and cotton plants, as well as the sugar cane in different stages of growth, and the process of sugar making. We likewise tasted, for the first time, the sweetness of this Southern reed, the negro in attendance peeling it with his knife, and handing it to us to be sucked, as do small boys their sticks, one end in paper, of molasses candy. It made a tropical and rather refreshing entertainment; though, to my taste, this is one of the few sweets of life which are a trifle too much sweetened. Meanwhile, our ears were likewise entertained with the novel cries and songs of the neighboring sugar house, and the clatter of the mules, as, driven by half-naked boys and girls, with whip in hand, they kept in motion this grand hurly-burly of the grinding. Servants everywhere attended us in our joyful progress about the estate, all grinning to do us pleasure. They gathered for us gorgeous bouquets of flowers; while one of the dusky damsels more comely than the rest, and, indeed, of blood almost purely Spanish, wore orange blossoms in her hair—the only ones we had seen so worn on the island. Specimens of tropical fruits were eagerly exhibited; and a nimble black boy, greatly to our amusement, shinned up a palm to cut some cocoanuts. A very sleek and happy-looking set of servants were they all at this chateau. The gobblers which greeted us in the courtyard, and spread their tails in honor of our arrival, were not more swollen and puffed than were these fellows, men and maids, all blown with hilarity and joy at the coming of the strangers from parts to them un known.

And so, after an excursion of three hours' length prolonged to six, we drove up to the doors of our *fonda*, as happy as the morning had been long, and as hungry as a man should be who sits down to the *tortillas* of mine excellent landlady.

CHAPTER XXXII.

A Cuban Railway.

FROM Matanzas to Havana I went by rail. Some Spanish gentlemen of my acquaintance endeavored to dissuade me from proceeding by land, inasmuch as the railroad, being a monopoly, is used principally for the transportation of sugar; and, so long as the freight trains can be kept on the track, small pains are taken about the comfort or safety of passengers. Three or four times in the week the passenger trains run off the road, or are delayed on it in consequence of the failure of the engines. To be sure, no lives are lost, the engineers always selecting soft places to go off on, and performing the operation in the very gentlest manner possible. But, though one's neck be not broken, he may be detained half a day in an open plain, parched by the sun of the tropics, or he may be kept over night where it will cost him a quarter of an ounce to order a supper, which, when ordered, will never be served, or, when served, will never be eaten. However, I went by the rail.

The train started at sunrise; and it would be superfluous to say that it was a fine morning; but it may be worth remarking, that we set off on the stroke of six, as punctuality is a rare virtue so near the equator. It made a very good start, but, before getting more than four or five miles out of town, suddenly came to a full stop in the open country. This was a halt requiring explanation; and, upon inquiry, it turned out that the conductor had received a signal at a certain point on the road, which induced him to stop, after he had got about a mile beyond it. He then sent back a man on foot, while the train was kept waiting. Why the train itself did not go back—as to have done so would have taken comparatively little time—it was not easy to guess. Indeed, the conductor himself finally walked back a quarter of a mile, and then, turning about, walked forward again. All these movements were very Spanish, and quite inexplicable.

But the long delay gave the officials having charge of the train an opportunity to inspect its condition, and see what might have given out in the course of the run of four or five miles. Nor did it take long to ascertain that something had gone wrong. We had broken a brake, one end of which lay upon the ground, and looked as though it had not succumbed a moment before its time. However, we got on quite as well without the brake as with it. Nothing more came to pieces during the journey; and we kept the track to the end. The Chinese appeared to make sufficiently intelligent brakemen; while some of them also supplied the passengers, from time to time, with peeled oranges. At one of the stations I bought most delicious cheese cakes, served on green banana leaves; so delicious, indeed, that uxorious husbands have been known to be tempted to repeat this journey simply for the sake of giving their wives another taste of them.

One more Spanish peculiarity, however, noticed in the running of the road, was, that, after the accident to the brake, the engineer backed the train a hundred yards or more, apparently for no other purpose than that of starting it; as when, in leaping, a man steps back a few paces, in order to give himself a better chance for accomplishing the feat successfully. So, at Guines, the train backed a full mile before leaving. It might possibly have been for the purpose of allowing another train to pass; but I suspected that the conductor thought it necessary to take unusual pains not to make a bad start, inasmuch as the day was Friday.

14

The country through which the road passes, being occupied chiefly by sugar plantations, is beautiful throughout, and, in some places, picturesque. The palm trees, of the sight of which one never tires, escorted us in groups and groves the whole distance to Havana, as the stars had previously done on our way along the coast to Matanzas. And scarcely less graceful than the palms were the thickets of reeds, which grew in clusters by the roadside. If the former trees reminded us, by the color of their stems, of the white birch of our Northern home, so the delicate leaves, slender branches, and bending heads of the latter brought to mind, also, the graceful foliage of this well-called lady of the woods. The mango tree resembles our chestnut, presenting a dense mass of green leaves, the extremities of which, at this season, are tipped with the orange and purple of the bursting buds. Interspersed together were everywhere to be seen magnolias, with their large, glossy, dark-green leaves; tall pines of a delicate shade of bluish green, and lightly fringed with needles; and orange trees at the same time golden with fruit and white with blossoms. Here towered the ceiba tree with its strong, graceful stem, and wore its crown of rich green leaves above the tops even of the palms. The darker mameys were loaded with fruit gray-colored; the sapota tree with fruit of brown; the tamarind drooped with pods; the calabash was hung with round balls; the leaves of the banana were swayed by the wind, revealing its fruit clusters and buds of violet; while only here and there the cypress cast from its mournful boughs a frown on the smiling face of the landscape. Up many a lordly stem climbed the female fig—*yuagua embra*—holding it in a beautiful though fatal embrace; the lovely convolvulus, entwining itself around the trunks of dead monarchs of the woods, decked them with palls of white flowers; and innumerable tops of tall trees were tufted with various parasitical plants, the orchids and the aloes, all their flowers laughing in the sunlight, or dancing in the wind. Many misshapen forms, indeed, come to view in these tropical woods; and in the midst of all this abounding life there is constant decay. But the grace of parasitical plants creeping everywhere, and beautiful with every tint of flowers, is hung like a veil over the deformity of nature.

The undergrowth of shrubbery, likewise, is most luxuriant, and shows much gorgeous coloring. The wild passion-flowers are of many different varieties; the hedges are covered with several kinds of convolvulus; the fever-flower flaunts in flame and gold; the species of aloe plant, called *peta*, burns a stately candelabra with fire of yellow; the mangroves hold out to the passer-by white chalices full of perfume; the apple rose scents the air around it so deliciously as to hold all footsteps, as in an enchanted circle, spellbound; the wild heliotrope runs modestly by road and path sides; while everywhere fly, amid the flowers and the sunshine, humming birds and butterflies, and countless insects, all flashing with the tints of precious stones and the bow in heaven. All the forms of nature were high colored—flowers, foliage, the sky, and even the very ground itself. Indeed, the red dust which occasionally filled the railway carriages painted as well as powdered all our faces, and imparted to our travelling dresses a tinge quite as warm as that of the landscape. But, in spite of the clouds of dust which we had to encounter at some few points on the road, it was a pure delight to breathe the air of the open country; and I remember that, after our luncheon of oranges, bought from the palm basket of the Chinese brakeman, we not only pronounced the juice equal in sweetness to that of the apples which tempted the first of women, but would have it that the island itself was not a very bad copy of the original Eden.

At any rate, 'tis hard leaving it. Indeed, the difficulty of getting away from Spanish countries is greater than persons who have never visited them can well imagine. To arrive, is, generally, no easy matter; but to depart—there's the rub. It costs just double the money to get out that it does to get in, and more than double the trouble. For example: the porter, when I went to the hotel in Havana, charged me a dollar and a half; when I left it, three dollars. The boatman asked one for landing, two for embarking. The passport fee was, on arriving, two dollars; on departing, four. Landlord, porter, boatman, official, all act on the principle of fleecing the parting guest, not speeding him. Nor, even after having satisfied the demands, just and unjust, of these worthies, can a man leave the island except by permission of his wife; for, under the Spanish law, she can stop him, by showing cause.

CHAPTER XXXIII.

Nassau—A Winter Newport.

IN eight-and-forty hours, or less, one may steam from Havana to Nassau, and see the tropical Englishman—a sight worth seeing. Leaving the island of the black-haired, olive-faced men, and making a short run across the northern tropic, the traveller is again among the blue eyes, and complexions which take on freckles. At the same time, he feels that he has reached once more a free country; that he has passed from beneath the law of military force, under that of liberty and a protecting public opinion. Here are no more stilettoes, no grated windows, nor the heavily barred doors of the Spaniards. The Nassauese have not, it is true, either *paseos*, or guitars at night beneath the moon; but, instead of Domenica's, here are the town library and reading room; instead of the opera, here are concerts and lectures once a fortnight at the Bahama Institute;

fashionable calls, between the hours of twelve and three, take the place of the midday *siesta;* and the stranger who has been entertained with ices and *volantes*, finds himself once more asked to dinner.

Indeed, my dear reader, you might even risk the voyage direct from New York, for the sake of exchanging, for once, your Northern winter for the perpetual summer of this green little island, so piously called New Providence, and so conveniently anchored just on the shady side of the Tropic of Cancer. Such a change of residence, once in half a dozen years, would cure all your chilblains, and even lengthen the days of your life; inasmuch as the winter's sun rises here an hour earlier, and lingers at evening an hour later above the horizon. Sitting, in the month of January, with open windows, and looking out upon the golden fruits hanging amid the leaves so deeply green, one can scarcely refrain from wondering why the frost-bitten nations do not every winter follow the sun to the south, pouring down into these Hesperides as formerly the rough Goths and Vandals descended into the sunny plains of Italy.

Come, then, once before you die—come along with the migratory birds to the islands of perpetual serenity, where the great god of day will have a chance to melt the icicles out of your beard, and cure your rheumatism, like a doctor. It will be a change for you, my hyperborean friend, second only to that of being born again. And do not think that you will see snakes here, or centipedes; do not be alarmed by the bugbear of bedbugs; and don't get unduly excited at the thought of a single mosquito buzzing at night under your curtains, or of a flea or two, instead of the good angels keeping watch and ward over you while you sleep. My word for it, nobody will see snakes here, excepting those persons who look for them; and nobody but the most determined sight-seers will be shocked at anything much worse than the beautiful chameleons, and the lizards, which from tree and wall do sometimes curse the passing negroes. So, throwing over your head your furs and muffler, your mittens and jack boots, your two top-coats and umbrella, come down here by the "Cunarder"—since Collins and the Yankees have gone to the bottom—and, making yourself comfortable in a thin jacket and slippers, get into one of these hammocks, slung on the cool side of the piazza, and rest yourself, after so many years of pacing up and down Broadway, and around the Boston Common.

But as to the tropical Englishman whom you have come to see, the most remarkable thing about him is that he is an Englishman still. He may be a little less red in the face, less heavy in the cheeks, shrunk a trifle in his calves, and bound about the loins with a somewhat narrower girdle—growing to look, in form, just the least bit in the world like a palm tree. In fact, owing to the greater dryness of the climate, the comparative toughness of tropical roast beef, and the diminished convenience of the ale tap, he has suffered, in most instances, considerable waste in his adipose cellular tissue; and his muscle has grown less juicy. For the greater part of the year, also, he wears linen instead of his natural woollen; and puts, moreover, so much starch into it, that his nightcap is sometimes almost as able to stand alone, when he goes to bed, as he is; while his sleeping-robe is liable to stalk about his chamber like a ghost, whenever the wind blows. The pith hat, the Panama, or a straw wound about with fine linen, makes here a partial disguise for an Englishman; as do also the morning jacket of white flannel, and shoes of white duck. The most careless observer, however, when seeing him going the round of fashionable calls in the tropical midday, dressed in black tail-coat and stovepipe, cannot fail of recognizing the original John Bull. Besides, he wears his gaiters, and leg-of-mutton whiskers.

Moreover, let the Bahâma Englishman dress or look as he may, he always regards the mother country—not the colony wherein he lives—as his home. Although well enough pleased, it may be, with this American side of the world, he nevertheless is seized every few years with a longing to revisit the other and better one. He must needs recruit his health, impaired by the excess of sunshine which nature never intended he should be exposed to; and goes back to the English climate, as to the wet sheet and vapor bath of the water cure. Particularly, if a North Briton, there is a sort of necessity in his constitution that he should be well drenched once every five or seven years in his native fogs; nothing sufficing so effectually as this to dilute his over-thick blood, and fill his shrivelled skin again. Thus the visit to the mother country, being the crowning joy of the colonist's life—and, in fact, the most fondly cherished hope of his heart being, one day, to take fortune and family back to the circle of well-remembered friends left behind in the imperial isle—he is no true West Indian. He cannot be said so much to be transported into the soil of these Bahamas, as to be temporarily set out in a pot of it; so that, at any convenient moment, he can easily be removed, and take all his roots with him. Hence, his colonial interest is almost entirely personal or official. All his public spirit, his patriotism, his national pride, centre in Old England. He has no colonial literature, but reads the London *Times.* Living on an islet of coral and limestone, in the midst of the democratic waters of the American ocean, he still maintains the spirit and the forms of monarchy, and goes almost as gladly to court in Government House as ever he did to St. James's. The old established institutions of neither church nor state are much modified to suit his colonial condition; but, bringing with him even to the New World his ancient true church, he loves, on Sundays, to wait for two long hours in a pew, though the mercury stand at ninety, while the hierarch, with three colors to his back, prays for sinners, and "all the nobility."

Not all the oranges and watermelons of the tropics can alter the Briton's native-born taste for old port, sherry, and malt liquors. He imports roast beef in tin from the mother country, rather than order fresh meat in ice from New York; and buys an English plum pudding hermetically sealed, sooner than eat one made in the colony. Having attached to his house a flower garden, fruit orchard, poultry yard, and sometimes a bit of a lawn, he surrounds all with a high stone wall, as beyond sea, and bottles it. Piazzas he must have to shelter him from the sun, as also green goggles to his eyes, and, over his head, a blue umbrella; but he does not need chimneys in his dwelling house, and has left all his coals behind in Newcastle. A steady though small fire, however, he keeps up in his kitchen; for the old English virtue of hospitality still lives and thrives in the Bahamas, where the well-accredited stranger finds open doors and groaning tables, being wellnigh as welcome as he would formerly have been to Robinson Crusoe. Indeed, the favored guest might almost be tempted to think that, although the cheeks of the Nassauese Englishman grow less and less to resemble shaddocks the more he eats them, yet his generous, sympathetic disposition does gradually secrete some additional sweetness from the tropical oranges and sapodillas. I myself have met persons here whose hearts ran over with sugary juices precisely like their mangoes. Even my shoemaker sent me a present of shaddocks, and my shopkeeper overwhelmed me with sweet oranges and grape fruit.

This New Providence, chief island of the Bahamas, and of which the town of Nassau is the capital, is only a small paradise, in extent some seven miles by twenty. On the side of the capital it has a horizon of islands and cays—Rose islands and Silver cays—with white-topped breakers rolling, in rough weather, between. Within, the harbor is as green as an emerald on a lady's finger; while the sea beyond, blue as lapis lazuli, and sprinkled with bright yellow gulf weeds floating on its surface, may bring to mind, perchance, the beautiful mantle of blue and gold which Carlo Dolce has thrown over the shoulders of his La Poesia.

Though a mere calcareous rock, composed of corals, shells, madrepores, and various deposits, and almost entirely destitute of soil, the island is nevertheless either tufted with palms, orange, and other fruit trees, or overgrown with tangled brushwood. Nearly everything grows directly out of the rock, wellnigh as great a miracle as when, in sacred times, water was drawn from it by the rod of Moses. But it takes a stone mason to set out a tree here; and it will grow all the better for the help of sponges and sawdust; while the farmer may

> "Lay down the shovel and the hoe,"

using, instead, crowbar, saw, and pickaxe. Still, the rock being highly porous as well as soft, the roots of trees run freely in all directions below the surface, and derive sufficient moisture from the reservoir of rain water, which, at the depth of a few feet, rests upon the salt water from the sea, rising and falling with the latter's daily tides. Every foot of the island is covered with verdure; so great is the vegetative power of nature in the tropics, spite of the lack of mould. The silk-cotton tree throws out its flat buttresses wide enough for the stabling of horses, and spreads its branches over an area one or two hundred feet in diameter. The cocoa palms and the Australian pines overtop the town. Many even of the larger trees bear flowers; while tall shrubs of various tropical varieties—oleanders, white, red, and pink, the yellow elder, the scarlet hibiscus, the white and golden jessamines, the coral flower, the plumerias and popinacs—projecting over the walls and peeping out of all the gardens, dash with bright colors the general green of the landscape. The air plant grows luxuriantly out of the rock; and the night-blooming cereus likes to climb a fence or gateway, on which it can get plenty of air and light, and see the world go by. It also runs up the trunks of tall trees, mingling its thick, fleshy leaves with the green foliage; and even scaling the sides of houses, it mounts to the chimney top, lifting its head above it as exultingly as, in continental Europe, does the merry, singing Savoyard. The sandy shores are fringed even to the water's edge with acacias, hops, and sea grapes. The moonlight flower, open at night, answers with its pure white to the silver light from the skies; and the morning glory is too happy to wish to fold itself in sleep before evening. Nature even preys upon herself, from excess of vigor; the wild fig strangling in its embrace the tamarind and almond trees; and the bindweed and the love vine hanging upon the highest branches of the groves their heavy drapery of leaves and innumerable filaments.

But the great charm of the island consists in its climate—so mild and soft, the expression in the face of your pet kid is not more so. During the season of winter, the ordinary range of the thermometer is between seventy and eighty degrees of Fahrenheit; the mercury going higher only occasionally, when the relaxing south wind blows, and not falling lower except during the prevalence of the bracing northers. The atmosphere is almost purely that of the ocean—soft, balmy, and having the fragrance of salt water in it. It is, in fact, the air of a ship's deck on a fine summer morning in the middle latitudes. The evenings, unlike those of Havana, are often moist with dew; though the stars shine with all the brilliancy of the winter night at the North, and the moonlight is very much brighter. Indeed, the silver crescent, when only two days old, brings out the shadows; while the full moon makes the limestone streets look as white as if covered with newly fallen snow. Day after day the wind blows here only a pleasant summer breeze, its pace not exceeding half a dozen miles the hour; though when, once or twice a month, the norther comes, he presses on at the rate of some twenty pounds to the square foot, making all things rattle; so that, for three nights in succession, no man can sleep without "spools" in his window shutters. Still, the north wind, in its passage over the gulf stream, loses much of the coldness which it possesses when, coming across the State of Florida, it reaches Havana. It is considered by the natives a good tonic—though rather an overdose, I thought.

Bright days, bright nights—they are together like diamonds strung with pearls. And the tropical fruits and flowers correspond with the brilliancy of the climate. The town is full of gardens, wherein the palm waves and the oleander blooms, and the orange hangs out its globes of gold, half hid among bridal blossoms. The sapodillas and the mangoes on the trees are, like the sands on the seashore, innumerable. The shaddocks grow to great size—as large as the heads of small black boys; and I have made the discovery that, if a man will eat a luncheon when he does not need any, there is nothing so good for him as grape fruit. Slightly acid, it rather creates an appetite than cloys one; and the stomach, after it, experiences a sense of gratification as after a glass of good Hock or Rudesheimer. Only beware of the rind; for the bitter and the sweet lie as near to each other in a grape fruit as they do in human life.

One goes to the tropics, of course, to live in the

open air, not to be comfortable in lodgings. So, at Nassau, I found but indifferent quarters, with only the promise of better ones in the future—a promise since happily realized. Yet my attic was an ample one; and of this I am quite sure, never was there so happy an attic before. We habitually sat with open doors and windows. And these looked to the four quarters of the globe; showing us, on one side, all the glories of the Government House, together with the statue of Columbus, painted white, and representing the great discoverer of these islands in the form and attitude of a dashing hidalgo. On another side, the view began with one of the numerous poultry yards, which fill this quiet little town with more crowing and cackling, gabbling and gobbling, than is to be met with in any other place in Christendom, I believe, not Spanish. It is a peculiarity of the Nassauese cocks, that they crow not only at daybreak, but through all the hours of the night. From sundown to the return of day it is a perpetual crowing, crowing, crowing. The instant any one of these feathery watchmen winds his clarion, he is answered by all his fellows throughout the town in chorus. The youngest chick will not be silent; nor can Bantam suffer himself to be outdone by the hoarsest and most guttural Cochin-China, or him of Shanghai. For what earthly purpose are so many cocks kept here? grumblingly asks the stranger, who, the first night after his arrival, tries in vain to sleep in such a rookery; or who, dozing in the small hours, facetiously dreams that the moral little town is full of secret cockpits, wherein, on Sundays, the good people clandestinely fight their birds between the religious services.

On still another side, our windows look toward the west, over orchards of bananas, oranges, and lemons, over gardens of climbing roses, jessamines, and oleanders, over pines and royal palms, toward the bright green harbor and the sea.

But the eastern window pleased me most of all, because from that I saw the sunrise. And know that this is a climate which forces, at least, all the lovers of nature out of bed before sunrise, simply by means of the beauty of the mornings, which, even in winter, open precisely like our Northern June roses. At this early hour I go to the shore for my bath; plunging into the pure, transparent water just at the moment when the sunrise is scattering its rose leaves over the surface. The deep sea water is like molten glass—for the moment turned Bohemian. Then, during the space of five blissful minutes, how lustily do I pull the old god Neptune by the beard; or more gently play with the tangles of some Naiad's hair! And all these marine divinities could testify that most gladly would I swim in the tepid waves from one Bahama to another—but for the sharks! These monsters give me pause. For, during my stay at Nassau, one of them swallowed his Jonah—a black man—and was found, after capture, to have digested the whole of him, excepting one hand, and his rum bottle. Dreadful!

However, the bathing houses offer their protection to the timid, or the more cautious; and on coming out of them, even, one feels regenerate, and as newborn as the day.

The winter midday, as well as the morning, is very fine here. The prevailing wind, at that time of day, is the trade, blowing pleasantly from the east; and such a breeze as in our sunniest May days at the North gently tosses the flowering tops of the apple orchards; or, in full-blown June, trips it lightly through the rose gardens; which makes the fragrant clover heads dance and nod to each other in the fields; and covers the growing meadows with rippling, grassy waves. At the noontide there is often not a cloud in the heavens, excepting the white canvas of ships' sails on the horizon, or in the harbor. The tropical sunlight gilds with leaf of gold the limestone streets, or paves them with the dark shadows of trees and houses. In the brilliant rays the façades of white marble buildings shine like burnished silver. And yet, though strongly marked the contrast between the lights and shadows of the town, how soft are the gradations of color where the verdant shore blends with the sea-green of the surrounding waves, and where the indigo-blue of the distant ocean passes without any distinct line of separation into the blue of the empyrean.

At this idle hour of the day I liked, sitting at the western window of my chamber, to look out upon a palm tree standing near by, which I selected from all other palms I had ever seen for my favorite. It is of the cocoanut variety, tall, and leaning gracefully—such an one as the wild Arab loves to call his bride. The tree seems almost a living form, animate with sense and feeling, and to stand there, its branches waving, and its leaves quivering in an ecstasy of delight. It appears to be enamored of the sun, toward which it aspires. It basks in the unclouded rays, like the black man lying asleep at its foot; and, like him, joyfully absorbs the midday heat. And as the sea breeze comes and goes, now lifting the branches gently aloft, and now letting them gracefully droop again, with what an expression of gladness the palmtop receives these soft caresses, toying and gambolling with the wind! The branches seem also at play with each other; harmoniously swaying to and fro, the topmost bending slightly, and the lower ones swinging themselves through wider curves, and with a more deeply impassioned motion. Surely, with such grace does a Venus move her limbs when she comes newborn out of the foamy waves; and so dance upon the stage the lithesome Spanish girls of Grenada, and the gypsies of Seville.

But the cuisine! Upon what food does a man live in such a clime, and on such an enchanted island? Does he, like the first of men and women, subsist on the fair fruits—on mere orange juices—on the perfume of his finger glass, scented, one day, with the green leaf of a lime, and, the next, with one of a pimento? Not quite so. But, to tell the truth, though the mutton will do for food, the beef is not succulent. It is, in fact, a little tough, and requires, in order to be masticated, to have been previously well *papawed.* "For the juice of the papaw," says Soyer, "makes meat tender, by causing a separation of its muscular fibres." Some of the more elderly chickens, also, will test the sharpness of the carving knife, as well as the power of a man's jaws, unless a pretty stiff dose of vinegar be poured down their throats just before their heads are cut off. Poor things! this must be the first; and the axe, the second death to them!

Accordingly, the stranger will find himself under the necessity of eating turtle twice a week here.

He can have turtle soup, turtle stewed; but the great dish of the island, and chief glory of the "conch" kitchen, is baked turtle. A small monster of about twenty-five pounds' weight is a good size; unless, indeed, you happen to be an alderman, in which case forty pounds would not be too much. He is brought to table in his own shell, which stands well up before you, and makes an ample platter. In its depths lie imbedded all the choice pieces. The fat and lean bits lie side by side; the eggs hug the liver; while the whole mass is moist with a delicious gravy, made of the juice of the animal, and hot with infinitesimal red peppers, each particle of which is endowed with a sting like that of the honey bee. An open space in the middle of the crust—for this great mystery of culinary art has a broad covering of paste around its entire edge—an open space, I say, in the crust, like heaven's gate standing ajar, enables you to get a peep at the feast of good things within, the moment it is set before you. Far off, too, the nostril anticipates the coming of baked turtle; for the whole atmosphere of the place is at once perfumed with the subtle essence and aroma of the dish; the very winds of heaven struggling to bear some of it off to their own caves.

After baked turtle, no Christian wishes to eat pudding. But if compelled to dine on a Nassauese beefsteak, one is certainly entitled to nothing less than either cocoanut pudding or banana fritters; and if he do not get the one or the other, he should consider himself robbed by his landlady.

In any event, you will drink a glass of uncommonly nice sherry with your turtle; for it is well known that this animal cannot crawl nor stir a fin in good sherry. I should have some hesitation, however, in recommending any one to adopt the local fashion of letting rum punch follow the soup. But no one should fall into the mistake of refusing, whether after turtle or anything else, the proffered glass of Madeira, known as the "Water Lily"—a wrecked wine, and named after the very unfortunate vessel in which it was cast away on these shores. The delicious sack had been sent to the West Indies for its health; and some of the casks bore, as I have been told, the names of venerable and right reverend English prelates, men supposed to know how to select good liquor. Alas for them! The only dash of bitter in the glass, whenever it was my good fortune to taste this juice of the grape, was the regret—impossible to repress it—that such good men should providentially have been cut off from the privilege of anointing their palates with so precious an oil of joy. For the wine is excellent, and must have received all the benefit from being sent to sea which its intelligent owners had anticipated for it. Well may the Nassauese, in describing this beverage, so fortunately rescued from the waves, speak of it with brightening face and uplifted eyelids, as more rainlike than rain water, more dry than the tropic Cancer, and yet more luscious than the grapes of Malaga or Muscat—the very aroma of aromas.

So you see this Bahama is what the Chinese would call a "little heaven." But you must know that three quarters of the saints are blacks. Seated on my piazza, morning and evening, when they go by on their way to and from the market, I have seen the street darkened with the number of them, and the tropical day almost put out as by an eclipse. They go by, many of them with tattooed, gashed faces, horizontal nostrils, and hair braided into rams' horns and corkscrews; nearly all possessing healthy, athletic forms, though not very heavily covered with muscle; all with the same loose, shuffling gait, as if their bodies were jelly, and going to pieces; with speech often resembling a kind of articulate grunting, and even their best English sounding a little like Congo. Up to the age of puberty the children are remarkably thin-limbed; and many of the smaller ones, having no other garment than a shirt, look like a large species of grasshoppers, and very much as did the children of Israel in the presence of the giants, the sons of Anak, who came of the giants. But, with the exception of one noted old beggar in sackcloth, these blacks dress as decently as do the lower class of whites in hot countries. Their garments are not often washed, nor always taken off at night; and most of the women have the habit of wearing their dresses very carelessly put on. Though many of the females cover their heads with turbans, and a hat besides, they are inclined to go barefoot, in spite of the "jiggers;" and hence the old song,

> "Jiggery foot, jump in the air—
> A bottle of wine, and a bottle of beer," etc.

But, on Sunday, every negro who goes to church comes fresh out of his bandbox; and he who, through the week, had worn a palmetto hat, price two cents and a half, will don a beaver, or a sky-blue cotton; and he who had worn nothing but a kerchief, will carefully protect his head from the sun under a family umbrella. Perhaps it is natural that the head should receive special attention, when it bears all the burdens; for there is nothing, from an empty barrel to a bottle of champagne, which is not so carried. I have seen a letter taken to the post on the head, with a small stone laid above it to keep it from blowing away; and, on the other hand, I have beheld negroes coming into town surmounted with as heavy a load of green corn blades as may be seen enveloping to their feet the Cuban donkeys which bring fodder into Havana. Everything goes naturally with them to the occiput; and there, too, not on the back of her head, does the ebony belle, on Sundays, stick the gay little bonnet of present fashion.

The Bahama blacks are generally well behaved and good natured. Their disposition is mild, passive, tractable; and, though often crossed with the English, they appear not to have a single hair of the bulldog on them. They rarely fight with each other, except in words; are not fond of fisticuffs, nor given to sedition; but, most of the time, have their mouths full of chat, laughter, and sugar cane. When meeting in the street or highway, they often converse together without stopping—both continuing on their way, while they exchange their jest and laugh, and neither turning their head. The commission of heinous crimes—the deed of blood and daring—does not comport with a character so soft and timid; but for petty theft, and all manner of lying, they have an extraordinary aptitude. Too many of them, I am sorry to say, are untrustworthy and unreliable. Capable, often, of strong personal attachments to the whites, when they have been long in their service, they are nevertheless, with exceptions, ungrateful, and forgetful of benefits. They pay comparatively little attention to the minor morals, and not too much to the major. Especially is the relation of the sexes badly regulated among them.

Yet this much can be said in their favor, that their faults of character and conduct do not spring from malice or uncharitableness, but rather from their heedless, thoughtless disposition, their natural indolence, and their habits of present self-gratification. Fond of the good things of life, they take scarcely more thought for the morrow than many of the brutes. So, in their speech, they never make use of the past or future tenses of verbs, but only of the present. Most of them are capable, if not of wearing all they possess on their backs, at least, of letting it all go down their throats at a single feast, and never think it any sin to run in debt to whoever may be imprudent enough to trust them.

Of all things, they do not like steady, hard work; and are not to be depended upon, therefore, for the carrying out of any large plan of active industry, or for securing a certain return of interest on any great investment of capital. They prefer odd jobs, as labor about the streets and wharves, or situations of easy service, or to catch fish, or to go on short trips in the wrecking vessels. Generally, when they get a few shillings together in their pockets, they lose all appetite for further toil until they have spent them. All their salvage money goes to the shopkeepers to pay old debts. Of the savings bank they make little use, but rely rather on their fishing banks, which furnish the greater part of their sustenance.

In general, it may be said of the Bahamian blacks, that they are as much inferior to their brethren in the "States," both morally and intellectually, as the climate of the tropics is hotter, and the fruitfulness of nature therein is more spontaneous than in our own. Although they have now been free for a quarter of a century, and, during this period, have enjoyed the superior advantages of English tuition and example, yet their improvement, whether intellectual, moral, or physical, has not been very great. I should say that, if the amount of white blood which has passed into their veins could be estimated, it would be found to be a tolerably exact measure of their progress. This, to be sure, is something; for the English have done considerable toward whitening the skin of the black population, and have straightened a good many heads of hair—with the help of pomatum.

The native Africans who, a few years since, were transferred to the island from slave ships captured at sea, are more industrious, and, perhaps, superior in morals, if inferior intellectually, to the Creole blacks formerly held in bondage. It is true that the children of the latter have acquired, in free schools, the rudiments of an English education, and that a few of them display, upon examination, as much cleverness as the young whites. Still it must be observed, that it is the faculty of memory, chiefly, which is developed by this early training, and that, the age of puberty once passed, the Africo-Bahaman mind appears to make but comparatively little further progress.

Of the purely abstract ideas, these tropical Africans, almost without exception, seem to have but an imperfect and dim apprehension. Even so simple an one as that of time they do not appear to conceive of with any considerable degree of clearness. When asked in what month of the year the different fruits of the island are in season, they can rarely give a precise answer; and I was informed by the son of an aged black woman, when I inquired the number of her years, that it was one hundred and sixty. A straight line, also, bothers them. I was told of a black gardener here, who could not be taught accurately to lay out his paths and spaces at right angles.

"This corner of the house is nearly a foot too high," once said a Nassauese gentleman to the mason who was erecting its walls.

"Oh! yas," was the reply; "dat massa say bery true; but folks isn't goin' to notice it."

"And the doors and windows," continued the proprietor, "are not quite opposite to each other."

"Well, yas—if massa will be so bery partic'ler."

In this difficulty of mastering a straight line, by the way, the inferiority of the negro to the lowest class of Irishmen is noticeable. For if you ask Patrick, in the tropics or out of them, what he considers to be the prettiest thing in the world, he will invariably make answer:

"An' shure, yer honor, 'tis a straight ditch!"

But the Bahama blacks are a healthy, prolific race. Out of four persons you meet in the streets of Nassau, three, at least, are blacks, or mulattoes. In church, one sits quite surrounded by his colored brethren and sisters; the whole congregation presenting a pepper-and-salt aspect. So, in places of both public and private entertainment, the impertinent question will often spring up in the mind of the stranger—like the roguish head of a truant child thrust through a half-open door—"Has not this estimable gentleman with whom I am so pleasantly conversing, or this most amiable lady, the line down the back slightly discolored?"

In the polite circles of society in the Bahamas there is a prejudice against the black or mixed color still prevailing, which surprises one, considering the liberal views entertained by English philanthropists in the mother country on this subject. But, in justice to the class of mulattoes, I feel bound to add, that I met, at Nassau, persons belonging to it whose intelligence, good character, and polite manners made them the peers of white men, whether there or in any other country.

It would be idle to speculate about the future destiny of the African race in the American tropics; or to conjecture whether, on the one hand, it is likely, after emancipation, to relapse into barbarism; or whether, on the other, after it shall have existed as long in these countries as did the Saxons in the woods of Germany, it may finally develop a new and original form of civilization. But one may, at least, divine enough of the immediate future of the Bahamas, to come to the conclusion that, in the natural increase of their black and colored population, it must soon crowd hard upon the whites, and gradually drive them out. They will either voluntarily take leave, or be sent away against their will, as formerly were the French from Hayti. Already the African element is so strong in some of the Bahamas —as, for example, in St. Salvador, Bahama, Andros, and Long Island—that, in spite of great natural advantages of soil and climate, white men begin to be reluctant to cast their lot there. And why, indeed, must not the same become true, at no very distant epoch, of all the West Indian islands? For, while the free African thrives in these tropics like a green bay tree, and willows by the watercourses, the Anglo-Saxon, and even the Spaniard, is a sickly exotic.

Time, unquestionably, will show it to be a law of nature, that in lands where the white man cannot sow, neither shall he reap; where he cannot himself labor, he shall not permanently dwell. So long, of course, as, by superior force and intelligence, he can retain the black men in bondage, or state of dependence, and make them perform the labor of sowing and reaping in his stead, so long he may hold the islands of the tropics; but not much longer.

I have before observed, that the Bahama blacks derive a portion of their support from the business of wrecking. The number of persons of all colors so engaged is between three and four thousand, and that of their vessels from two to three hundred. They are required by law to save life before property; and this they always do, as I am informed. The cargo to be rescued being often more or less under water, it is necessary that the sailors be also good divers, able to descend to the depth of even thirty or forty feet, and make bales of goods fast to tackle. The salvage of a single ship sometimes amounts to fifty thousand dollars, or upward, which is distributed one half to the captain and owners of the vessel, and the other to the officers and crew. Sometimes a considerable portion of a shipwrecked cargo is saved dry; but a great many boxes and packages get damaged, not only through fault of the waves, but also from being rudely opened, for the purpose of enabling the wrecker to judge whether they will yield a high rate of salvage. For the captains who arrive first at a wreck naturally desire to load, each his own vessel, with the most valuable part of the cargo.

In such a small, isolated town as Nassau, a little excitement goes, of course, a great way. So, when the fleet of returning wrecking vessels is seen coming into port with white flags flying, the little place is set all agog. Half the population stand, for the moment, on the tiptoe of expectation; the shopkeepers' heads stiffening like bristles, and the negroes' wool half uncurling from excitement.

"O Lord, massa!" said to me one of the latter, quite dancing with delight, and threatening to spit out all his ivory, as he pointed to the white schooners ploughing into the bright green harbor, "O Lord, massa! dere cum de rackers—full of drygood, silk stocking—eberyting!"

A wreck is a misfortune, of course, and great disappointment to somebody; but it makes a very pleasant holiday for the good people of Nassau. During my visit, there was a sale of an assorted cargo of drygoods, too much damaged to be forwarded to its port of destination. And never was such confusion seen before in mortal affairs, as in these rescued bales and boxes. All around the spacious yards of the consignee there were piles, a dozen feet high, of cottons, calicoes, muslins, linens, and flannels, all as full of salt water as ever was a sailor of grog and tobacco juice. Wet figs lay in juxtaposition with wet fire-crackers. Reams of tinted paper were deposited side by side with boxes of fine lace, tubs of mackerel, and barrels of yeast; the latter facetiously marked, in conspicuous letters, "Keep this dry." It was a scene of complete pellmell, with buyers going here and there in a high state of agitation, and negroes, who never could be made to lay out their strength before, now all in a lather.

The goods once distributed among the merchants, their shop doors and windows were festooned with cotton and woollen fabrics, which, hanging down to the sidewalk, were trodden under foot by the crowd of black and white purchasers. Even the sides of several of the streets and lanes were covered with wet goods, spread out to dry in the sun; fences and trees were hung with them; and the very roofs of the houses fluttered with muslins.

Truly, to enjoy a wreck, one must come to Nassau.

The white-stone days, it may be added, on which the fleet of wreckers sails into the harbor, have but one holiday in all the Nassauese year to rival them; and that is the one wherein occurs the august ceremony of the opening of the Bahama Parliament. Flags are then hoisted, guns fired, and the regiment of blacks mustered; while the band plays the national anthem, and other airs patriotic. Meanwhile, the Governor, having come down to the House in sword and epaulettes, the sergeant-at-arms holds aloft his mace, and brings up the honorable members of the House of Assembly into the presence of His Excellency. Thereupon the latter proceeds, sitting in his chair of state, and with his plumed hat on, to read to them, together with the gentlemen of the Privy Council, his gubernatorial speech. The honorables of the House stand during the ceremony, all in respectful tail coats; while the honorables of the Council sit during the same, clad in coats of blue broadcloth, set off with gilded buttons and linings of white silk, and matched with buff waistcoats. The reverend clergy occupy a corner of the scene, arrayed in black silk gowns; some having their hoods lined with scarlet, and some bordered with white down. But most conspicuous stands among them the chief prelate, sporting his doctor's cap and gown of flaming red, edged with black velvet; and having his under person set out in silk stockings and short clothes. Over against the men of God are seen grouped together the men of war—red coats all, spurred, also, and sworded, and some of them having their breasts decked with ribbons and crosses. Nor does the fair sex fail of being present; the roses in their hats, if not their cheeks, vying with the crimson of the priests and soldiers, and the unusual red in the face of some of the principal actors in the ceremony. Without the railing, however, hangs a cloud of dusky spectators, negroes and mezzotints; while one or two curly heads may, perchance, be noticed on the shoulders of the honorable members of the House of Assembly.

On the whole, this must be pronounced a very brilliant and high-colored scene, in miniature; and as thoroughly English as anything to be witnessed in Westminster Hall, or the Houses of Parliament.

CHAPTER XXXIV.

Santa Cruz and its Freedmen.

IN my search about the world for fine days, I thought that I had found the finest at Nassau; but I was compelled to change my mind after reaching Santa Cruz. The climate of this latter island is both dryer and more constant than that of the Bahamas. One may even spend the entire winter here without once encountering what, at the North, is called bad weather. There may be no storms; no entirely clouded skies; no rains, excepting showers; no winds, excepting the northeast trades. The island being destitute of high mountains or forests, the clouds are not detained on their courses by this speck of land; and one half the rain to which it is fairly entitled is drawn over to the well-wooded mountain sides of its neighbor, Porto Rico, lying to leeward. Moreover, the rain descending in occasional showers, is immediately absorbed by the thirsty ground;

while the dews of night are gone almost before the morning. The range of the thermometer, during the winter months, is between seventy and eighty degrees of Fahrenheit. The stranger, judging of the state of the atmosphere by his sensations, notices, at this season, very little change from day to day; but the Creole constitution, on the other hand, is sensitive to the slightest variations. The north wind, which the New Englander finds pleasantly bracing, brings colds, followed by mild attacks of chills and fever, to the natives. The negro now sleeps by night in a cabin as hermetically sealed as cracks and crannies will permit. The air within is never too thick for him; and he fears a draught of night wind as much as if he were a Frenchman. The whites, however, always sleep with either doors or windows open. And, with very few exceptions, they wear woollen clothes in winter, together with flannel next the skin. For, say they, we cannot move in this climate without getting into a state of perspiration; and we cannot stand still without being in a current of air. Hence, linen is worn outside, if worn at all, and wool beneath it. But the stranger in full health may dress differently; and, for my part, I found myself never so comfortable as when clad in a complete suit of light flannel, without under-dress of any kind—excepting a cotton shirt. My linen trunk proved to be a ponderous superfluity.

Quarantined by forty miles of ocean, this solitary island is rarely visited by epidemics. The cholera did not come here when formerly ravaging the West Indies; and though, in unhealthy seasons, there may be a few isolated cases of yellow fever, this disease does not prevail as in Cuba and Jamaica. The robust appearance of the native population is sufficient proof of the salubrity of the climate; and—what is remarkable—in the hotter part of the year the public health stands the highest. The men, especially, are neither sallow in complexion nor spare of flesh; but have, on the contrary, the glow of health in their faces, and are well covered with hard muscle. The climate agrees with both men and wine—makes good blood and good Madeira.

Yet the unacclimated invalid should not stand too much in the sun. Let him at all hours, excepting the early morning and evening, keep an umbrella over his head, or a carriage top, or the roof of a house. His physician, probably, will have sent him to Santa Cruz to live out of doors; but, with doors and windows always open, it is out-of-door life here in the house. Let the sick man rather beware of too much exercise in the open air—at least, for the first month or two; let him keep himself much more quiet than he would at the North; for, if he do not over-fatigue himself, nor commit imprudences, the mere breathing of the salubrious air will cure him—provided he be not past cure. In former winters there were hundreds of valetudinarians from the North in Santa Cruz, where there are now dozens. They have been enticed away to places in the South less favorable to their recovery, by the facilities of railroads and steamships. They have not patience enough for the slow sailing vessels. Made restless by disease, they prefer going to ports which they can with more ease get away from, as well as where they can receive more regularly advices from the home which they are all so apt to yearn for.

Well—it is a long voyage from New York to Santa Cruz. Eight days may, indeed, suffice for it; but, more likely, the good ship will take sixteen. Nor are there any regular packets. Generally, one can come only by sailing vessel to Saint Thomas, or by steamer to Saint Thomas, *via* Havana or Bermuda. Then remains the trip of forty miles across to this island in a small schooner, having state rooms on deck, fitly yclept doghouses. But do not be discouraged. If the invalid have only strength enough to get to the end of the journey, and also good accommodations secured in advance, his chance of recovery will be greater here than in most of the other islands.

Yet the stranger who comes to pass the winter in

Santa Cruz will do well to bring all his resources for killing time along with him. For the days are long and sunny; and there are no libraries, or bookshops, or magazines, or daily newspapers. The glorious sun is intent on ripening the sugar canes, and not on looking about Santa Cruz for poets or philosophers. The monotony of the livelong day may occasionally be broken by a morning call, or *matinée*, or birthday party. Once a month there may be pigeon shooting; and, once in the season, horse racing. Persons properly introduced into society will now and then be asked to dinners, balls, and parties. But riding and driving will be found to be far more ingenious inventions for whiling the time away; the roads being the best in America—smooth, hard, and free from dust. After getting acclimated, horses from the North thrive well here; while the native animals are both fleet and hardy, and will carry you, under the saddle, at a good round pace as carefully as if you were eggs. Their gait is the perfection of equine grace and rhythm.

For my part, while I preferred the evening hour for climbing, on horseback, the hills to "Punch" and "Mt. Victory," through the romantic ravine of Crai-crai, shaded by Thibet and mahogany trees, skirted by ipecacuanha, hybiscus, cactus, and fragrant log-wood hedges, and draped by every variety of tropical trailing plants, flower-bearing parasites, and mosses and creepers, half pendent from the overhanging precipices—the path winding gradually up out of the solemn gloom of the deep dell into the brilliant blue of the hilltop sky—I preferred, decidedly, the midday for carriage exercise. In the very brightness of the noontide we used to sally forth, two ponies in hand; and the eager animals apparently as much in love with the sun as ourselves; for away they flew over the smooth road, drinking in the eastern trade wind with distended nostrils, their long tails floating behind, their beating hoofs resounding like the waves of the beach by the side of which they trotted, and not more heated by the sun than cooled by the sea breeze. Protected by the carriage top from the direct rays of the great luminary in the zenith, and fanned by the soft airs which were invited in by the curtains rolled up on all sides, we found this rapid rolling over the road, at noon, a more delectable combination of the hot and the cold than the sitting in any summer cave or forest shade—more delicious than ices under the reign of the dog star, or champagne out of the cooler. And, indeed, the intoxication of the motion was as great as from mild wine. We were intoxicated with delight. The ponies, outflying the flies, were not stung by them; what little dust might have been raised on the hard road was left behind. The ladies had no fans, nor any shawls but scarfs, and ribbons fluttering. We looked out, on one side, upon the indigo sea, sometimes almost feeling the spray from its long-drawn waves breaking on the shore; and, on the other, upon lines of palms and groves of sugar cane. The little black children leaped out of the road, and threw up their caps, and opened on us their batteries of laughing ivory as we passed. The market women turned aside their "emancipation carts" far ahead, on hearing the coming rattling; and the men from the sugar fields—their ponies' sides projecting wide with their load of canes—carefully drew them almost into the gutter, in order to let the hurrying wheels go by. Did we not also hang out orange boughs from the carriage sides? And did we not bring home under the seats the big yellow shaddocks and grape fruit, more delicate to the taste than oranges? And had we not baskets stuffed with sapodillas and sugar apples? And did we not come back, too, with nuts in our cheeks, like monkeys, and no small part of the juices and the aroma of the tropics on lips and tongue? Of course we did.

And the ponies, likewise, fared well after such stretching of their legs. For their aged friend tied them under the cool India-rubber and frangipanni trees, without any fear of rheumatism before his eyes; and gave them big, succulent heaps of green corn blades, or the still sweeter leaves of the sugar cane. Doubtless they liked, too, the scent of the frangipanni.

Occasionally, the object of our noonday drives was to attend parties given by daylight. For here the custom is to give entertainments not only by night, but more frequently during the solid hours of sunshine—especially when ladies are to be present. The distances between the estates are, of course, considerable; so that the guests have to make a journey often of half a dozen miles or more. And though gentlemen, with or without a blanket over their shoulders, and perhaps the friendly company of a cigar, do not object, after having dined together at six o'clock, to a rapid drive across the island at midnight, ladies, who in this as in so many other things are more sensible, prefer the lively morning hours for such excursions. They are always ready for a dance by the light of the sun, and in spite of him. They are never too warm in dancing. The trade wind is their fan. They stand tiptoe as easily as a New Englander walks on his heels. And it would seem as though the hotter the climate, the more satisfactory was the pastime—just as the tropical gentlemen say that the hotter the day, the more rum goes into the punch.

Certain it is, the exercise puts the palates of all into a proper mood for receiving the cold turkey, or the hot guinea fowl of the luncheon. And perhaps few persons suspect what a jewel of a bird the tropical guinea fowl is, when, deprived of its voice, it appears on the table—for, if it still retained its preternatural screech, I think no one could eat it. The heat of an island so near the sun is always a good excuse for thirst. Accordingly, if you think the climate does not agree with the thin wines, you need not have any fear of swallowing a single glass of old sherry, or Madeira, after the guinea fowl. You might not drink it at the North for a variety of reasons; but here it is absolutely cooling to the blood; it gives great powers of resistance against the Southern heat; and your footing in the dance will be all the lighter for it. Neither disdain the sweetmeats. They will agree with your constitution as well as, at the North, do sourkrout and pickles. Sugar would seem here to acquire, by some gastric mystery of fermentation, the strengthening properties of alcohol; so that the more you eat of it, the more you partake of the nature of a lion with honey in his belly.

But, fasting or feasting, you must dance. For see how frantically Sambo's head is nodding with all its wool on it; and with what comic grimaces—his mouth a gash from ear to ear—he draws the fiddle bow! Old and young join in the graceful mazes. Meanwhile, buds of roses bloom on the maidens' breasts; and the delicate blossoms and fair leaves of noyau wreaths encircle their brows. Is it the scent of white jessamines, whiter for the contrast with the raven hair, which so pleasantly perfumes the summer breeze? Or do these sweets float in through the windows, thus gracefully latticed by passion-flower vines, from the lilies and the daturas, the oleanders and the fragrant cedars of the garden? Dance while the day lasts; for in the sunny courtyard a score of little darkeys are industriously improving the music, which sounds none the less sweet to their sun-burnt ears for passing through the open doors and windows; and are pirouetting, and knocking their naked heels, and crooking their elbows, until the perspiration runs down their faces like cane juice from the cylinders—literally enjoying their fun in the sweat of their brows, and laboring as if they thought every waltz and cotillon were a regular "breakdown." The merry fellows would be sorry to stop as long as they can have the sun to shine on them. So dance on.

"Juchhe! Juchhe!
Juchheisa! Heisa! He!
So ging der Fiedelbogen."

In the days of slavery, this island of the Holy Cross was called the Garden of the West Indies; and, though now partaking somewhat of the nature of a paradise lost, it remains still one of the most beautiful spots in the tropics. Riding, one afternoon, with a pleasant party of friends, to the top of the Bodkin—a height of a thousand feet or more—I thought the prospect one of the most lovely I had ever seen in any country. The hills, valleys, and plains upon which I looked down were nearly all green with sugar canes. On one side, the hills, round topped, and most gracefully curved, rolled away like the waves of a sea of emerald; on the other, stretched off toward a range of hills to the eastward, a broad plain of the greatest fertility, completely cane-covered, and dotted over with a large number of bright-colored plantations. These, having each one tall white chimney, resembled, in the distance, the small villages of the South of Europe, overtopped by spires. The windmills, too, on the lower summits, had a picturesque effect; while many dismantled ones might remind the traveller of the ruined towers which overhang the Rhine and the Danube. The prospect all around us was beautiful; but our hearts were almost too gay; for one of the company, having cut a bough from an orange tree full of fruit, and borne it in triumph to the summit,

I remember that our lips were running over with most delicious orange juice, at the same time our eyes were running over with delight in the beauty of the landscape.

The house in which I was so fortunate as to stay during my visit to the island, stood midway on a hillside covered with green canes, and sloping gracefully to the sea shore. It was therefore convenient both for the morning bath and the afternoon ride on the heights. Convenient, also, was it for seeing the sun go down in the sea; for the horizon of waters compassed, at this point, almost an entire semicircle. We found excellent companionship in the mild, tropical ocean, the waves of which were constantly making, both by day and night, a pleasing murmur, rarely changed to a roar. The ground swell brought up shells and corals. In the quiet bays the grave pelicans dived, rapid as the thunderbolt, all day long for sprats; and, returning at evening to their accustomed resting place, sailed sometimes directly over our heads, silently as the falling dew, and holding both wing and breath for a long distance. The shadows of passing rain clouds coming over the hills out of the northeast, often blackened the blue of the ocean in certain portions of it, while others were glittering in sunlight; and the April-like showers which fell from time to time were generally accompanied by brilliant rainbows, sometimes double, or triple, or even quadruple—rainbows in clusters, like the clustered pillars in Gothic cathedrals. Often rising out of the depth of a valley, climbing the hill-sides, and sweeping through the sky down into the ocean, they brought to mind the shining angel in the Apocalypse, who stood with one foot on the sea and the other on the land. On calm days, the shores, in places where there were coral reefs below the water, would be as green as the deepest emerald; at other times, the long line of rocks and beaches would be completely frosted with foam. Not only the colors of the sunset were reflected on the broad expanse of waters, but throughout the day a flitting purple light was often spread by passing clouds over the waves. In the early evening, the moon, when but one day old, drew a thread of silver from the horizon to the land; while the full moon poured a perfect flood of illumination over hills, valleys, and the sea. The limestone road which wound around the foot of the hill below us, running on the edge of the shore, shone then as if covered with hoarfrost; and the numerous forms of the palm trees bordering it were doubled by their shadows. So transparent, indeed, is the atmosphere in these latitudes, that, in calm weather, not only the islands of Saint Thomas and Saint Johns, lying forty miles to the northward, may be

16

seen distinctly by the naked eye, but Porto Rico comes into view, and reveals its mountains, at a distance of a hundred miles, floating among the clouds. Various other small islands also loom up, at such times, out of the misty distance; so that the beams of the chambers of the firmament seem to be resting upon them.

Directly behind the house was the garden. A door opening from one of our rooms into this, it was pleasant to sit looking, on one side, toward the sea, and, on the other, upon flowers and green leaves. It was pleasant to step out, as the morning was coming up behind the eastern hills, among the roses and the lilies, and many sweet-scented shrubs, and tall trees bearing flowers. At this hour I always realized best that I was in the tropics. As if in the natural state and condition of man, I stepped from my room into this little tropical Eden, wherein was no sin, but only the gushing light of the Southern morning; only the freshness of the sunrise air, in temperature just fitted to sense and feeling; only the green, glossy foliage, and buds and blossoms of every hue and fragrance. Here, from the tops of tall trees, the glowing scarlet cordia blossoms saluted, high in air, the rising sun; while those of the burning love shrub, and of the soldier's plume, equally full of fire, but growing lower, welcomed him to the ground.

Great clusters of oleanders, also, reddened the morning air; and groves of full-blown yellow cedar trees, mingled with high Spanish jessamines, gave back to the sky more than its own effulgence of molten gold. How gorgeous these tropical flowers! How strange to the sight these broadly spreading giant trees, and these puffed and swollen Guinea tamarinds, their trunks resembling in color the hide of the elephant! But the palm trees are the most beautiful of all, though now, unfortunately, more or less scathed by disease; and they may be seen, throughout the island, skirting the roadsides, and tufting, here and there, the hilltops.

In such groves and gardens strolling, during the first cool of the day, I was sometimes tempted to wish that there existed in our American tropics some great city worthy of their beauty and splendor—one that might indeed be called a Garden City, its houses being embowered in flowers, and having gardens hanging, if need were, like those of Bagdad, in the air. Of such a great capital, the architecture might be as light and graceful—as fantastic, too—as was that of the Moors in Spain. How splendid would be the pomp of arms and military parade beneath the sun of these tropics! How beautiful, likewise, the music of colloseums open to the air, fanned by the soft trade wind, and lighted by the full moon!

Here the costumes of the promenade and the dance might well glow in rivalry with the bright colors of the Southern vegetation. The domes and minarets might better be gilded than those of Moscow, situated beneath a sky of lead; while the inner walls of house and palace should be hung with colors caught from West Indian skies and seas, as were those of Titian from the waves and the marbles of Venice. No doubt, however, the delights of such a tropical seat of art and empire would be too luscious for our dyspeptic humanity; and, for some centuries to come, the highest civilization will be that which is fed on the gravel stones of the North.

So far, indeed, the West Indies have done little more for man than to develop the faculties and passions most nearly allied to sense. These islands have been cultivated for their sweets and their aromas. For a time, cotton was grown here, as well as coffee and cocoa; but the sugar cane has completely supplanted them; so that all the hills and valleys now drop with the fatness of sling and molasses. In Santa Cruz, however, nearly the whole of the latter article is sublimed into rum—potent, aromatic "Santa Cruz;" and, by feeding upon a little of this, and a good deal of cane juice, do the negroes, in crop time, fatten themselves. Even the cattle and horses grow sleek on the green cane leaves. The fields are full of rats and mice gnawing the stalks for dear life; and the very dogs and cats would become well favored from the drippings of the sugar kettles, did not the climate impose upon them the law of perpetual leanness.

With these two exceptions, all animals, human or brute, thrive on sugar—but most of all the negro. During the grinding season he is as full of juice as a cane in the field; while in the other seasons of the year he gradually becomes almost as thin as a cane which has passed between the cylinders. In the former period, his skin shines like the face of one anointed with oil. He is full of blood and marrow; and, when angry, will butt his adversary with his head like a ram. The senses bud, blossom, and bear luscious fruit; wellnigh overlying, even in the white Creole, the more spiritual faculties and sentiments. The latter eats less sugar, and even drinks less rum; but he has turtle, and oysters which grow on trees, and pork fattened on cane, and turkeys made tipsy with rum before killing, and mutton which is tender enough without being *papawed.* The Santa Cruzians are to this day drinking old Madeira ripened by their climate, while the rest of the world has scarcely a drop left of it. Unlike the Spaniards, their neighbors, they give dinners as well as balls. They dine, and dance, and have their rubber at whist. They also go to church on Sunday; but a man may live long on the island without listening to a public speech, or a lecture. One would be at a loss to know where to go to buy a book. Among the better class of whites, the children are sent to Europe, or the States, to be educated; but, where the sun is so hot as it is in the West Indies, a young man soon forgets his Latin. Twice a month the mails bring the English and American newspapers. A gentleman now and then receives odd copies of the reviews and magazines. Danish papers, also, come from Copenhagen a month or two old, and sometimes mouldy from sea fog and salt water. On such food does the public mind starve!

Happily, the Santa Cruzians are compelled to be reasonably industrious—the blacks by law, and the whites by necessity. Previously to the year 1848, the laborers were all slaves; and so heavily were they tasked, that the profits of sugar growing were very great. The planters lived in ease and luxury, and the island was filled with inhabitants considerably beyond its present numbers. But in that year the blacks, by a concert of action, and secretly instigated and favored, as is generally believed, by the Government in Denmark, suddenly ceased work, assembled in the two chief towns of the island, and declared themselves freemen. And after two or three days of interregnum, during which considerable property was destroyed, but no lives taken, the claims of the insurrectionists were allowed, on the one hand; while, on the other, they agreed to return to their estates, and resume their customary labors, on payment of wages by their former masters. From twenty-five to thirty thousand slaves forcibly recovered their rights from one quarter of that number of whites, without hurting a hair of their heads. At first, the home Government made fair promises of granting some small amount of compensation to the planters for their loss of service; but being, at the same time, of opinion that the island would, in the end, be rather a gainer than a loser by the change, it at first postponed, and finally withheld all remuneration. And if the very great wealth and prosperity of the planters has been materially diminished since the emancipation of the slaves, this unfavorable change is no doubt to be attributed much more to the lavish expenditure, and the practice of plunging recklessly into debt, on the part of the landowners, than to the diminished results of labor under the system of freedom. The planters, of late years, complain of the insufficiency of labor on the island, and have made some efforts to import free blacks from the more populous and more prosperous island of Barbadoes. But they at the same time admit that the freedmen are fairly industrious; and acknowledge themselves, on the whole, satisfied with the new order of things. If the summits of the range of hills which follow the whole length of the northern shore are not as green with cultivation as formerly, but many of them overgrown with the brush which now furnishes a home for the spotted deer, imported from Ceylon, still all the lowland—a stretch of some twenty miles in length by nearly half a dozen, on an average, in breadth—is crowded with waving canes; while the fair tropical sky above is blackened, in crop time, by the smoke of sixty or more steam engines. During the existence of slavery, the number of estates reached two hundred and twenty-six, each containing from two hundred and fifty down to six acres; but many of them, being heavily burdened with debt, have passed out of the hands of the old planters and their families; their number has been reduced to about ninety; and new men, in many instances, of moderate means, have come into possession of them.

If the Danish Government did not pay the planters for the loss of their slaves, it did what was much more for their interest—it established a code of laws which secured to them the willing service of the entire black population. Taking pattern from French rather than English legislation, in the West Indies, it placed the newly recognized freemen in a state of tutelage, preparatory to the future condition of absolute political liberty. They were not to be allowed to set up their castles of indolence under every cocoa tree and banana shrub, supporting themselves with little labor on the lavish bounty of nature in the tropics, and forming such habits of idleness and vice as the great heat of the climate would naturally engender; but they were required by law to perform a reasonable amount of daily toil —so much as would keep up their habits of industry already formed, and as would tend to secure their moral and physical well-being, as well as the general welfare of the white population. The new Labor Act was, in fact, a system of laws which at the same time guaranteed to the emancipated blacks all their rights, and minutely prescribed all their duties. In all important particulars, it described and established the relations to be sustained to each other by the two classes of laborers and employers.

The laborers were divided into three classes, according to age and capacity. They were required to work five days in the week, from sunrise to sunset—that is to say, from six in the morning until six in the evening—resting one hour for breakfast, and from twelve to two o'clock for dinner. The wages were at the rate of fifteen cents for those of the first class; ten cents for those of the second class; and five cents for those of the third class, per day. They were also allowed to claim twenty-five cents out of the amount of a week's wages, to be paid in corn meal and herrings at a fixed price, which, since the passage of the law, has proved to be considerably below that of the market. The laborers of the first and second classes were likewise granted the use of a house, or dwelling room, and the use of a piece of ground for raising vegetables, thirty feet square, or fifty feet, if on a hillside. They were to have, also, the privilege of keeping poultry, pigs, and ponies. When sick, they were to be entitled to medical attendance; if disabled, they were to be maintained on the estate; their young children were to be fed and attended to at the expense of the landowner; while women were not to be required to work during a certain period after childbearing.

For extra work on Saturdays, or other days, extra pay was given—the maximum being for the first class; as, for example, boilermen, in crop time, twenty cents per day. Any laborer, on the contrary, wilfully abstaining from work for a day, would lose the day's wages, besides incurring a fine of seven cents, if belonging to the first class; of five cents, if to the second; and of two cents, if to the third. Laborers not working faithfully, or committing any other offence against the laws, were to be punished by fine or imprisonment, on complaint made to the magistrate by the employer or overseer. On the other hand, owners and managers of estates convicted of violating any of the provisions of the Labor Act, or convicted of practices tending wilfully to counteract or avoid, either directly or indirectly, any of its provisions, were subject to a fine not exceeding two hundred dollars.

Gangs of laborers in the field are generally attended by a foreman, whose duty it is to see that all work is duly performed, as well as to maintain order at all times and places. He receives four dollars and a half per month. And any laborer resisting or insulting him is liable to punishment according to law.

The engagements of laborers with their employers are annually renewed on the first day of October. All blacks have then the privilege of changing their employers, and places of residence, at their own pleasure; and, at any other time during the year, the relation between laborer and employer may be dissolved by mutual consent, or by order of a magistrate, for cause—the laborer making, at the same time, an engagement on some other estate. In point of fact, however, the blacks are generally attached to their homes, and do not often pass from one plantation to another.

A military force of two or three hundred men, maintained in three small forts, suffices to overawe the sixteen thousand blacks and two thousand mulattoes; and enables the six thousand whites to live without apprehension of insurrection or disorder. Substantial and impartial justice seems to be administered by the magistrates between all classes of the population. Crimes are rare; there is but little drunkenness; and the few violations of the Labor Act occurring are the result, for the most part, of the general disposition to idleness and petty thieving. The Moravian missionaries, who have been in the island for upward of a century, devote themselves to the moral and religious care of the blacks, and the teaching of their young children. There are nine public schoolhouses; and all colored children—unfortunately, one half of them die in infancy, chiefly from neglect of parents—are compelled by law to attend school between the ages of six and twelve. Yet it must be confessed, so little time has the African nature had to improve itself in since the abolition of slavery, that not a quarter of these pupils, during all these years of attendance at school, can be truly said to learn how to read and write; and the passages of Scripture which all so fluently repeat from day to day, are acquired by ear. But they receive much excellent moral and religious instruction from their teachers. They are also taught one day in the week in Sunday schools; while all, both children and parents, are diligent attendants on public worship. They take great pleasure and pride in going to church, whether Moravian, Lutheran, Catholic, or Episcopal, in their clean clothes, especially on festival days; and it is said that many of the elderly dames are regularly confirmed every time the bishop comes to the island.

The more industrious and intelligent blacks acquire a competency; laying up their gains in savings banks, buying small plots of land, and building small houses in town. On market days, they may be seen driving to town in so-called "emancipation carts"—a kind of two-wheeled vehicle, without the ease of springs; while the little picaninnies who stay at home entertain themselves with riding on the backs of their fathers' pigs. Many of the blacks who have permission of the magistrates to live in town are mechanics; some are engaged in some petty trade; and others are fishermen, supplying the market, twice a week, with most delicious fish, and occasionally offering for sale to the stranger those delicate pink pearls found in the conch shell, which are so much more beautiful than corals.

Slowly, but surely, the African of this tropical region, set free from bonds, is attaining his majority

—his manhood. Not only does he go regularly to church, but he sits in a pew in the midst of white folks. The mulatto son of a white planter now and then inherits a valuable sugar estate. He begins, accordingly, to give balls, and is invited with his family to Government House. You do not yet meet him at every turn in society; but you do sometimes come on him suddenly, when not at all expecting it. And in many cases, it must be allowed, he appears every whit as worthy of a place in polite society as his Caucasian neighbor. Indeed, while the fortunes of the white man are gradually going down in the island, his are slowly going up. In another hundred years, the African blood will probably have thoroughly stained the Danish and English; and whereas now the fashion is for hair to be made straight by the use of pomatum, then, no doubt, it will be curled back again by the barber. With the progress of years, the number of educated mulattoes is constantly increasing; while the children of pure blacks are, day by day, learning something at school, if not always their letters. Almost every respectable cabin in the island will give convincing proof to the traveller that the inmates are more or less blindly feeling after a higher ideal of life; for in it he will see that they are the possessors of a nice clean bed—a high mahogany four-poster—covered with a snow-white counterpane, and not less than half a dozen pillows; though the whole family are, for the time being, in the habit of sleeping pellmell in their rags beneath it. No doubt the day will soon come when they will occupy the bed itself.

CHAPTER XXXV.

St. Thomas.

TO one approaching St. Thomas after, it may be, a long and wearisome voyage, the Virgin Islands, which stand in a group before it, seem to come out, like a company of fair maidens, to bid him welcome. Graceful forms all, they come with hands full of green wreaths and the gorgeous flowers of the tropics, scattering them on either side upon the blue, sunny waters. The eye, tired of gazing for weeks at the ocean's monotonous horizon and the unsympathizing waves, is so cheered by the sight of these fair isles, well named after England's famous queen, standing side by side in pleasant companionship, assuming every comely volcanic shape, and draped to the feet with the softest, freshest green, as were of old the eyes of the children of Israel when Miriam and her sisters came forth before them with timbrels and with dances. A few of these islands are cultivated, producing sugar, cotton, rum, and wild cattle; but the greater number are too mountainous, as well as too small to be inhabited. Swift and dangerous currents run between many of them. Others are guarded by reefs of coral, lying nearly level with the surface of the water; while the precipitous, rocky sides of a few of them equally repel the approach of man. The sea fowl enjoy here an undisputed home—or disputed only by their brethren, the high-colored land birds. Nature here reaps her own harvests of falling leaves and flowers, and receives into her own lap the spontaneous fruits as they drop. Here reigns silence, unbroken by the stroke of the axe or the dog's bark, and as perpetual as the summer which dwells on these shores throughout the year. What few sounds may chance to reach the ear of the mariner, while, borne by the currents, or propelled by the softly blowing trade wind, he floats silently through these narrow channels, are, doubtless, such voices of the syrens as in ancient times were heard by the voyagers through the Sicilian straits, when Calypso and her sisters dwelt on the shores. If, in the nineteenth century, one were ever liable to be bound by the spell of enchantment, it certainly might be when, coming up on deck in the early morning, he finds himself suddenly transported out of the blank of the ocean into the midst of this fantastic group of islands. Nor would the illusion be dissipated when, having passed through them, he catches sight, in the distance, of the hills of the town of St. Thomas, and sails up, between sheltering highlands, its beautiful expanse of bay and harbor. Alas! that it should be, the moment he sets foot in the streets.

Twice I was in St. Thomas; but each time I got away from it as soon as I could. It is no place for pleasure—only for business; for life here is entirely mercantile. Invited by its fine harbor, commerce hither brings, year after year, large stores for the consumption, not so much of the inhabitants of St. Thomas itself, as of those of the neighboring West Indies. This city is a great distributing point for both the windward and the leeward islands; a centre for numerous lines of sailing packets and steamships, and a supply station for vessels of war. Merchandise is brought to this mart from Europe and the United States, and various other parts of the world; and is sold by representatives of almost all the commercial nations, Jews and Greeks. The streets are a Babel of strange sounds; the faces of the merchants are of all colors; their costumes are a motley of all styles; but their occupation is one. It is to get money—to be rich—and, at the same time, to live luxuriously. No town in England can possibly be so shopkeeping, nor any Yankee population half so greedy of gain. There is a Spanish-Jew look in the general countenance, which makes one desirous of curtailing his dealings in the shops and market places, and even of bringing to as speedy a close as may be his residence in the town.

Of course, there must be many individual exceptions to this prevailing type of commercial character. I myself was personally acquainted with merchants of high intelligence and liberal sentiments. And it gives me pleasure to add, that one of the principal apothecaries of the town was a man learned in science, though self-taught, and had by his own efforts made a collection of objects in natural history, not surpassed, if equalled, by any similar collection in the West Indies.

There was, also, one noted person then living in St. Thomas, who was without any other occupation than that of seeking his own pleasure. This was the famous Mexican general, Santa Anna. Residing in a spacious house on one of the heights of the city, and overlooking the entire length of the beautiful harbor, he devoted himself exclusively to cock fighting —or rather, he had done so until just before the period of my visit. And the occasion of his suddenly throwing up his occupation was sufficiently characteristic of West Indian manners. The hero with one leg had for a series of years been passionately addicted to fighting cocks. The chanticleering of vast numbers of coops was music to his ears. He daily promenaded in the midst of his birds, admiring their strut, their cropped tails, and their haughty challenging of each other to the fight; and when Sunday came, he went into the pit with his pockets full of doubloons. So he lived year after year, feeding his cocks, and fighting all comers. But, at last, there arrived a party of Spaniards from the island of Porto Rico, bringing their trained champions to contend with him. During the first few days they lost, for the most part, their money and their birds; but as gradually the betting began to run higher, the luck began to turn in favor of the strangers. Their cocks rapidly improved in pluck and vigor; while the Mexican Don's heroes showed a disposition to turn tail, and were easily floored. After a few rounds, in fact, they fell dead; and, in consequence, the doubloons all passed across the pit into the pockets of the gay fellows from Porto Rico.

What was the meaning of all this? asked the valiant general, as he saw his ounces so rapidly leaving him. To his great disgust, he found, on inquiry, that the Spaniards' cocks had the feathers of their necks poisoned; so that their opponents, after pecking at them, soon became affected by the subtile venom, and were easily disabled.

"I'll never fight another cock in all my days!" exclaimed the incensed hidalgo. He thereupon kicked every Porto Rican out of sight with his wooden foot, and straightway shut up his cockpit. Unluckily for him, he had already lost, as the story went, several thousand ounces.

If St. Thomas cannot be praised for anything else, it must be for its situation, than which few cities can boast a fairer. For it is built on three round hills, of about equal size, which rise directly from the waterside; and from this triple height it looks down upon a harbor extending several miles in nearly a straight course out to sea. Beautiful in its natural features, this magnificent sheet of water is always enlivened by the white sails and black smoke of the coming and going sea craft. Huge steamers and ships of war ride at anchor on it; and great numbers of sail and rowboats are constantly dancing over its blue waters. Behind the hills on which the city is erected rises, at a little distance, a background of mountains covered with vegetation. Indeed, so close do the hills come down to the sea in the neighborhood of the town, and so mountainous is the whole surface of the island, that the inhabitants possess but one carriage road, a few short miles in length, and only one or two pleasant promenades. Of these they make good use on holidays, but are never seen on them when the shops are open.

There is but one farm on the island, and this lies hid, like a bird's nest, among the hills. All its products and supplies are transported to and fro on horse or mule back. The mountains stand for fences; there are no neighbors' pigs or cattle, hens or turkeys, to commit trespass; no outlying squatters to harvest the rightful owner's corn, or dig his potatoes in the night time; no vagrant boys to pilfer his grapes and oranges. The occupant of such an estate might lead a life which, in uninterrupted tranquillity, and exemption from the great world's annoyances, would be second only to that of Robinson Crusoe with his goats. At the time of my visit, the proprietor, like a Spaniard as he was, wished to dispose of his solitary estate by lottery. For thirty thousand dollars—I think that was the sum—he could be induced to part with this hill property, including all its furniture and equipage, its sheep, and cows, and horses, and asses. There was to be one prize, and I know not how many thousand blanks—say fifteen. In Spain, all things are liable to go into the lottery box. A man may draw anything out of it, except it be a wife. And why not, then, a farm in the mountains of St. Thomas? I have never heard who—if, indeed, the scheme did not fall through—was the fortunate holder of the prize. But most likely, if the proprietor happened to have a few tickets left unsold, as he naturally would, he must have been the man himself. San Fernando! if I could only put all my Spanish castles into lotteries! One need not be so very much greater a fool to buy the tickets, than to jump at the chance of those of a farmer on the mountain tops of St. Thomas.

One would naturally suppose that a city thus set on a hill would have good drainage, and be endowed with all the sanitary virtues; but, as is well known, it is not so in the case of St. Thomas. The thickly crammed quarters of the laboring classes are rarely free from the ravages of some form or other of pestilence. Fever, cholera, and smallpox are domesticated here; and often extend, also, to all parts of the city. Fair as it appears to one approaching it from the sea, St. Thomas is but an apple of Sodom—full of dead men's ashes.

Nevertheless, it is but simple justice to add, that, however much I had heard of its epidemics before visiting it, when there I neither heard nor saw any signs of them. I was well myself; while the indications at the table of the hotel where I staid, were that all the guests were in excellent appetite. Indeed, I was very comfortable in the great inn of St. Thomas. Its piazza could hardly have been cooler if it had been built by Moors instead of Spaniards; for it possessed ample space, an open colonnade, and only lacked a fountain in its centre. There was one in fact, in a small garden which the piazza directly overlooked, while, beyond this, the harbor lay so fully exposed to view, that, while sipping their coffee, or smoking their cigars, the patrons of the house beheld near by the active movement of boats and shipping. Here parties could sit at tea, eat ices, play at dominoes, talk, smoke even, all without interfering with each other any more than if they had been seated in a tea garden on the banks of the Elbe or the Rhine. In hot countries space is the chief of the architectural virtues. I never sat down in the vast dining room of this hotel without a cool sense of satisfaction. I was sure of a bountiful supply of fresh air, whatever else might fail at dinner; and that was certainly better than an extra joint and pudding. Could I have slept in a bedchamber of equal dimensions, I might perhaps have imagined that, in reaching St. Thomas, I had arrived at that emporium of delights which the dwellers in the neighboring islands fully believe it to be. But, alas! all places in this world fall, in some trifle or other, short of elysium.

CHAPTER XXXVI.

The Bermudas.

IN looking on the map of the world along a line of latitude eastward from Charleston, one sees, far off in the mid-Atlantic, five or six little dots. These represent the Bermudas. They are a cluster of small islands as numerous as the days in the year —spots of land surrounded by innumerable waves and boundless wastes of ocean, where the deep bottom of the sea has come up to take breath and greet the skies. Points of light are they, where the sun's rays are reflected by chalkstone and sea shells, and the still brighter habitations of men, all whitewashed even to the roofs; where the moon and stars are mirrored in tiny sheltered bays, more placid than the ever-rolling ocean around; and where the mariner, still afar off, descries wide circles of flashing foam, as the long Atlantic billows surge against the reefs of coral, which on all sides protect these solitary isles from the ravages of the angry main. Like angels' wings the breakers flash and shine, by day and by night, guarding the little sunny vales that lie nestling within their magic ring; nor completely shutting out the ships which seek for a refuge from the buffetings of the sea, but through secure, if narrow passages, inviting them in to rest in peaceful havens, and offering to famished crews their laid-up stores, and the fresh fruits of the land. A place of refuge in the midst of pathless waters, how many a shattered bark, since the day when Columbus sailed the sea, has sought in distress these hospitable harbors; how many an anxious mariner's eyes have strained their balls to discover through the blackness of tempest and hurricane the guiding lights of Hamilton and St. George's; how many land birds, driven off their course by gales, and exhausted by long flights over the weary waters, have folded their wings in joy and peace amid the succoring branches of these cedar trees!

I remember it as one of the most charming drives of my life, when, released from a four days' imprisonment on board the dirty, though stanch British steamer "Merlin," a Government mail packet running between St. Thomas and Halifax, *via* Bermuda, I was conveyed, one fine April day, by a sturdy pair of grays, leisurely through the centre of these islands. The road was a continuous curve. Now it wound up gentle ascents; now it followed the course of sinuous valleys; here it made a turn about a ledge of rocks; there it bent around the graceful half circles of the shores. But most of the turns were short; so that the way was full of surprises. At times I was in the midst of groves of low-growing cedars, which cover most of the higher grounds of the islands; then I descended into small valleys, mere dimples on the surface of the land, where there were little patches of cultivation; then again I came suddenly upon some inland bay, where the waves of the ocean were reduced to ripples, which broke in low whispers on the beaches. Such lovely, land-locked bits of sea water were they, and green as liquid emeralds—here pale, and there deep green, according as the depth of water above the coral bottom varied—sometimes purple even, especially where the prospect opened seaward, half revealing in the remote distance groups of islets, now darkened by the deep shadows of passing clouds, and now lit up by the returning floods of light, made doubly effulgent by the flashing and glimmer of the surrounding waves. To the silence of the forest succeeded quickly the murmur of the sea. From the dark-green foliage of the cedars the eye passed by easy gradation to the green of shallow waters, and the distant blue and purple of the deep. The solitude of nature was interrupted at intervals by the wayside cottages of the small farmers; and especially, on approaching the town of Hamilton, did I frequently come upon snug little villas, embosomed in trees, and shrubbery, and flowers. The hedge rows were composed of scarlet geraniums, and oleanders, and pomegranates, in full bloom. Nearer the town, what multitudes of roses were blowing in every garden, and climbing over the cottage walls! The very air was rose colored.

But neither of the two Bermudian capitals, St. George's and Hamilton, are particularly noticeable as towns. Their life is mostly seafaring. They being built directly along the harbors, the vessels come up close into town, their bowsprits projecting over some of the principal streets, and their masts peering over the chimney tops. From the sidewalks one beholds the sea-going vessels arriving and departing; the songs of the sailors ring out above the rattling of the carriage wheels; and gay little sail-boats are seen flying with birds' wings up and down the bays. Here is one of England's famous naval establishments; so that the streets are always more or less filled with uniforms, while the small parlors of society are crowded with epaulettes. Even the convicts, of whom there is here a large colony from the mother country, live and labor in huge hulks—great invalided sea monsters, which lie at anchor near one of the islands. When the commodore of the station, which, in company with an English friend, we were inspecting, politely asked us to luncheon, we found him living on a little island not so very much larger than a seventy-four gun ship. Received in a drawing room, built as much on the model of a ship's cabin as of anything else, we were served by boys in sailor shirts and jackets; and, on taking leave, were sent home in a boat which lay moored but a few steps from the door of the mansion house. But I remember well that, in spite of the huge round of salted beef which stood on one end of the table, as red as the face of the brave old commodore himself, the entertainment had the pleasant flavor of the land about it; and I was especially grateful for having the taste of the "Merlin's" sea biscuit taken out of my mouth by the April-grown strawberries. Have I said that the commodore's face was red, as of one who had faced in his lifetime many a breeze, if not a battle? Then I will add my belief that his heart was full of good red English blood also—redder than his beef and strawberries, if possible; for he showed kindness to me, who was a stranger; and, according to his opportunity, gave proof that he was endowed with that fine sense of hospitality which is so generally the crowning gift and grace of an Englishman in his own home.

The Bermudians are not always following the sea; but, when on shore, are busy raising onions and potatoes. Generally, sailors make poor farmers; yet here they succeed in producing early vegetables in such perfection, that it is to be feared lest the Bermudas, instead of being famed as the oleander isles, may become known in common parlance as the spring kitchen garden of New York. Certain it is that, early in the season, the Bermudian brigs and schooners, all built of red cedar, are annually setting off for the "States," laden down to the gunwale with these useful fruits of the soil. A certain amount of the best arrowroot in the world likewise forms part of their cargo. The soil and climate must be remarkably adapted to the cultivation of these products; for I never tasted, in any other part of the world, vegetables of such good quality. Nature excels here, not in trees, for the cedars are scrubby; nor in men or women, for the best of these, as well as the worst, are imported from England; but in flowers, and especially in onions, tomatoes, and potatoes. She produces the latter in such exhausting perfection, that they are incapable of perpetuating their species with any similar degree of excellence; and every year the farmers are obliged to import for seed our own "Western reds." Imported in the body, they are here endowed with the soul of goodness. So the most luscious pears often yield imperfect seeds; and, in order to obtain new varieties, the pomologists raise their seedlings from somewhat inferior sorts, in the production of which nature stops short of her utmost possibility of pulp.

If it is not to be supposed that these small-islanders have developed any great degree of mechanical genius, still it must be allowed that they are tolerable ship builders. To be sure, the old English hulks, which lie at anchor about the islands, set before the eyes of the ship carpenter a sorry lot of models; and sometimes, as I was told, when the British admiralty produces some naval abortion, like their first iron-clad frigate, they send it to the Bermudas, in order to have it moored well out of sight. However, the colonial brigs and other small craft, though clumsy-looking enough, are good sailers, and manage to run over to New York with their potatoes before the rot gets into them. There are also to be met with here a few cunning artificers in cedar wood, who out of this fair and pleasantly scented material fabricate various articles of furniture and the toilette. The delicate palmetto work of female artists, likewise, is to be set down to the credit of the colonists; for their skilful fingers weave the prettiest of baskets, and the lightest and jauntiest of hats and bonnets. As the convicts are not allowed the freedom of following the seas in their penitentiary hulks, they, too, contrive to relieve the monotony of life by occasionally working in the petrified water which is found in the stalactite caves of the islands, and from which they manufacture very pretty brooches, and other ornaments. Loafers permitted to go at large sometimes search the shores for a species of seaweed, which, after it has been buried in the sand long enough to get rid of the congealed salt water with which it is incrusted, they make a fanciful kind of riding whips. The stranger is expected to make small investments in all these specimens of handicraft—to say nothing of his bags of potatoes, strings of onions, boxes of tomatoes, and bottles of arrowroot.

In Hamilton I found two or three of my countrymen, eating their potatoes, and recruiting their health. But I do not think the climate can be recommended for invalids at any season of the year, excepting, perhaps, the spring. In summer, the south winds too much prevail, bringing intense heat, accompanied with humidity—a sultry, stifling atmosphere—and, consequently, both languor of body and depression of mind. In winter, the weather is chilly and variable. The Bermudas are then the vexed

Bermoothes of the poet. For the winds then course after each other around these islands as a goal; while they breathe out of their nostrils dire mists and vapors. The atmosphere is so constantly charged with humidity, that the inner house walls emit a cold perspiration worse even than the stone walls of Paris. The paper hangings are discolored; articles of dress mould as in a ship's cabin; the inhabitants live in a perpetual vapor bath, and one which is as much too cold for comfort as that of the Grand Turk is too hot. Unhappily, there is but little fuel in the islands wherewith to repel the cold and dampness; for there is no coal, and but a moderate supply of wood. The natives, of course, fight out the battle of the winter as best they can with flannel and strong beer; but valetudinarians of other lands should leave them to do it alone.

And yet it may seem almost ungenerous in me to write in such disparaging terms of a climate which to myself was so agreeable. The few days of my sojourn in—shall I call them the oleander, or the rose islands?—were days without stain or blemish. Coming from the tropics, to me the coolness of this more northern atmosphere was more exhilarating than could have been any tonic from the doctors' shops. I felt refreshed and invigorated by breathing this air, as one does after taking a cold bath. From morning until evening the sun shone out of a clear blue sky, with only occasional white clouds floating through it, and happily tempered by its genial heat the sharp coolness of the sea air in spring time. During the period of my visit, all the vexing winds had withdrawn to their caves—probably the remarkable stalactite caves which exist in some of these islands. Only the zephyrs were at large, gambolling on the water, and frolicking among the cedar trees; while Boreas and his dire crew kept their secret orgies far under ground. The mornings and evenings were perfectly calm; and at midday the faint breezes served only to waft through open doors the fragrance of flowers blooming in the fields and gardens.

I recollect with special pleasure the beautiful calm of the Sunday morning after my arrival. No Sunday could be more sabbatical, more hushed, more full of heavenly light, or pervaded with a more genial warmth. As I walked out under the thick cypress trees, and along the roadside, the silence of the morning was broken by no noise of business, or even sounds in nature. Not even a cow lowed, nor a dog barked, nor a cock crowed, nor hardly a cricket or a grasshopper chirruped.

Here and there, the dark thickets were lighted up by the flash of a cardinal grosbeak, which uttered a carol or two, and then was still again. The red-breast now and then added a few melodious notes to its early morning song; and the gorgeous bits of humming birds made, occasionally, a low murmur in the hedges. Otherwise, nature lay as silent as if entranced; while the most brilliant sunlight bathed all the isles of cedar, checkering the ground beneath them with sharp contrasts of light and shade, and spread its gilding over the circumambient waters and the coral shores.

If every day in the Bermudas were like this, men, whether invalid or robust, would be attracted to them as formerly to the Happy Islands of ancient fable; and I am glad to be able to bear witness that there may be such in the month of April.

CHAPTER XXXVII.

Cape Cod.

THERE is always a second summer in the American year. When the September gales have swept over the woods, and shaken the first leaves of autumn to the ground; when from the gardens the more delicate buds and fragrant blossoms have passed away; when the earlier fruits have ripened and been gathered; when evening begins sooner to draw the curtains of the day, and the sun's horses start later on their morning courses; when the pleasure parties of the season are breaking up, and words of farewell are being said, and over the most buoyant mind a certain pensiveness steals, and regrets fall upon it as from out the autumnal air, then the year, which had begun to withdraw its face, turns again with a parting smile, and kisses its hand to us. Then comes a succession of golden days, when the air is still, and the heavens, slightly veiled with purple haze, are without a cloud. The autumnal flowers are arrayed in all their glory. The orchards yield up their red-sided, gold-colored apples for the winter's store. The grapes are turned to purple. The latest pears melt upon the devouring lips, and the last drops of sweetness are being distilled into the yet unplucked peaches. Now the diligent housewife gathers from out the leaves, still green, the yellow, shining quince, and, correcting its tart juices with melted sugar, lays it by for winter tea drinkings. The farmer husks his corn, making the greensward shine with the long, broad line of glittering ears. He piles up, also, the yellow pumpkins, or hangs the squashes against the wall, by their necks. His boys bring home at night the cows from still green and thickly matted meadows, with udders wide distended. The poultry yards are full of cackling, and youthful attempts at chanticleering. Fleets of geese and ducks float down the brooks, or lie moored on the ponds; and the half-grown turkey cocks gabble, and spread their tails over vast spaces of yard and pasture. This season is the mellowing of the year. In sunny European lands, and beneath sacred Oriental skies, the grapes are now trodden in the winepress; and even in our own New Jersey, the bounty of nature runs to sweet cider. The earth has put forth her great productive power, and rejoices as a woman after childbearing; the sun has done his year's work, and ripened all seeds and grains; there is food garnered up for man and beast; and the great God seems to look down out of heaven upon what He hath wrought, and pronounce it good.

It is a season to be enjoyed as one does old wine. As we bring this out of the cellar on high festal occasions, to celebrate the rite matrimonial, or to honor the anniversary of a birthday, to greet the coming of long-absent friends, and freshen the memories which run far back to days of "auld lang syne;" so this brief second summer of the year should be filled up with unusual joys. Then make a holiday. Then telegraph to your best friend to come with wife and child. Let boys and girls be let loose from school, that they may go a-nutting. Let there be picnics in the glens and on the hillsides. Climb the mountains. Coast the shores. 'Tis the hunter's moon, and you may follow the path of the buck and the doe, or hey on pointer or setter. You see the breaking of day as you go on your way to lie for wild fowl, which, when it is yet dark, fly overhead with whistling wings; while far off is heard the scream of the coming wild geese. Now let the reel hiss, as the line is cast from the rocks for tautog. It is the season, also, for bass fishing. Now let the lover of nature and mushrooms prevent the sun, and gather his breakfast with the dew on it. Let all men—all Yankees—eat pumpkin pie. The full moon favors husking by night; and he who finds brindled ears may kiss his partner, though he may no longer drink milk punch, for it is contrary to law. Now is "training" time; and there will be cakes at the muster for old and young—and, surely, pop beer. Now pack into country wagons, three on a seat. At morning, wind the horn, and let the hounds bay. At night, draw the bow, dance, sing, and make merry, giving God thanks; for this glorious second summer, called Indian, is given us but for seven days, or it may be ten. Then get quickly out of doors—be off—and caps in the air!

Happy harvest days! and happily did I spend them, ankle deep in thy golden sands, Cape Cod!

Perhaps I should have done better still to have gone in rough weather. The scene here, doubtless, is more characteristic when nature frowns, than when she smiles. For the Cape is decidedly tragic. Its great mood is when nature is angry, and all her elements are at war. When the east wind is rising out of the sea, and the pine woods begin to sigh for pain; when the ocean, fretted to madness by the gale, lashes the long sandy beaches, and breaks high over the rocks on the shore; when the drift sand flies like snowflakes, and the whirlwinds, in their rough play, bear it aloft in the air; when the rain, bursting the clouds, contends in its turn with both winds and waves, and beats them down; when, in winter, the sharp sleet cuts the air, and the snow-blast shuts out the light of heaven, and night, setting in, adds the terrors of utter darkness to those of the storm, and the signal gun of the East Indiaman, drifting upon the leeshore—a few hours before so near the wished-for haven—is heard faintly booming through the uproar of the elements, and vainly calling upon the wrecker, who sits idle by his blazing fireside, pitying the poor souls whose imaginary cries ring in his ears, but whom he cannot save from the jaws of the devouring waves. For no mortal arm can stay the implacable wrath of the Almighty when He bids the sea roar, and engulf in its depths the impious mariner and his ship. Then the traveller, on this long arm of sand vainly stretched out to embrace the unwilling, untamable ocean, and marry it in loving wedlock to the land, sees and feels what Cape Cod is. With awe he hears the sublime moaning of the long, flat beaches, and the more angry resounding of the coast, where it is bolder, and rocky. The north shore answers with its uproar to the uproar of the south. As, at sea, the wind whistles and sings in the cordage of the scudding ship to the deep bass of the roaring waves, so, here, the howling of the winds among the branches of the oaks, and the loud lament of the pine woods, are added to the bellowing of the strands. How weak does man appear when tossed on these waves! Yet how strong, when, in his snug cot on the shore, he sits reading by the unflickering candle, and heeds not either the outcries of nature or the wrath of God!

But, at the period of my visit, the stormy Cape was lying as calm and placid in the midst of the sea, as, in midsummer, rise the round tops of the Alleghanies in the untroubled southern heavens. The sun looked with warm, enamored beams upon the bosom of the earth; the winds lay reposing in the depths of the pine woods, scarcely breathing audibly; and the tired waves slept on the shore. At evening, as the full, round moon rose from the Atlantic, it spread out a level, silvery carpet to the horizon, almost tempting the beholder to walk forth on the high sea; as, on solemn festal occasions, the gold-spangled tapestry invites the feet of the guests who go up into the lighted palaces of kings. And all night long, when at intervals I awoke out of my dreams, I heard, at the distance of a stone's throw, the innumerable ripples breaking on the sand, as if the uxorious old ocean were kissing, even in his sleep, the softly breathing lips of the shore. At midnight, I arose from my bed, and walked out into the air, feeling an irrepressible curiosity to listen to the whispering of the night winds, and overhear the telling of their secret loves. I beheld, also, the dance of the waves, which were keeping up their revelry beneath the light of the moon, tripping it as gracefully as fairies on the greensward, and quickly dissolving in mutual embraces, like hearts in the joined breasts of lovers. How refreshing and wholesome was the salt in the air from the ocean! "There can no malignant spirit or goblin walk this strip of earth," said I, returning to my couch; "the air is too pure." And, indeed, it can scarcely be credited that a real, *bona-fide* ghost was ever seen on Cape Cod. There are Quakers here, but no witches. It is not possible.

But by day my eyes feasted, through all the hours, on the richly colored autumnal landscape. Here stretch, for miles beyond miles, the salt meadows of Barnstable, watered not by rains and dews only, but by the monthly flowing of the tides; and these level tracts are now as tawny as the lion's skin. This, likewise, being the season when the pine trees shed their needles, the earth beneath them is no less tawny than the open marshes. And everywhere the sand of the shore is as yellow as the breast of a robin. In the warm rays of the sun it even shines like beaten gold, making the whole Cape gilt-edged.

But on the uplands, the yellow runs into a russet, a richly tinted brown, and forms a background which is covered with a glory of autumnal tints, the purple of oaks and whortleberry bushes, the orange and scarlet of maples, the green of pines and cedars. There is color everywhere—on the fields and trees; on the meadows and the shores; in the hollows and around the edges of pools. Not a bush but glows, not a stone but shines. The very particles of sand, if closely inspected, flash like diamonds by candle-light; and, though held in your hand, seem almost as far off and as glittering as the stars in the blue twilight of the night. And these colors are all dashed together—a beautiful variety in unity—making a kaleidoscope in the eyes of every man. Still, it must be acknowledged that, as one proceeds farther upon the Cape, he notices a gradual falling off in the tone of nature's coloring, as old pictures in travelling down the course of time lose, during each century, more and more of their first blush and gorgeousness. The brilliancy of the reds and purples fades, and the browns grow duller. Even the fine gold of the pumpkins becomes tarnished; the color of animals runs to sorrel; and the habitations of man, partaking of the tendency of nature, show only the unpainted gray, or the stains of the original red and green, or the blank white of modern fashion, which makes the pupils of the eye instinctively contract to look at it. There is evidently a deficiency of coloring materials on the great painter's easel; and, at last, whether the power of nature be diminished, or this part of her work be yet raw and unfinished, there remain only the green of the pines and the yellow of the sands, wherein is no harmony.

And yet there is a notable exception to this law of gradual fading. There is more red in the face of the Cape Codders, all the way down to Provincetown, than of any other people in the States. It is the old English red—blood-red. Though the skin be generally pretty thoroughly sunburnt, bronzed often by the glare from the salt water, yet the vermilion shines through, giving evidence of good blood and vigorous arteries. The race is, indeed, purely British. For the inhabitants are all direct descendants of the Puritans, or, at least, of early emigrants from Great Britain. There has been no mixture of races here. While the Cape has always been a fruitful womb of men, sending her sons out into all the broad American earth, there has, on the contrary, been no reflex tide of immigration. The Cape, therefore, is all of one blood, of one face, of one speech, of one homogeneous heart. True, there are Indians still in Marshpee; but are they not also red men? Their faces are, indeed, not a little smutted by a dash of negro blood in them; but some, fortunately, still show the reddish glitter of the original copper. At least, they are not pale faced, but high colored, and come not without a degree of grace into the autumnal landscape.

And this red-facedness of the people is a great point in the description of Cape Cod. For, while the earth gradually loses its color and all its signs of vigor, as we travel toward the end of his path in the sands, we see that the lord of nature, on the contrary, remains ruddy and strong featured. Neither the weakness of the land, nor the extraordinary strength of the circumambient waters and winds has been able to produce degeneracy of the race of man. He has buffeted the waves, and overmastered them. He has sailed in the very eyes and teeth of the winds. He has fixed the floating sands, by planting them with beach grass; has sown the pine trees in furrows; has set oaks on the hilltops, that when the winds, rising in their might, threaten to tear him from the land, he may have something to hold on to; has planted the barren shore with Indian corn, putting a dead "horse foot" in every hill; has grown potatoes from seaweed down to the very line of high-water mark; has turned the mud of flats to oysters; has dried the cod from the great deep into codfish; and, finally, has manufactured the sea itself into salt.

Thus has man made himself master; and though, in struggling with the earth to till it, he has sometimes come upon his hip, like Jacob wrestling with the angel, and though he has often been pinched by the wind, and jammed against the leeward shore, yet, after all, he has fought the lifelong battle with the natural elements triumphantly, and still hangs out his flag of victory in the red of his face.

The Cape Codder is hardy and vigorous, and may emphatically be said to be a self-made man—external nature having done so little for him. If the bone of this young country may be considered as yet somewhat in the gristle, it is not so with that of this Cape. Its bone is mature, and its muscle, also, is as hard as rope's end and bowline. Oft pelted by storms and riddled by gales; now buried in snow banks, and never quite sure of his footing in the sands; now petrified by east winds fresh from Greenland and the ice islands, and then, in hot summer days, when there is not a breath of air to break the glazed surface of the surrounding ocean, baked as if he were an ostrich egg; obliged constantly to harass the surface of the earth, in order to extort from it even a niggardly increase; and, finally, driven in despair to the wall of the sea, and in straits compelled to sound the depths of the ocean with line, hook, and sinker, and to vex its surface with his keels, the Cape Cod man has to fight his way through existence as a gladiator his way out of the ring. Of course, the feebler children die early; but the grown man is all thews and sinews. His nerves are of whalebone, and his skin will keep out water like oakum.

But while this hardness of nature seems only to develop a superior hardness in the frame of man, all lower animals are ground down in the face against it. I saw but few of them anywhere, and these mostly stunted. Scarcely a dog yelped at me from one end of the Cape to the other; for dogs do not thrive well on fish; and, besides, the waves are there to do the barking. But one would suppose it a very paradise for cats; yet, as there are no mice but water rats, so all the cats are catfish. And, accordingly, in all my lying awake to listen to the vespers which the waves on the beaches chanted through the livelong hours of the night, I heard not a single charivari. Sailors, too, are notoriously hard on horses; and drift sand, like Jordan, makes a hard road to travel. Shanghae fowls do not thrive well here. Their tails do not grow, and they become so stupid as scarcely to know how to set one foot before the other; making awkward, uncertain movements, as if they were on stilts, or even walking on their own eggs. At the cattle show in the county town where I happened to be present, the native breeds were all inferior. Whatever was big and fat was foreign born, or, at least, of blood not strictly Capish. Such was their great Ayrshire bull—as huge a monster as the Trojan horse, or the whale which, in attempting to jump the Cape, landed himself, with all his tusks and blubber, high and dry on the sands. All the fat pigs were Lady Suffolks; all the battering rams were Southdowns; and all the hens that laid golden eggs were born Poles. In fact, the only native animals at all worth the showing were the men themselves. One in particular there was at the ploughing match, who reminded me of that Triptolemus of Eleusis, to whom, first of mortals, Ceres taught the use of the plough. Cincinnatus himself could not have bent over the tails with broader shoulders, nor a nose more truly Roman. Between his legs and the length of his furrows there was a certain correspondence. When standing upright, he cast a shadow over half the scene, and dwarfed the oxen before him till they looked scarcely bigger than rats.

The inhabitants of this ridge of drift sand are remarkably thrifty. One sees nowhere indications of extreme destitution. But while most of the people are independent in their circumstances, there is not much wealth, and no show of it. The Grecian column will, indeed, follow the traveller all the way down the Cape, though Greece may seem farther off than ever; nor can all the window blinds on the houses make the place appear in the least degree like Venice. Here he will see a Doric entablature pierced by five small windows, and there a court house in the form of an antique temple, but with its roof bristling with half a dozen stacks of tall Yankee chimneys. Yet this show of Grecian architecture, if it does not always indicate good taste, is a certain sign of thrift. The man who builds his house with a front like an Athenian temple, is sure to be a financially successful one, and, generally, a man who has earned his own money; for they who inherit fortunes, being often travelled men, or cultivated by some considerable amount of reading, know that the public edifices of the old Greeks do not suit the purpose of our modern housekeeping. Thus, every successful captain of a ship who comes home to build a house in the sands, must have Grecian pillars. He has got the money, and he will have a cottage front like the Parthenon. Nothing can stop him.

But the thrift of Cape Cod is not of that kind which follows fawning. Here dwells evidently an independent race of men, and all living at arm's length of each other. Even in the towns the houses do not touch, but stand apart. Every one has its separate enclosure, with plot of greensward, orchard, and garden patch. House and grounds form a distinct and independent establishment, leaning on no other for its support; and though, unfortunately, there are no plank roads in these sands, yet every front door is approached from the street by a plank pathway. Nor do these people generally occupy the whole of their houses. They have vacant apartments, though none to let. The front rooms are all furnished, and shut up. The family live in the kitchen. And they can afford to do so; for the back part of the house is large enough to accommodate all the members, while the other half is kept as neat as wax, for tea drinkings, and the use of company. Hence, the stranger who goes stumbling through the unlighted streets at night, may fancy himself in a Turkish town, or an aoul of the Circassians. He can no more descry the light of a candle than if he were in the centre of Ethiopia. Accordingly, to stir much abroad after nightfall in these streets filled with painted wooden posts, is to set mantraps for one's self, and present the very sorest temptations to Providence. For, inevitably, at this corner you bark your shins; at that, you break your neck. A Chinese lantern here would not be an unmeaning joke. Still, every native, doubtless, knows the way to his habitation in the darkest night, as well as a bee to its cell in the hive.

And no Spaniard goes to bed earlier. He does his work by daylight, and economizes candles. All his habits are simple and natural. He dines on the stroke of noon. He takes his tea—rather weak—at the hour when the merchant in the city sits down to dinner; and he gets up in the morning just as the town snob is going to bed. His fare, too, is simple: at breakfast, fish; at dinner, fish—fish fried, broiled, boiled, baked, and chowdered! Though, probably, there is not one housewife in ten that has not a pie, or a loaf of cake, stowed away somewhere. And you shall nowhere eat such delectable "apple slump;" nowhere such doughnuts, scarcely even in Connecticut; nowhere such baked clams, out of Rhode Island and Providence Plantations. There is, also, a love of junketing and tea drinking, when neighbors come together in winter evenings, and when lassies assemble of an afternoon at a "quilting," making the bridal bedspread with innumerable stitches, and squares of white calico, upon each of which is written, in indelible ink, the name of the fair sempstress who presented it. On these occasions the number of hot biscuits and sweet cakes served up is almost incredible; and, the next morning after one, I have seen with my own eyes a small Cape boy make a hearty breakfast of pound cake with plums in it.

After all, life on the Cape is more like holiday than one might suppose who had never been there. For the men, being mostly seafaring, they do their work in all parts of the world rather than at home. The Cape Codder is omnipresent. He casts his line wherever there are codfish. If there is a school of bass or mackerel on any coast, he is after them with his seine. He chases whales from the southern frozen zone to the northern; and will, some day, throw his harpoons in the open sea at the pole. In all the steamers, liners, packets, he is captain and first mate. On the high seas, or the coast, there is no better man to handle a ship. You find him in all the crack clippers; and if a fore-and-aft schooner runs her nose into any strange place, ten to one there is at her helm a Cape Codder. He has also been in his day a fighting man. Some of our proudest frigates have been sailed by him. He was on the lakes in the last war with England, and threw up his cap there; and as for privateering, it is that one among all the trades of which he is Jack that he likes best to turn his hand to. Though not much of a fist at marching on the land, the Cape Codder, nevertheless, was at Bunker Hill and Saratoga, besides having fought the French and Indians in the old wars, and shouldered arms at Quebec.

But when, having sailed all the seas, and roved

the world over, he comes back to his cot in the sands, the short season he spends at home is a holiday. Then give him a fast horse, and his good wife or sweetheart by his side. He must go to see all his cousins. Nor does any man have so many uncles and aunts, and kindred of various degrees. In fact, nearly all the inhabitants are first cousins, or call themselves such. Therefore, when the mariner comes home, there must necessarily be a good deal of shaking of hands and merry making. Everybody must tell him the news; and he, in return, must tell everybody of his adventures on sea and shore. He has probably seen the sea serpent—at least, a mermaid, a whale, the elephant in his own country, or the Grand Mogul. Undoubtedly, the longest yarns are spun on Cape Cod which are spun anywhere in this country. And be it observed, that the Cape Cod man, let him go to whatever part of the world he may, is sure to come back. His local tastes never die out; and where'er he roams, at every step away he drags a lengthening cable. If he run a packet between Boston and some other of our principal seaport cities, he does not remove his family to town; but, the moment he gets on shore, hies away to the Cape. He does not like the air of great cities, and cannot really feel at home anywhere that there is not sand under his feet, or even a little of it running over his shoe quarters.

This disposition to keep holiday I could not but notice at the county cattle show. There was, indeed, not much to be seen or heard—only the farmer's old "Bright" and "Gelding," with his everlasting "gee-up" and "haw-tu;" only a few pumpkins that might make the native mouth water a little to look at, a few cranberries as big as your thumb and dark as mahogany, which it is mischievously said the Cape girls stain their cheeks with; only a show of Mexican flint cornstalks a dozen feet high, just to show what the Cape sand *could* do; a specimen or two of "quilting" and domestic stocking knitting; some curious attempts in worsted fine art, and even the beautiful vanity of cotton lace, and *crocheting.*

But, notwithstanding the little to be seen, everybody came to see it. They came three women in a gig, and whole families in carryalls with tops of painted canvas. There were farmers in homespun, Quakers in drab, sailors in tarpaulins, and retired captains in black broadcloth. Besides a few great ladies in silks, and bonnets worn falling in the neck, there were any number of good, plain, buxom housewives in their best bombazines and calicoes, most of them with bevies of daughters, all high rigged, in curls, in flounces, with petticoats trimmed with lace, and all their ribbons flying. I saw very pretty girls in swings; and very eager youths buying jack knives, whips with whalebone in the handle, and razors warranted to shave, for twenty-five cents apiece. Every small child's mouth was running over with sugar candy, every man's with tobacco, and every good-looking woman's with smiles. All — men, women, and children—were most busily doing nothing; staring, and seeing nothing; moving hither and thither, and going nowhere; and all appeared to be excessively delighted. Whoever had no baker's gingerbread in his pockets, had peanuts in them; and if any father of a family had neglected to stuff his coat tails with buns for the children at home, be sure his better half had not forgotten to fill her "working bag" with lions and elephants in cake, and dogs and cats in sugar. Almost every one seemed to have bought something, and nobody looked as though he had been "sold." They that had got rattles were tickled, and so were they who had only straws. And when, finally, at the close of the day, the brass band came down the street, playing the old tune of "The girl I left behind me," I remember to have said to myself, that it was the happiest holiday I had seen since I was in Spain.

It is not strange that locomotive civilization should not yet have reached the end of the Cape; and the only wonder is, that the railroad should have gone as far as it has before being effectually run into the ground. At any rate, I reverted to the old, cast-off stage coach at a point on the Cape very nearly amidships. The day being as beautiful as the last rose of autumn, I was naturally tempted to take a seat on the coach box; and, seeing no person present at all resembling a driver, I waived the ceremony of asking leave, and straightway invited myself up. But as I sat there quietly looking at the different cut of the tails of the four horses, I was taken by surprise at seeing a small boy climb to the seat by my side, and gather up the reins, as if he were really going to drive the coach himself. I looked at the boy again, and thought, surely, he could not be turned of ten, though I afterward learned that he was twelve, being small for his age. And this boy, said I to myself, is evidently going to drive this coach-and-four to Orleans! I immediately took out my glass, and inspected him closely. Was he Phaeton? If so, he would doubtless set the Cape on fire before getting to the first stopping place. An old whip he certainly was not. Was he a whip at all? There he sat on the box, a boy apparently ten years of age, and his legs barely long enough to reach the footboard. By and by he encouraged his team up a hill with his voice, for whip he had not yet taken in hand; but his chirrup had the clear, decided ring of a full-grown hostler. "Get along, Chandler Bob," said he, at length, addressing the nigh wheel horse; "and you, Jaques," calling to the off leader. But I, meanwhile, had not said a word, and, in fact, had scarcely made up my mind what to say. "Eh, there, Lizzie! what are you doing?" called out the young Jehu to the rather restless mare on the nigh lead. Still I said nothing; but, screwing my glass firmly into my right eye, looked, at intervals, sharply at the boy. Besides his thick buckskin gloves, there was nothing in his appearance in the least degree professional. He neither wore a pea jacket, nor was he in his shirt sleeves. His single-breasted jacket, buttoned close in the neck, was a plain drab; and around his neck was a clean, modest turn-over collar, such as is commonly worn by boys of tender age. "Hunter!" he exclaimed, threateningly, and at the same time offering to strike the off wheeler with the slack of his reins. Whereupon "Hunter" mended his pace, and I continued my observations. The boy's hat was a nice felt, and of a modest color corresponding with that of his dress. A bourgeois, well-to-do in the world, would not dress his son any better. And his looks were in keeping with his dress—his complexion being a healthy brown, almost an olive, but with no red in it, more like the bark of the rose than its flower. Being so young, his features, of course, were not yet very definitely chiselled, but showed, indistinctly, the outlines of a future manliness. Only his eye was already perfect —being a large dark gray, and thickly shaded by long black lashes.

"Steady, Lizzie!" he cried, for the mare, which was a little gay, was still inclined to fret occasionally.

And now, taking down my glass, I entered into conversation with the young expert—for such he was, beyond all question. The first inquiry one generally makes of boys of this age is, "What is your name?" I used a little circumlocutory politeness, but managed to find out that the lad's name was James. The second question naturally is, "How old are you, my boy?" And I also contrived to get this information from the little man without giving offence. Then, as James occasionally threw out his foot with a sideward motion, in making his appeals to "Hunter," I was curious to know the reason of it.

"Hunter," said he, "keeps an eye on me from behind his blinder, and whenever he sees this motion of the foot, he thinks I am going to kick him."

"And how long may it be since you began to drive a coach?"

"I go to school; but I have driven more or less since I was eight years old."

"But how could you drive a coach when you were only eight?"

"My father began with lashing me on to the box, to prevent my falling off—for I couldn't then reach the footboard—and I drove so."

By this time my interest in James had risen to a high point, and I afterward learned from others that this account of himself was strictly true. Should I ask him to take a cigar with me? Plainly not. Here was a specimen of "Young America" whose patriotism evidently did not consist in smoking and chewing. He talked familiarly with his horses, but did not swear at them. There was nothing of the vulgar stage driver about the lad, no taking on of airs, no slang in his language, no brag. He had not even the usual frolic and roguery of his years. He did not crack his whip—using it only to threaten the little vagabonds who attempted to climb up on the rack behind; and there was no laughing in his eyes, which indicated that he was going to tip the coach over. His face was that of one who had taken responsibility upon himself, and felt equal to it. It beamed with intelligence; but the expression of it was firm, self-restraining, and even demure. The impending shadow of a coming man darkened in it the brightness of the schoolboy. I afterward learned that, for pluck, the little fellow had not his equal in all the country round. If, by chance, there was a horse in the stable that nobody dared drive, he would beg his father to let him do it. And, long before leaving the coach box, I came distinctly to the conclusion that James—I never should have thought of calling him Jimmy—by the time he was twenty-one years of age, would be "up" for Congress. For surely the boy who, at twelve years, can drive a four-in-hand, with a mettlesome "Lizzie" among them, will, in the course of another ten, be competent to manage such an ass as the sovereign people.

So, hurrah for the Cape Cod boy, James! He took me into Orleans in good style, having made his time to a minute; with "Lizzie" only a little frothy, but scarcely a wet hair on either "Chandler Bob" or "Hunter."

I left the Cape not without a certain feeling of regret. Perhaps it was because of the termination of the Indian summer; and I had to exclaim:

"Die schönen Tage in Aranjuez
Sind nun zu Ende."

And, possibly, the unusually neat and pretty quarters in which I had spent the last night of my journey might have had something to do with it. The fact was, that, there being a press of company in the inn, some kind-hearted lady had surrendered the use of her apartment for the accommodation of a tired traveller. Taking note of this on my entrance, I should have been strongly tempted to refuse taking advantage of such generous hospitality, and have contented myself with the use of three chairs, or a sofa, had it not been for the lateness of the hour; but, under the circumstances, nothing else could well be done than to put off my shoes as quickly as possible in such a sanctum—which I accordingly did, and gave them to the "boots." And when he had departed, the mortification of my gallantry at having taken possession of the room was so great, that I exclaimed:

"What a pretty pickle of codfish I am in now!"

But I endeavored to persuade myself that the fair occupant was, at least, not a person of tender years; and seeing a shoe case hanging against the wall, I asseverated that the shoes in it—of course, I did not presume to examine them—were certainly a foot long; and that the hoops which, doubtless, were standing up in the closet, instead of being, as they should be, no larger than strawberry baskets when they first come, had been taken from one of the biggest hogsheads that had ever drifted ashore on the Cape. These suppositions, to be sure, were very ungenerous, and would not have much helped to pacify my mind, had I not happened to notice a few verses from a newspaper pinned on the wall, the concluding line of which ran as follows:

> "As we journey through life, *let us live by the way.*"

This seemed to hit my case pat. Yes, said I, this is the true philosophy of life. Especially, let a man on his travels live as he goes along, and sleep where he can, giving God thanks first, and next to woman. So, laying my head on the pillow, I likened myself to a Mungo Park, succored by the hand of woman in a strange land, where was none else to help him. I slept well. And the next morning, on opening my window toward the east, and seeing the dear Cape lying stretched out far into the sea, I gave to the sands my parting benediction—not forgetting the fair ones who inhabit them, but wishing them all sorts of good things, down even to plenty of cranberries wherewith to make their pretty red cheeks still redder.

THE END.

N. B.—The new Tax on Books and Stereotyping, and the further advance in the cost of manufacture, render it necessary to add to the prices in the annexed Catalogue, viz.:

25 cents per volume on 12mos.
50 cents per volume on 8vos.

The above addition will be made *on the 1st of July*, 1864.

LIST

OF

CHOICE BOOKS,

PUBLISHED BY

G. P. PUTNAM, 441 Broadway,

Near Howard Street, NEW YORK.

N. B.—COMPLETION OF SETS.—All persons having incomplete sets of IRVING'S WORKS, HOOD'S WORKS, BAYARD TAYLOR'S WORKS, or the REBELLION RECORD, are requested to order immediately the volumes or numbers required. After a reasonable time the Publisher cannot undertake to furnish uniform volumes to match sets heretofore supplied.

BOOKS ARE THE WINDOWS THROUGH WHICH THE SOUL LOOKS OUT. A HOUSE WITHOUT BOOKS IS LIKE A ROOM WITHOUT WINDOWS. NO MAN HAS A RIGHT TO BRING UP HIS CHILDREN WITHOUT SURROUNDING THEM WITH BOOKS, IF HE HAS THE MEANS TO BUY THEM. IT IS A WRONG TO HIS FAMILY. HE CHEATS THEM. CHILDREN LEARN TO READ BY BEING IN THE PRESENCE OF BOOKS. THE LOVE OF KNOWLEDGE COMES WITH READING AND GROWS UPON IT. AND THE LOVE OF KNOWLEDGE, IN A YOUNG MIND, IS ALMOST A WARRANT AGAINST THE INFERIOR EXCITEMENT OF PASSIONS AND VICES. * * * * A LITTLE LIBRARY, GROWING LARGER EVERY YEAR, IS AN HONORABLE PART OF A YOUNG MAN'S HISTORY. IT IS A MAN'S DUTY TO HAVE BOOKS. A LIBRARY IS NOT A LUXURY, BUT ONE OF THE NECESSARIES OF LIFE.—*H. W. Beecher.*

Washington Irving's Writings.

Alhambra.

By Washington Irving.

A Residence in the celebrated Moorish palace, the "Alhambra," with the historical and romantic legends connected therewith.

Popular Edition, 1 vol., 12mo, green cloth, ...	$1.50
Tinted Edition, Illustrated, cloth, gilt, extra, ...	2.25
" " " half calf, antique, ...	3.00
" " " half calf, extra, ...	3.00

"*The beautiful Spanish Sketch Book, the Alhambra.*"—W. H. Prescott.

Astoria;

or, Anecdotes of an Enterprise beyond the Rocky Mountains. By Washington Irving.

"*It is a book to put in your library, as an entertaining very well written account of savage life on a most extensive scale.*"—Rev. Sidney Smith.

This volume describes the first great explorations of the Oregon and adjacent territories, and the foundation of the great wealth of Mr. John Jacob Astor.

Popular Edition, 12mo, green cloth, ...	1.50
Tinted Edition, large 12mo, half calf, extra, ...	3.00
" " " " half calf, antique, ...	3.00

Bonneville's Adventures.

The Adventures of Capt. Bonneville, U. S. A., in the Rocky Mountains and the Far West. From his own journals, and illustrated from other sources. By Washington Irving.

Popular Edition, 12mo, green cloth, ...	1.50
Tinted Edition, large 12mo, half calf, extra, ...	3.00
" " " " half calf, antique, ...	3·00

"*Full of exciting incident, * * with the power and the charms of romance.*"—Chancellor Kent.

BRACEBRIDGE HALL,

or the Humourists. By WASHINGTON IRVING.

POPULAR EDITION, 12mo, green cloth,	$1.50
TINTED EDITION, Illustrated, large 12mo, gilt, extra,	2.50
" " " half calf, extra,	3.00
" " " half calf, antique,	3.00
ILLUSTRATED (large paper) EDITION, 8vo, cloth,	3.50
" " " " 8vo, gilt edges,	4.00
" " " " 8vo, morocco, extra,	6.50
" " " " 8vo, morocco, antique,	6.50

"*It is very ill-natured, however, to object to what has given us so much pleasure.*"—LORD JEFFREY.

CHRONICLES of the CONQUEST of GRANADA.

By WASHINGTON IRVING.

POPULAR EDITION, 12mo, green cloth,	1.50
TINTED EDITION, large 12mo, half calf, antique,	3.00
" " " " half calf, antique,	3.00

"*It has superseded all further necessity for poetry, and, unfortunately for me, for history.*"—W. H. PRESCOTT.

COLUMBUS AND HIS COMPANIONS.

The Life and Voyages of Christopher Columbus: to which are added those of his Companions. By WASHINGTON IRVING.

POPULAR EDITION, 3 vols., 12mo, green cloth,	4.50
TINTED EDITION, Illustrated, 3 vols., large 12mo, half calf ant.,	8.00
" " " " " " half calf, extra,	8.00
OCTAVO EDITION, Illustrated, 3 vols., 8vo, cloth, extra,	10.50
" " " " 8vo, half calf, extra,	15.00
" " " " 8vo, half calf, antique,	15.00
" " " " 8vo, full calf, extra,	18.00

"*In treating this happy and splendid subject, Mr. Irving has brought out the full force of his genius.*"—ALEX. H. EVERETT.

"*The noblest monument to the memory of Columbus.*"—W. H. PRESCOTT.

"*It will supersede all other works on the subject, and never be itself superseded.*"—LORD JEFFREY.

CRAYON MISCELLANY.

Comprising a Tour on the Western Prairies; Abbottsford and Sir Walter Scott, and Newstead Abbey and Lord Byron. By WASHINGTON IRVING.

POPULAR EDITION, 1 vol., 12mo,	1.50
TINTED EDITION, large 12mo, half calf, antique,	3.00
" " " " half calf, extra,	3.00

DIEDRICH KNICKERBOCKER'S

HISTORY OF NEW YORK, from the beginning of the World to the end of the Dutch Dynasty: Containing, among many surprising and curious matters, the Unutterable Ponderings of Walter the Doubter; the Disastrous Projects of William the Testy; and the Chivalric Achievements of Peter the Headstrong—the Three Dutch Governors of New Amsterdam; being the only Authentic History of the Times that ever hath been or ever will be published. [By WASHINGTON IRVING.]

POPULAR EDITION, 1 vol., 12mo, ...	$1.50
TINTED EDITION, with Plates and Cuts, large 12mo, gilt, extra,	2.50
" " " " " half calf, extra,	3.00
" " " " " half calf, ant.,	3.00
ILLUSTRATED (large paper) EDITION, 8vo, cloth, . . .	3.50
" " " " " mor., extra, . .	6.50
" " " " " mor., antique, . .	6.50
" " " " " calf, antique, red edges,	6.50

"*The most excellently jocose History of New York.* * * * *Our sides have been absolutely sore with laughing.*"—SIR WALTER SCOTT.

"*A book of unwearying pleasantry.*"—EDWARD EVERETT.

"*The most elaborate piece of humor in our literature.*"—H. T. TUCKERMAN.

"*Manly, bold, and so altogether original, without being extravagant, as to stand alone among the labors of men.*"—BLACKWOOD'S MAGAZINE.

MAHOMET AND HIS SUCCESSORS.

By WASHINGTON IRVING.

POPULAR EDITION, 2 vols., 12mo, green cloth, ...	3.00
TINTED EDITION, EXTRA PLATES, 2 vols., half calf, extra, .	5.50
" " " " " half calf, antique, .	5.50

OLIVER GOLDSMITH: a BIOGRAPHY.

By WASHINGTON IRVING.

POPULAR EDITION, 1 vol., 12mo, green cloth, ...	1.50
TINTED EDITION, Illustrated, large 12mo, gilt, extra, . .	2.50
" " " " half calf, antique, .	3.00
" " " " half calf, extra, .	3.00

I have read no biographical work which carries forward the reader so delightfully. * * *I know of nothing like it.*"—WM. CULLEN BRYANT.

SALMAGUNDI.

By WILLIAM IRVING, JAMES K. PAULDING, and WASHINGTON IRVING.

POPULAR EDITION, 1 vol., 12mo, green cloth, ...	$1.50
TINTED EDITION, 1 vol., large 12mo, green cloth, . . .	1.75
" " " " half calf, extra, . .	3.00
" " " " half calf, antique, .	3.00
LARGE PAPER EDITION, 8vo, morocco, extra, ...	6.00
" " " " morocco, antique, . . .	6.00

"*Full of entertainment, with an infinite variety of characters and circumstances, and with that amiable, good-natured wit and pathos,*" *&c.*—R. H. DANA.

SKETCH BOOK

OF GEOFFREY CRAYON, GENT.

By WASHINGTON IRVING.

POPULAR EDITION, 1 vol., 12mo, green cloth, ...	1.50
TINTED EDITION, with Woodcuts, cloth gilt, extra, . .	2.50
" " " half calf, antique, . . .	3.00
" " " half calf, extra, . . .	3.00

[☞ SEE *the Artist's Edition of the Sketch Book.*]

"*It is positively beautiful.*"—SIR WALTER SCOTT.

"*This exquisite miscellany.*"—J. G. LOCKHART.

TALES OF A TRAVELLER.

By WASHINGTON IRVING.

POPULAR EDITION, 1 vol., 12mo, green cloth, ...	1.50
TINTED EDITION, large 12mo, with cuts, gilt, extra, . .	2.50
" " " " half calf, antique, . . .	3.00
" " " " half calf, extra, . . .	3.00
ILLUSTRATED (large paper) EDITION, 8vo, cloth, extra, . .	3.50
" " " " 8vo, morocco, extra, .	6.50
" " " " 8vo, morocco, antique, .	6.50

WOLFERT'S ROOST.

By WASHINGTON IRVING.

POPULAR EDITION, 1 vol., 12mo, green cloth, ...	1.50
TINTED EDITION, large 12mo, gilt, extra, ...	2.50
" " " " half calf, extra, ...	3.00
" " " " half calf, antique, . . .	3.00

"*We envy those who read these tales and sketches of character for the first time.*"—WESTMINSTER REVIEW.

WASHINGTON IRVING'S WHOLE WORKS,

Including LIFE OF WASHINGTON, SALMAGUNDI, and all the Miscellaneous Writings.

Complete in Twenty-two Volumes, 12mo.

SUNNYSIDE EDITION, Tinted Paper, with Vignettes,

(a)	22 vols., 12mo, extra cloth,	$33.00
(b)	" " extra sheep, [white.]	37.00
(c)	" " half calf, plain,	55.00
(d)	" " half calf, extra,	60.00
(e)	" " half calf, antique,	60.00
(f)	" " half morocco, gilt edges,	65.00
(g)	" " full calf, extra,	70.00
(h)	" " full calf, antique,	70.00
(i)	" " full morocco, extra,	75.00

WASHINGTON IRVING'S WRITINGS, exclusive of "WASHINGTON" and including "SALMAGUNDI." *Complete in 17 Volumes.*

(k)	SUNNYSIDE EDITION, cloth, extra,	25.50
(l)	" " half calf, plain,	40.00
(m)	" " half calf, antique,	44.00
(n)	" " half calf, extra,	44.00
(o)	" " full calf, extra,	48.00

"*I cannot hesitate to predict for him a deathless renown.* * * *He whose works were the delight of our fathers and are still ours, will be read with the same pleasure by those who come after us.*"—WM. CULLEN BRYANT.

WASHINGTON IRVING'S WRITINGS, NATIONAL EDITION. Illustrated. On superfine tinted paper.

☞ *This edition is printed only for Subscribers.*

Complete in Twenty-two vols., extra black cloth, bevelled edges.

*** These may be subscribed for to be delivered monthly or oftener, for $1.75 per vol.

(p)	A Complete Set,	37.00
(q)	The Same Edition, cloth, uncut,	37.00
(r)	" " extra green cloth, cut edges, not bevelled,	37.00
(s)	" " half calf, extra,	65.00
(t)	" " half calf, antique,	65.00

WASHINGTON IRVING'S WRITINGS, with his LIFE AND LETTERS. Beautifully Printed, and mostly Illustrated. LARGE PAPER EDITION. Twenty-six volumes. 8vo, Folded and coll., 86.00

Cloth, gt. tops,	92.00
The same, in half calf, extra,	140.00
" in half morocco, gt. tops,	145.00
" in full morocco, extra,	175.00

*** Early application should be made for these, as only 100 sets are printed, and no more will be done in this style.

WASHINGTON.

THE LIFE OF GEORGE WASHINGTON.

By WASHINGTON IRVING.

"His Life of Washington is a marvel."—GEO. BANCROFT.

I. POPULAR EDITION, 5 vols., 12mo, green cloth, ...	$7.50
" " " 12mo, sheep, extra, . . .	8.50
II. SUNNYSIDE EDITION, with plates, 5 vols., 12mo, cloth, . .	8.00
" " " " 12mo, half calf, extra,	13.50
" " " " 12mo, half calf, ant.,	13.50
" " " " 12mo, hf. mor., gt. ed.,	15.00
" " " " 12mo, full calf, extra,	16.00
" " " " 12mo, full mor. gt. ed.,	17.00
III. UNION EDITION, steel plates, 5 vols., small 8vo, cloth, uncut,	8.50
" " " " " " hf. cf., extra,	15.00
" " " " " " hf. cf., ant.,	15.00
" " " " " " full cf., ext.,	16.00
" " " " " " full mor. ex.,	18.00
IV. LIBRARY EDITION, octavo, 5 vols., cloth, ...	10.00
" " " " sheep, ...	12.50
" " " " half calf, antique, . .	16.00
" " " " half calf, extra, . .	16.00
V. MOUNT VERNON EDITION, 100 Steel Plates and 40 Wood Cuts, on tinted paper. A new and superb edition. 5 vols., square 8vo, cloth, ...	17.50
half calf, extra, . .	26.00
half calf, antique, . .	26.00
half morocco, gilt tops,	26.00
full calf, extra, . .	28.00
full morocco, gilt edges,	30.00
full morocco, gilt, extra,	30.00
VI. ILLUSTRATED (large paper) EDITION, 5 vols., royal 8vo, half calf, antique, ...	30.00
half calf., extra,	30.00
full mor., extra,	36.00

*** *In this edition the pages are enclosed in lines.*

VII. AMATEURS' (Quarto) EDITION, with 102 Steel Plates, proofs on India Paper, 5 vols., quarto, morocco, extra, . . .	110.00

*** *Of this superb edition only* 110 *were printed, and but* 3 *copies remain unsold.*

AN EDITION FOR CANVASSERS is also printed in ONE large volume, double columns, with Twenty Steel Plates. Price, $5, in cloth. Also, in Twenty-Six Numbers, with Fifty-Two Plates. Price, 25 cents per number—making two handsome volumes. Price, ...	7.50

WASHINGTON ILLUSTRATIONS.

Comprising 102 Steel Plates, Proof-impressions on India Paper, including 70 Portraits of eminent men of the Revolution, and 30 Historical Scenes by Darley, Trumbull, &c.

Quarto, in portfolio, ... $25.00
Any Plate may be had separately, price 40

WASHINGTON ILLUSTRATIONS to match the 8vo edition, 1 vol., cloth, 6.00

BAYARD TAYLOR'S WRITINGS.

"*There is no romance to us quite equal to one of Bayard Taylor's books of travel.*"—HARTFORD REPUBLICAN.

ELDORADO;

OR, ADVENTURES IN THE PATH OF EMPIRE, (Mexico and California.)

12mo, cloth, ... $1.50

CENTRAL AFRICA;

LIFE AND LANDSCAPE FROM CAIRO TO THE WHITE NILE.

Two plates and cuts, 12mo, ... 1.50

GREECE and RUSSIA;

WITH AN EXCURSION TO CRETE.

Two plates, 12mo, ... 1.50

HOME and ABROAD;

A SKETCH BOOK OF LIFE, SCENERY, AND MEN.

Two plates, 12mo, cloth, ... 1.50

HOME and ABOAD—(Second Series.)

A new volume, just published, (1862.)

Two plates, 12mo, cloth, ... 1.50

INDIA, CHINA, and JAPAN.

Two plates, 12mo, cloth, ... 1.50

BAYARD TAYLOR'S WRITINGS—*Continued.*

LANDS OF THE SARACEN;

OR, PICTURES OF PALESTINE, ASIA MINOR, SICILY, AND SPAIN.

With two plates, 12mo, cloth, ... $1.50

NORTHERN TRAVEL;

SUMMER AND WINTER PICTURES OF SWEDEN, DENMARK, AND LAPLAND.

Two plates, 12mo, cloth, ... 1.50

VIEWS A-FOOT;

OR, EUROPE SEEN WITH KNAPSACK AND STAFF.

12mo, ... 1.50

HANNAH THURSTON:

A STORY OF AMERICAN LIFE, ... 1.50

BAYARD TAYLOR'S TRAVELS.

POPULAR EDITION, complete in 9 vols., 12mo, cloth, extra,	.	13.50
" " " " " sheep, extra,	.	15.50
" " " " " half calf, extra,	.	22.50
" " " " " half calf, ant.,	.	22.50

BAYARD TAYLOR'S PROSE WRITINGS.

CAXTON EDITION, printed for subscribers. In 10 vols., on tinted paper. Issued monthly. Price, per vol., . . . 1.75

The volumes are issued as follows:

I. HOME AND ABROAD.
II. VIEWS A-FOOT.
III. HOME AND ABROAD. SECOND SERIES.
IV. ELDORADO.
V. CENTRAL AFRICA.
VI. LANDS OF THE SARACEN.
VII. INDIA, CHINA, AND JAPAN.
VIII. NORTHERN TRAVEL.
IX. GREECE AND RUSSIA.
X. HANNAH THURSTON.

A Magnificent and Valuable Work.

THE ARCHITECTURAL INSTRUCTOR;

Containing a History of Architecture from the Earliest Ages to the Present Time; illustrated with nearly 250 Engravings of Ancient, Mediæval, and Modern Cities, Temples, Palaces, Cathedrals, and Monuments; also, the Greek and Early Roman Classic Orders, their principles and beauties; with a large number of Original Designs of Cottages, Villas, and Mansions of different sizes, accompanied with practical observations on Construction, with all the important details, on a scale sufficiently large and definite to enable the Builder to execute with accuracy; and further Designs of Churches, Monuments, and Public Buildings; together with a Glossary of Architectural Terms; the whole being the result of more than Thirty Years' Professional Experience. By MINARD LAFEVER, Architect.

1 vol., large quarto, half morocco, gilt tops, ... $16.00

*** *This handsome volume is, probably, the most comprehensive single volume on architecture ever published—embracing a full History of Architecture from the earliest times, and also a complete treatise on its theory and practice, with designs for modern houses, public buildings, churches, &c. It should be in every good library for general reference, as well as in the hands of every architect. Mr. Lafever was one of the most eminent and thorough architects in the country.*

AMERICAN HISTORICAL AND LITERARY CURIOSITIES;

Consisting of Facsimiles of Original Documents relating to the Events of the Revolution, &c., &c., with a variety of Reliques, Antiquities, and Modern Autographs. Collected and Edited by JOHN JAY SMITH and JOHN F. WATSON.

Sixth edition, with improvements and additions.

Large quarto, cloth, gilt tops, ... 8.00
" " half morocco, gilt edges, ... 10.00

A SECOND SERIES (COMPLETE IN ITSELF) OF

American Historical and Literary Curiosities;

Consisting of Facsimiles relating to Columbus, and Original Documents of the Revolution, with Reliques, Autographs, &c. Edited by JOHN JAY SMITH.

Quarto, cloth, ... 8.00
" half morocco, gilt edges, ... 10.00

WASHINGTON PORTRAITS.

The Character and Portraits of Washington. By HENRY T. TUCKERMAN. With 12 Portraits, proofs on India Paper. Only 150 printed.

Quarto, cloth, ... 6.00
" in a portfolio, ... 6.00

REBEL RHYMES AND RHAPSODIES—

The Curiosities of Southern Literature of the Times. Edited by FRANK MOORE.

24mo, Black and Yellow, ... 1.00

New Romance of Real Life.

UNDERCURRENTS OF WALL STREET;

A ROMANCE OF BUSINESS. By RICHARD B. KIMBALL, Author of "ST. LEGER." 1 vol., 12mo, 5th Edition. . $1.50

ST. LEGER; THE THREADS OF LIFE.

By RICHARD B. KIMBALL. Ninth Edition, 12mo, cloth, . 1.50

"*I find great power and beauty in your book, and a fertility of invention almost prodigal.*"—WASHINGTON IRVING.

"*A brilliant book, full of suggestions of wisdom.*"—NEW YORK TRIBUNE.

"*A book of great strength.*"—N. Y. EVENING POST.

"*Who is the author of this powerfully-written book?*"—PHILADELPHIA EVENING BULLETIN.

"*Here, there, and everywhere, the author gives exhibitions of passionate and romantic power.*"—LONDON ATHENÆUM.

"*A very extraordinary book.*"—LONDON MORNING POST.

The American Robinson Crusoe.

KALOOLAH;

A ROMANCE. By W. STARBUCK MAYO, M. D.

In 1 vol., 12mo, 512 pages, with illustrations by Darley, . . 1.50

"*The most singular and captivating romance since Robinson Crusoe.*" —HOME JOURNAL.

"*By far the most fascinating and entertaining book we have ever read since we were fascinated by the graceful inventions of the Arabian Nights.*"—DEMOCRATIC REVIEW.

*** Mr. Washington Irving considered Kaloolah to be a work of decided genius, and of extraordinary interest. The description of the magnificent city of Killoam, the capital of the great nation in the heart of Africa, includes a capital commentary and satire on the municipal regulations of American cities, and especially of New York.

ANGLO-SAXON GRAMMAR.

A GRAMMAR OF THE ANGLO-SAXON LANGUAGE. By L. F. KLIPSTEIN. 12mo, cloth, ... 1.25

*** *The best Anglo-Saxon Grammar in the language.*

MANUAL OF POLITICAL ECONOMY.

By E. PESBINE SMITH. 12mo, cloth, ... 1.25

*** *Used as a text-book at Princeton and other colleges, and well adapted for popular reading.*

ELEMENTS OF GEOLOGY.

Intended for the use of Students. By SAMUEL ST. JOHN, Professor of Chemistry and Geology in the College of Physicians and Surgeons, New York. Eleventh Edition. 12mo, cloth, . 1.25

THE WORLD'S PROGRESS;

A DICTIONARY OF DATES: *From the Creation to A.D.* 1861. Edited by G. P. PUTNAM, A. M., Hon. Mem. Conn. Historical Society, Wisconsin Historical Society, &c.

[An entirely new edition, with copious additions; including the most important facts in the History of the World, down to the Inauguration of Abraham Lincoln.]

The volume now contains more than ONE MILLION FACTS, on all topics connected with the progress of society, from the earliest period to the present, arranged for convenient reference.

1 vol., large 12mo, over 800 pages, ...	$2.50
half calf, extra, . .	3.50
A few copies on large paper, ...	4.00
do do interleaved, half morocco, . .	7.00

"*A more convenient literary labor-saving machine than this excellent compilation, can scarcely be found in any language.*"—NEW YORK TRIBUNE.

"*It has been planned so as to facilitate access to the largest amount of useful information in the smallest possible compass.*"—BUFFALO COURIER.

"*The best manual of the kind that has yet appeared in the English language.*"—BOSTON COURIER.

"*An exceedingly valuable book; wellnigh indispensable to a very large portion of the community.*"—COURIER AND ENQUIRER.

"*It is absolutely* ESSENTIAL *to the desk of every* MERCHANT *and the table of every* STUDENT *and* PROFESSIONAL MAN."—CHRISTIAN ENQUIRER.

Uniform with the Above.

CYCLOPEDIA OF UNIVERSAL BIOGRAPHY.

By PARKE GODWIN, Esq., Author of the "History of France." New edition, with continuation to 1863.

1 vol., large 12mo, ...	2.50
The same in 8vo, ...	4.00

The Best and Most Complete Edition.

PAPERS FOR THE PEOPLE.

A Series of Popular and Instructive Papers on History, Archæology, Biography, Science, Industrial and Fine Arts, Civilization, Fiction, Personal Narrative, and other branches of Elegant Literature. Edited by ROBERT CHAMBERS.

12 vols., 12mo. Bound in 6. Red cloth, in a box. Price, .	6.00

⁂ These admirable volumes comprise about 3,500 large and substantial pages, including a great variety of valuable and entertaining information on the subjects above indicated, interspersed with attractive narratives and tales, and all written with eminent ability by some of the most competent authors of the day.

The work is, in fact, a little LIBRARY IN ITSELF, eminently worthy of a place in every household, and attractive alike to young and old.

It is probably the CHEAPEST WORK (considering its eminent excellence and value) ever published.

Every FAMILY, and every PUBLIC LIBRARY and SCHOOL LIBRARY, should have a copy.

The above work is also issued in parts, royal 8vo, each part containing two distinct works, with a steel plate, ...	.25

RUTTAN

ON

WARMING AND VENTILATING

PUBLIC BUILDINGS, RAILROAD CARS, &c.

WITH PLATES.

Royal 8vo, ... $3.50

FRANCIS'

HISTORY OF THE BANK OF ENGLAND.

EDITED BY J. SMITH HOMANS.

8vo, cloth, ... 3.00

*** This work includes a comprehensive FINANCIAL HISTORY OF ENGLAND.

The Illustrated Edition of the

LIFE AND LETTERS

OF

WASHINGTON IRVING.

A few copies, on large paper, with extra engravings on steel, elegantly bound in morocco, gilt edges. 4 vols. 8vo, . 32.00

The People's Edition of the

LIFE OF WASHINGTON;

With 52 steel plates. Complete in 2 vols., Royal 8vo.

Half calf, extra, marbled edges, ... 11.00
Half morocco, gilt edges; or half calf, gilt edges, ... 12.50
Morocco, extra, ... 16.00

The most popular book of the year.

BAYARD TAYLOR'S NEW NOVEL.

HANNAH THURSTON:

A STORY OF AMERICAN LIFE.

1 vol., 12mo, ... $1 50

*** *The success of this book at home and in England has been so remarkable and so thorough, that the publisher deems it quite unnecessary to quote any more of the criticism, almost unanimously in its favor as a book of unusual merit and interest.*

The "RED, WHITE, AND BLUE" SERIES of

NATIONAL SONGS AND BALLADS.

Collected and arranged by FRANK MOORE.

Neatly Printed by HOUGHTON, on laid paper, and bound by MATTHEWS. 24mo. viz.:

(1.) Lyrics of Loyalty.
(Now ready), ... $1.00

(2.) Songs of the Soldiers.
(In Press), ... 1.00

(3.) Personal and Political Ballads of the Times.
. . . . 1.00

The "BLUE AND GOLD" SERIES

FROM THE RIVERSIDE PRESS.

IRVING'S SKETCH BOOK.

Complete in one Pocket Volume, "Blue and Gold," $1.00

Uniform with the above are:

LONGFELLOW'S PROSE WRITINGS. 2 vols., ... 2.00
" POETICAL WRITINGS. 2 vols., ... 2.00
TENNYSON'S POETICAL WORKS. 2 vols., ... 2.00
LOWELL'S " " 2 vols., ... 2.00
WHITTIER'S " " 2 vols., ... 2.00
HOLMES, SAXE, MOTHERWELL, &c. Each, per vol., ... 1.00

The KNICKERBOCKER SERIES.

*** *The page and type of this series have been carefully studied, with a view to attain a page most attractive to the eye, in a snug, portable, and elegant volume, which shall be the best size for the fireside or the traveller's bag.*

The first of the series is

IRVING'S KNICKERBOCKER—

With new Vignettes by DARLEY. 16mo, vellum Cloth, gilt tops.